A Woman Among
All Those

A Woman Among All Those

Lessons in Christian Womanhood

Mary Middlebrooks

BBCG Publications
Goodland, Kansas

All Scripture quotations taken from the King James Bible

ISBN – 10: 1502837064
ISBN – 13: 978-1502837064

BBCG Publications
Goodland, Kansas
www.biblebaptist goodland.com

Printed in the United States of America
By Createspace ©

Table of Contents

Foreword

This book is compiled from a series of lessons that I teach in Christian Womanhood in our Bible Institute. It has been the work of quite a number of years. The Lord has blessed it in ways that to my mind are amazing! I never intended to write it in book form and never intended to use it for any but our own folks. But the Lord had other plans. I am sure that there will be many things that many ladies will not agree with as they peruse the pages. I don't ask that everyone agree with me. All I ask is that you take it to the Lord, and love me anyway.

A number of pastors' wives have chosen to use the lessons in teaching their ladies – I welcome that and you are free to copy the lessons. All I ask is that you be honest.

I have included the review sheets, just as I use them in class. If you wish, you may copy the review sheets and send them to me. If you do them all, I will send you the same certificate that our ladies receive from our institute. My email address is: mrs.mary1611@yahoo.com.

May the Lord richly bless you.

mrs.mary

John 6:37, Colossians 3:17, Romans 8:28

It is well, it is well with my soul!

A Woman Among all Those
Lessons in Christian Womanhood

Lesson 1

During this course we will be memorizing Proverbs 31:10-31. We will also be referring to a lot of references that are not written out - so grab your King James Bible and keep it close by!

Scripture memory for lesson 1: Who can find a virtuous woman? for her price is far above rubies. Proverbs 31:10

A virtuous woman is a crown to her husband: but she that maketh ashamed is as rottenness in his bones. Proverbs 12:4

Spiritual growth takes a different path in every Christian's life. As her Saviour works in her heart, the God fearing woman will eventually ask, "What kind of woman does God want me to be?" Yet when we begin to search the Scripture for an answer, or when we hear preaching on the subject, many times the old nature flares up in instant rebellion. This is not medieval times! Women today are different! What happened to independence, equality and all those wonderful, fought for ideals??!!

Behold, this have I found, saith the preacher, counting one by one, to find out the account: Which yet my soul seeketh, but I find not: one man among a thousand have I found: but a woman among all those have I not found. Ecclesiastes 7:27-28

Remember, this was Solomon talking - he had 1,000 of them to make his comparison with! What a sad, but true testimony. In God's eyes a virtuous, godly woman is a rare and precious jewel. "Why should we care?" some would ask, or "We're all right compared to some women we know, better than most…" but what's the yardstick?

For we dare not make ourselves of the number, or compare ourselves with some that commend themselves: but they measuring themselves by themselves, and comparing themselves among themselves, are not wise. 2 Corinthians 10:12

So, if we try to claim that we are all right by saying that we know others that are worse, the Bible says we are not wise. Our comparison is supposed to be the Word of God - how do we measure up to what God wants us to be?

There are many different ways and methods that have been used to teach virtuous womanhood. The method that I believe God has given me to use in this study came from Romans 15:4:

For whatsoever things were written aforetime were written for our learning, that we through patience and comfort of the Scriptures might have hope. Romans 15:4

The Lord gave us the Scriptures as a guideline for our salvation and our Christian lives - to introduce us to His ways that we might be conformed to His will. Many people want to discount the things that are written in the Old Testament, saying that they are not relevant for the New Testament Church. Romans 15:4 and 2 Timothy 3:16 say differently. There was a reason for every word that was placed between the covers of the Word of God. Yes, some things were put there specifically for the Children of Israel. But all of Scripture can be applied to us spiritually. One of the ways that it applies is in example. So I have taken each of the characteristics of the Proverbs 31 woman (our outline of the woman God says is virtuous) and some examples from Scripture that teach us how those characteristics are applied and can apply directly to our lives, today, now. One of the great beauties of the Scripture is that it is never outdated. Our Marvelous, Wonderful God has given us a Book that is for all time. We can learn everything that we need to know about being the woman that God wants us to be (and who He does not want us to be) right from the pages of this Book. Other people may choose to teach it differently, but this is what God gave to me. Have I arrived? No, not by any means. I am not in any way worthy to teach such a course. But, God being my helper, we will learn together.

There are books enough to build a library on this subject. Why?? "Who can find" is the issue. She's rare. We, as women who love the Lord Jesus, have to seek to become that treasure spoken of in Proverbs 31:10. Our life should reflect our desire to be the one whose value is far above rubies, the rare treasure of being a crown to her husband. Why is a virtuous woman so hard to find? Why did Solomon say he had not found one among a thousand? To search out the answer to this we must look at the word virtuous.

According to Webster's 1828 dictionary the word virtuous is defined: Moral goodness, the practice of moral duties, and the abstaining from vice, or a conformity of life and conversation to the moral law. Virtue is nothing but voluntary obedience to truth.

Virtue and Virtuous are found 9 times in the Word of God. Mark 5:30, Luke 6:19, Luke 8:46 - These refer to Jesus healing. There went out a virtue (a goodness) from Him and healed them. Philippians 4:8; 2 Peter 1:3; 2 Peter 1:5 - These refer to virtue that we as Christians should strive to display in our lives. Ruth 3:11, Proverbs 12:4, and Proverbs 31:10 all refer to women.

Nine is the number of fruit in the Bible: "By their fruits ye shall know them" the fruit of the Spirit - This should show us that virtue is an outward display of the moral goodness that the salvation given to us has planted in our hearts. This is living our salvation for all to see.
The question to ask yourself at this point is: Do I really want to be the woman GOD wants me to be, or do I want to be the woman I want to be? If your attitude is a desire to have your own way instead of God's way then we are wasting our time with this study. Take a good, long look at your heart and if you believe you want to be God's woman, pray. Ask God to help you, as you study, to fight against the rebellion that is a natural part of our lives and to develop the attributes HE desires. You will need, if you are at all like me, to return and pray again and again for that attitude of submission to God's will as we go along. So, taking a closer look:

Proverbs 31:10 - Who can find a virtuous woman? For her price is far above rubies.

So rare is the woman who will display voluntary obedience to the truths found in the Word of God that she is a treasure compared to rubies. The only other thing in the Word of God that is compared to the value of rubies is wisdom. Job 28:18, Proverbs 3:15, 8:11, 20:15 (there is only one other place that the word rubies is mentioned at all - Lamentations 4:7 - and that is a comparison of color.) Rubies are the highest priced gem known to man. (Not diamonds, as is usually supposed - - real, quality rubies are rarer, and when they are found, of higher value.) How highly does God prize wisdom? All the things that may be desired are not to be compared to it. And God gives a virtuous woman the same words of comparison. A price above rubies. So a virtuous woman is, in God's sight, a rare and priceless jewel. One so difficult to find that there is not one among a thousand.

Since the example the Scripture gives us of a virtuous woman is found in Ruth 3:11 let's look at what it says.

And now, my daughter, fear not; I will do to thee all that thou requirest: for all the city of my people doth know that thou art a virtuous woman. Ruth 3:11

Contrary to all propriety, then and now, this woman had just approached a sleeping man in the middle of the night and asked him to marry her!!! Looking in verse 14 we see that he was not anxious for it to be known that she was there. But, he said that all of the city knew that she was a virtuous woman. She had proven herself. What had she done?

The first thing she had done, in Ruth 1:14-18 was that she left everything familiar to her to care for an elderly widow, because she felt it was the right thing to do. She showed selflessness. Someone else's welfare was more important to her than staying with the loved and familiar and looking out for number one. The Word of God makes it plain that selfishness is a sin.

Fulfill ye my joy, that ye be likeminded, having the same love, being of one accord, of one mind. Philippians 2:2

For all seek their own, not the things which are Jesus Christ's. Philippians 2:21

Let no man seek his own, but every man another's wealth. 1 Corinthians 10:24 (referring to spiritual wealth),

Even as I please all men in all things, not seeking mine own profit, but the profit of many, that they may be saved. 1 Corinthians 10:33

Sometimes doing right may mean that you have to leave the "familiar zone". What did Ruth leave behind? Her family, her mother and father. Plainly her parents were still alive - Ruth 1:6. Her culture, her gods verse 15. The Moabites were not worshipers of the one true God, they worshiped Chemosh, who was an off scouring of Baal worship. Yet, we see in Ruth 1:16 that Ruth had embraced Naomi's God and had no desire to turn back. If you desire to be the woman God wants you to be, you might have to leave the familiar zone. You might have to be willing to stand out in your community, and even in your own family as the one who goes against what is accepted and expected. You may have to answer questions as to why you dress differently, why you do or do not participate in certain things. Why are you raising your children this way? You might even have to turn away from the loved and familiar and go where God leads you to go. Many missionaries' wives have had to face the fact that when they follow their husband to a foreign field they may never see loved ones again. It is the same sacrifice that Ruth made. Her first step toward virtue was to follow the Lord's leading at the expense of the loved and familiar.

The next thing that Ruth did was to display industriousness. She showed that she was not lazy. Chapter 2 verse 2. Have you ever gleaned? It's not exactly rewarding work. I was a teenager before I knew that more than six green beans grew on a bush. My mother used to take me to the fields to glean after the pickers. We would work together for hours to pick a few bushels of green beans or pick up a few sacks of tiny new potatoes. It's hot, back breaking work for not much reward. Ruth's job was even less rewarding. She was picking up stalks of barley dropped by the reapers. Her next step toward virtue was to labor, without murmur or complaint, at a job that seemed endless and thankless.

Do all things without murmurings and disputings: Philippians 2:14

And that ye study to be quiet, and to do your own business, and to work with your own hands, as we commanded you;   1 Thessalonians 4:11.

She stuck with the work without stop and without complaint. Boaz noticed her and was told in Ruth 2:6-7. "She hath continued from the morning until now."

He was plainly told that she was not lazy, and not a quitter. She didn't get in the middle of the task and say "this is too much work for too little results." Not only did she keep at it that day, she kept at it though all of the barley and wheat harvest. Verse 23.

Laziness is a sin. Proverbs 6:6-11; 10:5; 13:4; 18:9; 20:13; 23:21; 24:30-34; 26:15-16; Ecclesiastes 10:18; 2 Thessalonians 3:11-12 ; Hebrews 6:12

Well, there you have it. These are the two things that Ruth displayed before the inhabitants of the city that gave her the tag of a virtuous woman. She showed kindness to her mother-in-law in not leaving her destitute, Chapter 2 verse 11, and she showed diligence and consistent hard work throughout the harvest. You might say, "Surely there must be move than that?!" No - that's all it says. Now, we can make some other suppositions. One is that they did not find her in the local night spots. Another is that they did not see her immodestly dressed or displaying unladylike attitudes. But we don't know that. All we know is that she left her home to care for a widow and worked hard at that task. All we know is that the tasks that she took on, she took on willingly and performed with all of her heart.

And whatsoever ye do in word or deed, do all in the name of the Lord Jesus, giving thanks to God and the Father by him. Colossians 3:17,

And whatsoever ye do, do it heartily, as to the Lord, and not unto men; Knowing that of the Lord ye shall receive the reward of the inheritance; for ye serve the Lord Christ. Colossians 3:23-24.

God gives each one of us a task to do. One designed especially for us. Now that task is not going to always be the same - but in the barley field I'll bet Ruth wondered if she'd be gleaning the rest of her life. God had something special in mind for her, but her job at that point was to be obedient about picking up the grain.

While we wash dishes and sweep floors, while we wipe noses and brush out tangles, while we try to shop on an impossible budget - we are slowly picking up the barley grain that builds the name "virtuous woman." It doesn't happen overnight, and it doesn't happen with a reluctant, defiant, complaining attitude. As you "pick the grain" that God has designed for you, what is your attitude? Do you fight against the field he's placed you in, looking for greener grass on the other side of the fence? Do you wish for an easier lot? Is your mind always looking back at the things you have left behind in order to serve Christ? Jesus' rebuke for that attitude was very pointed.

And Jesus said unto him, No man, having put his hand to the plow, and looking back, is fit for the kingdom of God. Luke 9:62

Remember there was nothing glamorous about Ruth. Her life was plain hard work and dedication. She was the real Cinderella story, but she had no guarantees that Prince Charming would ever come into her life. She was not seeking a man.

The next thing that Ruth displayed that can help us understand why she was called virtuous was her submission to authority. Look at Ruth 3:1-5 - Naomi was the one who made the strange suggestion to her. She told Ruth just what to do. And Ruth was willing to follow her advice, knowing that Naomi was more knowledgeable in the customs of the land, and was seeking for her good.

The way of a fool is right in his own eyes: but he that hearkeneth unto counsel is wise. Proverbs 12:15

It was Jewish law that when a man died childless his nearest relation would take his wife, and his lands. The first born son of that union would bear the first husband's name instead of the father's so that the first husband's name would not die out in Israel.

What was Boaz's comment when Ruth told him why she was there? "thou hast shewed more kindness in the latter end than at the beginning, inasmuch as thou followedst not young men, whether poor or rich." Boaz knew she was not "on the catch" for a man. He knew that she was a stranger to their customs and probably knew from the way she worded her request that Naomi had sent her.

Nothing turns a man off more than a woman who is out to catch a man. He does not want to be pursued, he wants to be the pursuer. Man chasing is immodest behavior. It used to be considered a scandalous thing for a girl to chase boys. Girls who would call a boy on the phone, or ask him for a date, or seek to get close to him were behaving "loosely". And they got a reputation to match - anything but virtuous.

Proverbs 7:5-27 gives us a picture of the harlot - the loose woman. We will probably refer back to this picture many times, because just as Proverbs 31 is a picture of what we should be, this is the opposite contrast - what we should not be. It gives us an overview of 4 things about her: Her dress, her speech, her actions and her attitude. Notice that in verse 10 she has the attire of a harlot (it was easy to see what her morals were by the way she was dressed.) She is subtil of heart. She's sneaky (on the make.) She's loud and stubborn and her feet abide not in her house. All attributes that we should avoid. If you have a natural tendency to talk loudly and boisterously, learn to temper it. Study to be quiet. If you have a tendency toward stubbornness, practice submission. Seek for ways to be submissive. If you always have to have your own way, stubbornly, seek for an opportunity to do things someone else's way. If you look for every opportunity to get away from home so you can be around the wilder side of life, you are in a real danger zone! Seek for ways to be contented at home, doing the things you are supposed to do. The Proverbs 7 woman is running the streets, looking for men. She is the pursuer here. She kissed him. And with an impudent face.

The word impudent means: Shameless; wanting modesty; bold with contempt of others; saucy.

She's sassy and bold. We must teach young girls to have a modest, virtuous attitude toward young men. Not to be bold, or pushy in their relationships. They need to be taught to let the young man take the lead. Many young men will be ready enough to accept a bold, forward, pushy girl like that - - for the wrong reason. If a young man is interested in a girl for the right reason - he does not want one with character like that unless he's stupid, because he'll never be able to trust her.

Ruth was right in her obedience to Naomi, but also right in following the next advice she was given. Chapter 3 verse 18 "sit still my daughter." Naomi was telling Ruth to step back and let the man take the lead in the situation.

Then came the reward. First she was unselfish, willing to leave her comfort zone, and follow where God would have her to go. Then she was willing to work, at drudging labor, and do so with the right heart and attitude. She kept herself morally pure and modest. Then was willing to follow wise counsel in spite of its strange nature. Her reward? She found rest, as was promised, in the house of her husband, and became great-grandmother to David the king.

What attributes of the virtuous woman can we glean from this for our lives?

#1 - Unselfishness - A Christ like attitude we're told to have all throughout the Word of God.
#2 - Submissive dedication to the will of God
#3 - A diligent hardworking attitude
#4 - Moral purity for all to see - modesty
#5 – A willingness to listen to Godly counsel

Lesson One Review

1) Ecclesiastes 7:27-28 states that "one man among a _____ have I found, but _____

2) Define Virtuous_____

_____

_____

3) Virtue and Virtuous is found _____ times in the Bible. _____ of those times it refers to women.

4) Only one other thing in the Word of God is compared to rubies. What is it? _____ .

5) List the two things that Ruth had done to prove herself to all the city as a virtuous
woman._____

_____

6) Her first step toward virtue was to leave her "_____" And to follow _____In doing so she displayed _____

7) Her second step toward virtue was to show she was not
_____She displayed _____ by working consistently without complaint throughout the harvest.

8) Did Ruth have a promise that things would ever get easier?_____

_____

9) Her third step toward virtue was to _____

_____

She displayed _____

10) Ruth was not _____ for a man.

11) The Proverbs 7 picture of an harlot speaks of 4 things:

_____
_____
_____
_____

12) Young women should learn to allow the man to

_____

13) Define impudent _____

_____
_____

14) What was Ruth's reward?

_____

15) Ruth was King David's _____

16) List 5 attributes that Ruth had that we can apply practically to our lives to make us virtuous women

_____
_____
_____
_____

A Woman Among all Those
Lessons in Christian Womanhood

Lesson 2

Scripture Memory for this week: The heart of her husband doth safely trust in her so that he shall have no need of spoil. She will do him good and not evil all the days of her life. Proverbs 31:11-12

House and riches are the inheritance of fathers: and a prudent wife is from the LORD. Proverbs 19:14

The definition of prudent is "Cautious, circumspect, practically wise, careful of the consequences of enterprises, measures or actions; cautious not to act when the end is of doubtful utility. Frugal, economical."

Simply stated a prudent woman thinks before she acts. She's careful about the end results of what she does. "Look before you leap." Trust is a very fragile thing. Can your husband (your future husband, your heavenly bridegroom) trust in you? Safely trust in you? Will you do him good all the days of your life? It takes years of faithfulness to build trust; yet it takes only a few moments of time to erase the trust of years. A man must never, ever have to worry about the whereabouts or activities of his wife. A safely trusting man would rather have his wife do an important job or run an important errand for him than have someone else do it. A safely trusting man feels no need to check up on or check behind his wife. Let's look at some areas where we should be able to be trusted.

#1 He should be able to trust our love.
#2 We should be able to be trusted with his good name, his convictions.
#3 We should be able to be trusted with his money and possessions.
#4 We should be able to be trusted with his home and children.
#5 We should be able to be trusted to perform the tasks he sets for us.

This boils down to two areas of our life - Purity and Submission. We don't have time to cover all 5 of these areas in this one lesson, so we'll just cover the first. The others will all be covered in future lessons, and we'll refer back to these 5 things.

Look at the phrase "so that he shall have no need of spoil." The word spoil in this passage refers to the goods taken in battle. When an army would come through and take over an area, they would "spoil" the people. They would take whatever there was for the taking. One of the sad pictures of the battlegrounds of man was (and let's face it - is) that part of the "spoil" involved was the vanquished women. The picture God gives us here is a man so in love with, and so wrapped up in, the beauty of, his virtuous woman that no other woman can tempt him. Even alone on the battlefield for months and with women for the taking - he's not interested. The reason for his contentment and total commitment is that he has no reason to worry about his wife. She is completely trustworthy. He knows without a doubt that she's there waiting for him, and worth waiting for. Now let's look at the opposite side.

As a jewel of gold in a swine's snout, so is a fair woman which is without discretion. Proverbs 11:22

Look at the picture Solomon paints. Can you imagine how foolish and worthless it would be to take a ring of pure gold, worth a great deal of money, and place it in the snout of a muddy, sloppy, grunting sow? This is how he compares a pretty woman who does not show discretion.

Webster's 1828 dictionary describes discretion as "Prudence or knowledge and prudence; that discernment which enables a person to judge critically of what is correct and proper; united with caution and primarily regarding one's own conduct."

In other words discretion is being careful to act in a proper way. Again, look before you leap - this time in regard to what other people think of you. There is an old phrase used by many mothers that is oh, so true. "Pretty is as pretty does." That certainly applies here.
The woman who does not show discretion does not care how she acts. She's the one who says "I don't care what people think of me, I'm going to do as I please." Solomon compares her to a ring in a pig's nose. A worthless ornament that is GOING to get dirty. Solomon should know, remember he was Bathsheba's son. Compare this to Ruth 3:11 and you'll know why the virtuous woman's husband is known in the gates - - not on his own merit - - on hers. "Now that's a man with his house in order. His wife is a sweet, modest lady, his children are in submission and obedient, etc." The reverse is also true. The husband of an immoral woman carries a

terrible stigma around with him. That of a fool. Surely a study amongst Christian women would not have to go "there". Or would it? Every day of our lives we hear of not just Christians but preachers who have fallen into immorality. There are churches who do not preach the whole counsel of God and have couples as members of their church who are not married, but are living together. There are teen groups who are not properly supervised and the young people are living immoral lives – sometimes participating in hands-on behavior during youth activities. There are adulterers and adulteresses sitting in prominent places in the church. The immorality in Bible colleges has become so commonplace, that I have seen some of the young people shrug their shoulders at it and comment, "It's to be expected, you will have that wherever you go." The church has become so morally corrupt that the world looks at it with a snicker and a sneer. And the devil hugs himself - because the wicked testimony of the immoral ones overrides those who are trying to live pure lives, as God would have them to be. People are going to hell excusing themselves by pointing at the rotten testimony of the church. So yes, unfortunately we must go there.

Who was Bathsheba? 2 Samuel 11:1-5; 26-27 There have been a hundred arguments about whether or not Bathsheba was guilty in this situation. God judged David very firmly for his sin. It is plain to see that the greatest part of the guilt lay at David's door. He was the king. She could hardly have refused him, could she? Maybe not - but what I see here is that there is no indication that she even tried. She was taking a bath on the roof top. She had to have known that she could be seen from the palace. Simple directional sense - if she had to look up to see the palace windows, then someone looking out the palace windows could see her (showing a lack of prudence, no discretion.) In the dark of the city in order for her to be seen in the night she must have had a light illuminating her. Okay, maybe she was dumb enough not to realize she could be seen. I doubt it. However, notice the wording in verse 4 "he lay with her." This was not rape. In cases of rape the Bible says "he forced her." What did she do when she found she was pregnant? Did she send a message to her husband telling of the horrors of having been forced into this relationship with the king? No, she told David. David was a very handsome man, the king of Israel, wealthy beyond dreams, and a charmer. Bathsheba was lonely. Her husband was at war. She was obviously flattered by the king's attentions, and a willing participant in this adultery. We don't know that we can accuse her of being intentionally immoral, but she certainly was indiscreet and easily enticed.

Let's look at another woman. Genesis 39:1-20 The wickedness of Potiphar's wife is very easy to see. She cast her eyes on the good looking young Hebrew slave and intended to have him. When he rejected her attentions she persisted to the point of it being an obsession with her. Then when finally spurned she responded with malice and hatred. She was lewd, loose and immoral.

Both of these woman could not be trusted with the love of their men. A godly woman will never give her husband cause to doubt her love, any more than she would want her Lord to doubt her love. I have known of women who keep their mates in constant turmoil by wishing to create jealously. I have even known of a few who get their amusement by creating such jealousy in their husband that he is willing to pick a fight over her. A lot of the time they have no intention of following through with immorality - they're just toying with their husband's affections. This is childish and selfish. It's not a funny game, it can ruin a marriage. It is also an ungodly attitude. He must safely trust her love.

So what can we learn from these two "less than ladies?"
Bathsheba was indiscreet. She was either not cautious about uncovering herself where she could be seen, or she did it with design. Most of the time, I believe, a woman who indiscreetly uncovers herself is ignorant of the reaction she gets from the men around her. Some do it by design, but many simply don't fully understand what they are doing to the men around them and the sin that they are involving themselves in. I'm not referring to bathing on the housetop. I'm referring to the way that you dress, or don't dress. We will go more in depth into what God expects in this area in a future lesson but now we'll touch it lightly. You probably are aware by now, and if you are not let me inform you, that a man is sexually stimulated by sight. That is not his "dirty mind" it's the way that God made him. And when God made him that way he was in a perfect environment. When his environment became sinful, God put clothing on them. A woman many times overlooks this, because that is NOT her stimulus. You may appreciate the look of a good looking man but it will not cause the same thought processes in you that the sight of a woman's body does in the men around you. Please don't even begin to give me the cop-out attitude "that's his problem." No, my dear, if you are wearing

revealing clothing, or very little clothing, you may as well be bathing on the rooftop and in God's opinion it's just as much your problem as it is the man's. (Remember that it is God's opinion that counts here - we're seeking godliness. Our opinion of the make-up of male minds is not the issue here, in fact our opinion is not, *at all,* what counts here. What counts is what God expects from us if we are to be virtuous women.) Caution should be taken also in the way you conduct yourself around men. Bathsheba accepted the attentions of a man that was not her husband without resistance or complaint. Proverbs 26:28 says that a flattering mouth worketh ruin. Not only should you, yourself, never be guilty of flattering, you should not stand around and accept it from men you to whom are not married. Flattering and flirting walk hand in hand and neither has a place in a Christian woman's life. Whether you are married or not, if you find yourself around a man who is overboard with his compliments, particularly about your physical appearance, this is a man you need to get away from. As soon as the conversation begins to get too personal, it needs to end. A Christian woman should never be indiscreet enough to participate in fleshly conversation. Dirty jokes and off color comments should be met with cold disapproval. When you are around men who do such things, and they find out that your Christianity is real enough that you do not approve of such behavior, they will not only honor it - they will respect you for it. Even if they don't, you will be honoring your Lord and building the trust of your husband. When you are around men who do such things and they find out that your Christianity is NOT real enough for you to disapprove of such behavior, they will ridicule your faith behind your back, tag you as an easy mark for immoral behavior, mock your husband as a fool, and use you as an excuse to discredit Christ and the church. If you do not make your stand for Christ plain and clear in this respect, do not be shocked if a man makes unwanted advances or suggestions to you. Behave at all times like a Christian lady and you will be amazed at the considerate treatment you will receive. Participate in fleshly conversations and the treatment you will receive will be fleshly.

Young women and girls should be taught to be discreet around young men. Discretion is an almost unheard of thing in our society, even in churches. An unmarried girl should not be "hanging around with the guys." At a church meeting that I attended not long before writing this, I noticed a girl around sixteen or seventeen years old. She was dressed in the style that is typical right now, her clothes appeared to be about two sizes too small. She was following close on the heels of a whole crowd of boys about her age. She was the only girl in the crowd. As I watched, I noticed several things. One was that she was loud, with a high pitched, overdone laugh. Another was that she was constantly slapping at, touching, or leaning over the boys. The other thing that I noticed was the look on the faces of those boys. They were amused by her attentions but behind her back they gave smug, sarcastic looks at one another, quietly ridiculing her lack of discretion. This is a girl headed for trouble and there are many, many more just like her. Girls should be warned that if they present themselves in an indiscreet manner toward boys they will gain an ungodly reputation and never have the respect or real affection of the boys whose attention they are trying to gain. We should also warn our boys and young men about a girl who behaves like this. The Bible gives a stern warning to young men to stay away from such a woman. Proverbs 7:5-23.

We do not know if Bathsheba would have been allowed to refuse the king's invitation to the palace but as we are short on kings around here we know there's not an invitation to any private audience that *we* cannot refuse. Never, ever, allow yourself to be alone with a man to whom you are not married. This is part of the prudence and discretion we are talking about. If you find yourself accidentally alone with a man, calmly and firmly excuse yourself, and leave, or if your leaving is impossible, gently request that he leave. If you will make it a standard in your life to never be alone with a man other than an immediate family member you will not only keep yourself from temptation, you will preserve your testimony.

Abstain from all appearance of evil. 1 Thessalonians 5:22.

Testimony: Your Christian walk - what others see. Is it important? A lot of carnal Christians use the excuse that, "God sees my heart, it doesn't matter what the outside looks like" Wrong, Wrong, Wrong!!

Sanctify yourselves therefore, and be ye holy: for I am the LORD your God. Leviticus 20:7

That he would grant unto us, that we, being delivered out of the hand of our enemies, might serve him without fear, In holiness and righteousness before him all the days of our life. Luke 1:74 -75

Having therefore these promises, dearly beloved, let us cleanse ourselves from all filthiness of the flesh and spirit, perfecting holiness in the fear of God 2 Corinthians 7:1

Because it is written, Be ye holy; for I am holy. 1 Peter 1:16

Seeing then that all these things shall be dissolved, what manner of persons ought ye to be in all holy conversation and godliness.   2 Peter 3:11

What about Potiphar's wife? She was openly immoral. An adulteress. She was the enticer here. Not only should you never accept flattery, you should never be guilty of using it.

The Bible warns a young man: "To deliver thee from the strange woman, even from the stranger which flattereth with her words; Which forsaketh the guide of her youth, and forgetteth the covenant of her God." Proverbs 2:16-17

A lying tongue hateth those that are afflicted by it; and a flattering mouth worketh ruin. Proverbs 26:28

A foolish woman is clamorous: she is simple and knoweth nothing. For she sitteth at the door of her house, on a seat in the high places of the city, To call passengers who go right on their ways: Whoso is simple, let him turn in hither: and as for him that wanteth understanding, she saith to him, Stolen waters are sweet, and bread eaten in secret is pleasant. But he knoweth not that the dead are there; and that her guests are in the depths of hell.
Proverbs 9:13-18

Such is the way of an adulterous woman; she eateth, and wipeth her mouth, and saith, I have done no wickedness. Proverbs 30:20

Flattery is defined this way: To soothe by praise; to gratify self-love by praise or obsequiousness; to please a person by applause or favorable notice by anything that exalts him in his own estimation or confirms his good opinion of himself. (2) To please; to gratify; as, to flatter one's vanity or pride. (3) To praise falsely; to encourage by favorable notice

The world has picked up the phrase "male ego" and used it to death. But it is true that men are easily flattered and a loose woman uses that to his destruction. NEVER should a Christian woman be guilty of flattering a man AT ALL, much less one to whom she is not married. Flattery is dishonest at best and immoral at worst. So - what to avoid. Do not make personal comments about a man's physique. He does not need for you to notice and comment on how strong he is, how well cut his clothes are, etc. If you appreciate his character or wisdom, thank God for it. There's nothing wrong with a well-timed PUBLIC word of appreciation for something done or for a message preached, etc. But earnestly avoid going overboard with praise. If he is skilled with his hands and helpful step back and thank him for his helpfulness sincerely and as simply as possible. Never make any comment to any man that is designed to pump up his ego for your own benefit. It is wicked for a woman to flatter a man (even her own husband) with the motive of getting her way.

Potiphar's wife went out of her way to seek to get Joseph alone. She openly propositioned him, then hated him for rejecting her and decided to destroy him.

For a whore is a deep ditch; and a strange woman is a narrow pit. She also lieth in wait as for a prey, and increaseth the transgressors among men. Proverbs 23:27-28

I cannot stress enough that you will destroy your own testimony and that of the man involved if you seek opportunities to be alone with him. Even if you never commit an immoral act - remember that the devil is very real and loves to spread dirt on the faces of Christians. If you do not carefully guard your testimony he will take advantage of your lack of prudence. A person's testimony is as fragile as fine china. Once broken the scars remain and in a lot of areas make a person useless for the cause of Christ. Don't foolishly toy with your testimony.

If you have no control over your fleshly passions then I would strongly suggest that you carefully and prayerfully consider whether or not you are truly saved. God plants within a saved person's heart a burning desire to please Him. Sometimes we smother that desire with our own selfish wants and sometimes we become frustrated with our weaknesses and throw up our hands and want to quit trying - but the desire is still there. If you will allow the Lord to work in your life He will build that desire into victory.

If, however, there's no desire to please Him, there's probably no salvation.

In summary, we can learn from Bathsheba and Potiphar's wife to:
1 - Show discretion in the way that we dress and to be careful about who we are affecting in the way we present our bodies.
2 - Never allow ourselves to be alone with a man other than a family member.
3 - Never accept the flattery or attentions of a man to whom we are not married.
4. - Guard our own testimony and the trust of our husbands by not flattering other men.

Purity is an indispensable element in godliness. We must keep ourselves pure - unspotted from the world - in order to please the Lord. That's going to take a good measure of prudence and discretion on our parts

Lesson Two Review

1) Write the Scripture memory portion for this lesson

_____

_____

2) Proverbs 19:14 says: "House and riches are the inheritance of fathers: and a _____ wife is from the LORD."

3) Define Prudent _____

_____

4) It takes years of faithfulness to build _____ yet it takes only a few moments of time to _____ the trust of years.

5) List the five areas in the lesson where your husband should be able to trust you:
A)_____
B)_____
C)_____
D)_____
E)_____

6) Proverbs 11:22 says "As a _____ in a _____, so is a fair woman which is without _____ .

7) Define discretion _____

_____

8) Solomon was _____ son.

9) A godly woman will never give her husband cause to

_____ .

10) It is childish and selfish to try to create _____ in your husband.

11) Bathsheba indiscreetly _____. From this we can learn to be careful how we

_____.

12) Bathsheba accepted the _____ of a man that was not her husband without resistance or complaint. We should never be guilty of encouraging the attentions of a man to whom we

_____.

13)_____ and _____walk hand in hand.

14) Dirty jokes and off color comments should be met with

_____

15) Never, ever allow yourself to be _____

_____

16) God expects us to be_____.

17) Not only should you never accept flattery, _____

_____

18) Define Flattery: _____

_____

_____

19) Potiphar's wife was _____. An _____. She was the _____.

20) Do not make personal comments about

_____

21) It is wicked for a woman to flatter a man (even her own husband) with the motive of

_____

22) Don't foolishly _____ with your _____.

23) List 5 things we can learn from Bathsheba and Potiphar's wife:

_____   _____

_____   _____

_____

_____

_____

_____

A Woman Among all Those

Lessons in Christian Womanhood

Lesson 3

Scripture Memory for lesson 3: She will do him good and not evil all the days of her life. Proverbs 31:12

Wives, submit yourselves unto your own husbands, as it is fit in the Lord. Colossians 3:18

In a lesson on Christian womanhood we have to address the subject of Biblical submission. This class is where we tackle the monster. Yes, a thousand times, yes! We are required by God to be in submission. Let's get the history behind it.

Unto the woman he said, I will greatly multiply thy sorrow and thy conception; in sorrow thou shalt bring forth children; and thy desire shall be to thy husband, and he shall rule over thee. Genesis 3:16.

At that point woman was put under the authority of man. If you will look at the passage, you will see that mankind has been trying to wiggle out from under that curse ever since it was established. Man tries to do everything in the world rather than work for his bread. Woman tries to assert herself and take a man's role in everything, and snakes climb trees! But we're still bound by the curse that Adam's sin brought upon us until the Lord comes back.

However, in Christ Jesus, He turns our curse into a blessing. In Ephesians 5:21-33 we are given the picture of the God blessed, God ordained order of the home. We are told that, if done correctly, it is a picture of Christ and the church. Remember as we study that we are speaking of a Christian home here. It becomes an entirely different picture when you are dealing with a woman married to a lost man. A woman is still required to be in submission in that instance, but her situation is vastly different. There are a lot of Scriptures that deal with that area, that we will cover later, but not in this particular class.

Submission is defined: The act of yielding to power or authority; surrender of the person and power to the control or government of another.

The two areas of our lives that will spark rebellion faster than anything else is in the area of clothing, and the area of submission. Why? Both require a giving up of our own identity in order to identify with Christ. It's a matter of surrender. I talked with a young unmarried woman just this past week who said that she did not think that she would have any difficulty with submission to her husband. I responded by telling her she thought so because she had not had to do it yet. Then I asked her how difficult it was for her to submit to her parents' authority. That put it in a different light, because she's had to deal with submission to them in day to day life. We may believe in submission in theory - how much do we believe in it when submitting to our husband crosses our desires?

Our last lesson dealt with purity in the manner of trust.
#1 - We should be able to be trusted with his love.
#2 - We should be able to be trusted with his good name, his convictions.
#3 - We should be able to be trusted with his money and possessions.
#4 - We should be able to be trusted with his home and children.
#5 - We should be able to be trusted with any tasks he sets for us to perform.

Let's take a look at #2. His good name, his convictions. As I said in our last lesson, there have been many, many a man who would have stood for God but his wife dragged him down in the battle. Susanna Wesley was a godly mother of 19 children. She taught them purity and Biblical holiness. John and Charles Wesley, two of her sons, were two of the great preachers of the 1700's. However, John Wesley married a woman (Molly Brown) who hated the gospel and grew to hate him for his stand for Christ. She would show up at meetings and heckle him while he preached. She publicly accused him, falsely, of being unfaithful, a drunkard and other sins in an effort to smear his reputation and cause him to fail as a preacher.

I know, personally, of a young man who God called to preach while he was still a teenager. In his 20's he became so desperate for a wife (just any wife) that he attached himself to a young girl who was looking for a ticket away from the "oppressions" of home. He married her when he was

27 and she was 17. Shortly after their marriage, she began to find fault with the church they were in and eventually dragged him out of the church. Grieved and wanting to do right he found another church, only to have the same thing repeated. Over and over again he would begin to get right with God and she would dislike the change and drag him down and out. She declared she "would not be married to a preacher." He was afraid of losing her so he turned his back on his call - and lost her anyway. She left him for another man. I wish I could tell you that he got right and went on to live for God after that, but the truth is that he instead began to look at another woman, this time a lost one - and God had enough of his rebellion and took him home.

I know of another young man who lost his wife in a tragic car accident while he was on deputation. He had two young sons, was lonely and felt he needed a wife to go with him to the mission field. He found one - the wrong one. She married him, went to the mission field with him and within a year couldn't stand it and pulled the whole family off the field.

Another older man of my acquaintance lost his wife of many years to cancer. Within a year he married again. This woman claimed to be all that he was looking for. As soon as the ring was on her finger, she began to boss the house and change everything about him. This was a dedicated man, one who believed in separation and holiness, but this new wife would be seen in public immodestly dressed, with vulgar language and behavior. He became so ashamed of her that he withdrew from all of his former friends and dropped out of the ministry to which God had called him. She eventually took everything he had and left him. Praise God, the last I heard, he was picking up the pieces and going on for God.

These are true horror stories of failures in God's service, I could go on and on. I know of many women who run the home and husband and dictate if, when and where they go to church (these usually also try to run the preacher and the church.) These scenes are repeated every day by women who will not dedicate themselves, first of all to God then to their home and family. These are women who will not, in obedience to God, submit themselves to their husbands.

If God works in a man's life and calls him to a work or a ministry, a woman's job is to follow. If He does not call to a specific service, her job is still to be in obedience and to support him as he labors in his local church. It is the man's responsibility to make major decisions in the home.

A woman's job is clearly outlined in Titus 2:4-5 and in 1 Timothy 5:14 and in Colossians 3:18.

In this lesson we are going to make a comparison of two unnamed women in the Bible. God does not give us either of their names or much about them at all. We must glean what we know about them from their circumstances and the outcome of their lives. We need to read quite a bit of Scripture to even get a small amount of information about them but what we glean will be worth it. Genesis 6:8 - 7:7; 8:15-22; 13:8-13; 19:1-26; 2 Peter 2:5-8, Luke 17:26-32.

The first one that we will look at is Noah's wife. Noah's wife was never mentioned by name but her influence is plain to see. Sometimes the position to which God calls you may mean that you will be an obscure "support person" – it is a blessed calling. Noah found grace in the eyes of the Lord. Suppose his wife had been another Eve? Or Job's wife? The natural tendency of woman is NOTICE ME!!! We hate to be overlooked. Even those who are shy like to be noticed. Sometimes it might be you who does all the work or has the plans and implements them, only for someone else to get the credit. Are you willing to take a back seat - even to the point where no one knows your name? (Oh, that preacher's wife, what's her name? My, that missionary has done a great work! - Is he married? I don't know, I guess he's got a wife around there somewhere.) That preacher's wife or that missionary's wife may carry twice the load of any woman you know and she's got the preacher to live with, too. What of those who are not called to such a service? That Bro. _____ is such a giving man. That Bro. _____ gives so much and does so much for the church - what of the Mrs.? Are you willing to be that Mrs.? Or do you have to have recognition and a front row seat for everything you do?

So what did Noah's wife do? All we know about her is that: #1 she was his only wife in a day of polygamy. This may have been simply Noah's righteousness, but probably not. Under most (not all) circumstances the physical purity of a man is in his wife's safe keeping. Proverbs 31:11. If you seek to meet his needs, a godly man (and even most lost men) will not turn elsewhere. 1 Corinthians 7:1-5. The comment has been made "When a man has a Cadillac in the garage, he's not going to steal a Volkswagen." This is not just true in personal matters, but also in pleasantness. Many a man has been unfaithful to his wife, not because of sexual need, but because of the need for a pleasant companion. Most men are funny creatures. They love to debate, argue and wrestle with each other, but distractedly hate to argue with a woman.

It is better to dwell in a corner of the housetop, than with a brawling woman in a wide house. Proverbs 21:9 (this is repeated almost in the same exact words in Proverbs 25:24)

It is better to dwell in the wilderness, than with a contentious and an angry woman. Proverbs 21:19

So what do you do if you have one of those rarities, a husband who does love to argue and picks fights?

Not rendering evil for evil, or railing for railing: but contrariwise blessing; knowing that ye are thereunto called, that ye should inherit a blessing. 1 Peter 3:9

We are told not to render railing for railing, we are not to fight back - ouch! This is a part of studying to be quiet.

Only by pride cometh contention: but with the well advised is wisdom. Proverbs 13:10

If pride is the only source of contention, and pride is a sin, then contention is the result of sin in the life of one or both individuals who cannot get along. A woman sets the mood in her home. Your attitudes will reflect in the attitudes of your husband and children. If you have a cheerful, pleasant attitude, your family will in almost every instance "catch it" from you. If you have a gloomy, depressed attitude they will catch that too! If you wake up looking for a fight, you'll probably get one before the day is over.

In cleanliness and comfort. Make his home as comfortable as possible. He should feel like a king when he walks through the door. He should know securely that he is the most important person in your life and you should seek to keep him as such in the eyes of your children. More than one godly man has given the testimony of being able to step away from the snare of unfaithfulness by God renewing a vision in his mind of his wife at the door and his children running to greet him. This is a scene that is nearly extinct in our age and to a great deal mocked by modern women.

How do we apply this practically? Seek to please him. Learn what he likes to eat and fix it the way he likes - not to please yourself or because this is the way Mom always made it. Arrange things to please him. This might mean sometimes leaving things where you don't want them. Keep your home clean and free from unwanted clutter, but don't keep it sterile and untouchable (unless he likes it that way.) Talk to your children about him positively. Seek his opinion. Follow his orders. Let your children know 'this is daddy's ruling and we're going to follow it - cheerfully.' Get involved in the things he does and likes to do. Be a companion. Learn his likes and dislikes. Big order? Yes, and practice makes perfect. Remember that God's primary job for you is to be a completion of this man's life. So study him, learn him, and work on it day by day.

#2 She lived in an age of horrible wickedness and lived with a preacher of righteousness. Could she have ignored him and have followed the world around her? Without a doubt - everyone else was doing as they pleased and so can we in this present evil world.

For the time past of our life may suffice us to have wrought the will of the Gentiles, when we walked in lasciviousness, lusts, excess of wine, revellings, banquetings, and abominable idolatries: Wherein they think it strange that ye run not with them to the same excess of riot, speaking evil of you: 1 Peter 4:3-4

Do you have what it takes to stand? I cannot tell you the ridicule I have received and other ladies that I know have received because of the stand for submission. Noah's wife surely had some things to put up with. She was the wife and mother of the only men on the face of the earth who were standing for God. Her relatives, perhaps her own parents or sisters and brothers, her neighbors - all of them thought Noah was crazy. They surely thought that Noah's wife was crazy right along with him. A woman who did not love and believe God herself would have left him to build that crazy boat by himself. It had to have meant some self-denial and hard work for her, as well as enduring constant ridicule. Yet, she got on that ark.

You may have to toil at seemingly endless, backbreaking and thankless labor. You may have to take some ridicule. Noah had NO converts except his family. I recently found out that one of my close relatives was witnessed to by someone that I know. When she responded in anger, our names were brought up in the conversation. Her reply was, "The whole family knows about them, they are brainwashed, and just crazy." Are you willing to take your place on the ark? They'll think you are a weirdo. "You don't work? You believe in submission? (They say it like it's a dirty word.) You want children? Home School? Of all things!! What do you mean? You are an intelligent human being! Stand up for your rights!!"

#3 She had 3 sons (married to one wife each.) She and Noah must have had a great influence on their children. They stayed home and helped daddy build that ark instead of joining the crowd. How important is it that you submit to your husband? Only as important as the lives of your children. It is very difficult for a child to submit to authority when they have a mother who will not submit to her husband. A child reared by a rebellious mother will, themselves, almost without fail challenge authority all of their lives.

#4 She received the victory - safety! A new world! A promise from God! – **and we still don't know her name.**

Now - Lot's wife. We don't know her name either but her character shouts glaringly. How in the world did Lot go from living securely as the nephew-pet of the friend of God to dwelling as a political figure in Sodom? We don't know that it was his wife's influence that got him there but we do know that she did not want to leave. Perhaps it was the love of possessions that made her turn back or perhaps it was the children she was leaving behind. But, her turning back was in direct rebellious disobedience to the command the angels gave her in Genesis 19:17. We're told to remember her. What was Jesus warning about when he said "Remember Lot's wife?" Look at Luke 17:26-32. When the judgment comes upon the world, don't consider any of your possessions -- obey God. We have a very longsuffering and gentle God who is absolutely no nonsense. Her judgment was swift and without remedy. Proverbs 29:1. So what do we know about her, and what can she teach us?

She was the only wife of a man who lived in the wickedest of all cities. He tried to live righteously among them. Perhaps she supported him, perhaps she didn't - we don't know - but look at her children. At least two daughters who were married to men in Sodom who laughed at the coming judgment and two daughters who lived at home with horribly wicked minds and hearts. The Bible says that Lot was a righteous man, vexing himself with the evil surroundings of Sodom. It never mentions that his wife was righteous. It is possible to raise lost children in a Christian home. However, the fact that all of her children were lost and that she herself hesitated to leave, even to the point of having to be dragged from the house by the hand, then looked back in a sinful reluctance to leave what was behind gives a clear reflection of her as a wife and mother. Her mind was on her possessions. I do not believe that I am too far off base in assuming that Lot would not have been living in Sodom, vexed, if his wife were not a factor.

What was there about Sodom for her to love?

#1 Prestige - Her husband sat in the gate. He was one of the political figures in Sodom. He had 'standing' in the community. Many women sacrifice their children on the altar of a love for the limelight. **Shame** on a mother who will enter her impressionable young daughter in a beauty or talent contest or set her on a stage dressed like a harlot for perverted men to gawk at and imagine evil toward. All because she has a desire for fame. **Shame** on a mother who will convince her husband to live in a wicked place when she has the opportunity to raise her children in a quiet peaceful community because she has a desire for the fast lane. A mother who does that is a Lot's wife, sacrificing her children on the altar of her fleshly desires.

#2 Wealth - Lot started out as a sheep herder. He had plenty, but now he was wealthy. Would you disobey the commandment of God to follow your husband - reluctant to go where He commands and look back on 'things,' because you might have to leave some earthly possessions behind?

#3 Family - This is a hard one and it is a whole lot easier to say than it is to do. If family will not follow you away from the path of destruction, they have to be left behind. If family must be left behind to follow your husband to God's field of service, then go and don't look back. Imagine what (or who) Noah's wife left behind when she got on the ark. And God shut the door. There was no opening it. There were no last minute conversions, no last chances. You cannot refuse to follow the will of God because your family will not follow as well. Luke 9:59-62; Matthew 10:37

So what do we learn here? Looking back at Ephesians 5:22 and Colossians 3:18 we see several things that we need to take note of. The first is that a wife is to submit to her OWN husband. This phrase is listed in two separate Scriptures exactly the same way. Any time God repeats Himself in exactly the same words it is something to sit up and take notice of. Your husband, not your boss, your father - etc. Your husband is your authority. No other man - except your pastor - and he is required go through your husband - is your authority. This avoids any conflict of interest and any confusion. If you have ever worked a job where there were several bosses, all of which had different ideas of how the job was to be done, you know the problem that arises from having more than one authority.

The next thing to note is that the wife is to SUBMIT HERSELF. This is the most overlooked part of this scripture - by men and women alike. The typical picture in our minds is of the huge gorilla type husband beating the poor little dear into shape, or else. This is NOT, repeat NOT, what the Bible says. We do not have the dubious pleasure of being martyred in such a fashion. Just as Salvation is of your free will, just as service to Christ is of your free will, this is another item you must choose to do on your own. It is not your husband's job to place you under submission. (He couldn't really do it, even if he tried. He might cause the outside to submit - but submission is not real if it does not come from the heart.) It is your job to submit yourself. You must be in voluntary obedience if you would be right with God.

Next, notice that this submission is 'as unto the Lord.' You must submit yourself to your husband as if he held the same position of authority over you that the Lord does. Your submission to your husband is in direct correlation to your submission to God. An un-submissive wife is not right with God. No excuses, no ifs, ands or buts - she's simply not right. Also note that Colossians says "as it is fit in the Lord." You must not only submit to be godly, you must also submit in a godly manner. It is not enough to simply do what your husband says to do, you must do so in a manner that is pleasing to him and to the Lord. A sour attitude is not real submission, no matter how closely you follow the "letter of the law." Unwilling obedience is still only half surrender.

There are some serious results to un-submissive behavior - a home out of order, children raised in a rebellious atmosphere, a rocky unhappy marriage relationship and most serious of all, Titus 2:5 says that if we are not obedient to our husbands we could cause the Word of God to be blasphemed.

No one - absolutely no one - can force you into submission to your husband. It is your responsibility and your **privilege** to place yourself in the position of submission. Is it easy? NO! It will take prayer, putting down the flesh, repenting, and practice. Then you will have to repeat those steps over and over again. Is it worth it? A thousand times, YES! What a blessed relationship you can have, both with your husband and with the Lord, when you seek to be in submission to the will of God and to your husband.

Lesson Two Review

1) Write this lesson's Scripture memory portion:

_____

_____

_____

2) #2 in our list says that we should be able to be trusted with

_____

3) Define Submission:

_____

_____

3) If God calls a man to the ministry the job of his wife is to
_____. If he is not called to a specific service, her job is
to be in _____ and to _____ him as he
labors in his local church.

4) Noah's wife was never _____ but her
_____ was plain to
see.

5) You may be called to be an "obscure _____ it is a
blessed calling.

6) List 4 things that we know about Noah's wife.

_____

_____

_____

_____

7) Seek to meet your husband's needs in_____ in
_____ and in _____.

8) A child reared by a rebellious mother will usually _____
authority all his life.

9) Lot and his wife had _____ daughters who married men who

_____ at the coming judgment and _____ daughters at home with wicked, corrupted minds and hearts.

10) List 3 things that Lot's wife may have set her affections on that caused her rebellion.

_____

_____

_____ _____

11) A wife is to submit to her _____ husband.

12) A wife is to submit _____.

13) This submission is as unto _____.

14) Unwilling obedience is only _____.

15) No one can _____ you into submission.

16) Submission will take repeating these steps over and over in your life._____, _____, _____ and
_____. But the result is very much worth the effort.

A Woman Among all Those
Lessons in Christian Womanhood

Lesson 4

Scripture Memory for Lesson 4: She seeketh wool and flax, and worketh willingly with her hands. She is like the merchants' ships, she bringeth her food from afar. She riseth also while it is yet night and giveth meat to her household, and a portion to her maidens. Proverbs 31:13-15

Every wise woman buildeth her house: but the foolish plucketh it down with her hands. Proverbs 14:1

We have three "W's" to look at in this lesson: Work, Willingly, and Wisely. In our list of "trusts" we mentioned that we should be able to be trusted with the home and children. Let's look at some areas of responsibility where we should work willingly with our hands, and wisely build our house.

In all labor there is profit: but the talk of the lips tendeth only to penury. Proverbs 14:23

Penury means: want of property, indigence; extreme poverty.

Work has somehow become a dirty word in our society. We sometimes spend more effort getting out of work than we would spend to just go ahead and get the job done. The truth is this: good old fashioned hard work honors God.

An example of a woman who was not afraid to work is Tabitha (also called Dorcas.) She was full of good works and almsdeeds - she sewed for others. Acts 9:36-41

In Genesis 24:15-28 Rebekah is an example of a woman who was not afraid to work willingly. She hasted to let down her pitcher, she hasted to empty it into the trough, she ran to the well. She willingly drew gallons and gallons of water for those camels. (According to Wikipedia one camel is capable of drinking 26 gallons of water!) Why was she willing to do this? She had been taught all of her life that God is pleased when we meet the needs of the weary traveler. Not only is God honored when we work, everything that we do for God should be done with the right attitude.

And whatsoever ye do in word or deed do all in the name of the Lord Jesus, giving thanks to God and the Father by him.   Colossians 3:17
And whatsoever ye do, do it heartily as unto the Lord and not unto men. Colossians 3:23

There is the issue. What we do is not for ourselves, not even primarily for our families, it is our service to our King. If we will take the attitude that the work with which He has entrusted us is His royal command and fulfill it as such, then we will have a much better attitude about the work we are required to do. We'll work willingly.

The best of examples in the Word of God of a wisely working woman is our Proverbs 31 lady. Let's take a look through the passage and see the things that made her diligent and wise.

#1 In verse 13 - She seeketh wool and flax, and worketh willingly with her hands. This lady is out looking for raw materials for her labor. We live in a society that has instant everything. We have instant potatoes, instant pudding, instant this and instant that. We can even microwave minute rice! If you (and, more importantly, your husband) like instant foods and you can afford them, go ahead. However, remember that instant foods do not taste as good as food prepared naturally, have about half the nutritional value of natural foods, are full of additives and preservatives that are slowly killing off our society and they cost more for less quantity than preparing food from scratch. A wise woman will put some effort into old-fashioned homemaking. I have never met a man who really wanted a modern bride. There may be one around but I've never met him. I have met many men who brag about the old-fashioned abilities of a wife who can cook from scratch, sew and keep a home comfortable.

Notice in the same verse that she is not pushing the task off on someone else. She is not only carrying out her responsibilities, she's doing it willingly. She's not afraid to dirty her hands. She doesn't think she's too good for manual labor yet if you look further in the passage you can see that she's not poor - she has servants. But she's still willing to work. This is not a lazy woman. Laziness is a sin. There's no way to sugar coat it. There's no way to get around it. The Bible never has a bad thing to say about good, old fashioned work. It does have plenty to say about laziness and slothfulness, and none of it is good.

By much slothfulness the building decayeth; and through idleness of the hands the house droppeth through. Ecclesiastes 10:18

Slothfulness is defined as: The indulgence of sloth; inactivity; the habit of idleness; laziness.

Slothfulness casteth into a deep sleep; and an idle soul shall suffer hunger. Proverbs 19:15

The opposite of slothfulness is diligence.

Diligence is defined as: Steady application in business of any kind; constant effort to accomplish what is undertaken; exertion of body or mind without unnecessary delay or sloth;

(In other words, diligence is doing the job with a faithful attitude, without having to be prodded, and without putting it off.) A simple truth to remember is: Do not expect God to bless laziness. He will not.

The soul of the sluggard desireth and hath nothing, but the soul of the diligent shall be made fat. Proverbs 13:4

(I always get the picture here of a person who will not work and spends their time dreaming of winning the lottery.)

For even when we were with you, this we commanded you, that if any would not work, neither should he eat. 2 Thessalonians 3:10

In fact there are so many Scriptures about this subject that we do not have time nor space here to cover them all. The Bible says that a man who will not work does not deserve to eat. By the same token, a woman who will not work in the home and for her home will have a chaotic household. Proverbs 24:30-34 gives us the picture of the lazy man's field and vineyard. The picture is clear - if you want to have good things you must work for them - not sit around and wish for them. We have a tendency in this country to equate poverty and dirt, and think that the two go hand in hand. This is not true! I have been in nice suburban brick homes that from the outside would give you the ideal of middle class perfection, but on the inside resembled a garbage dump. I'm not referring to that "lived in look" that comes with having a family. I'm referring to piles of sour laundry strewn on the floors, dishes from days past overflowing the sink with flies and roaches everywhere, dirty babies who haven't been changed or bathed in days. Yet from all appearance the family has the ability to do much better. I have also seen a cinder block "hovel" in Mexico that from the outside would spark pity to the coldest heart but inside was clean, polished, and decorated with the obvious love of the woman of the house shining from every little corner. Four walls do not make a home. The love and care contained within those four walls is what makes the home. A dear little godly lady in Florida recently gave a young friend a one sentence piece of advice that says more than a whole page - "attitude is everything."

What am I saying? Do not excuse laziness by thinking that if you had more money you could do better. Take what you have and do the very best that you can. Early in my marriage I adopted a phrase that my children heard so many times that they laugh about it now. "We're going to do the best we can with what we've got." That little motto has seen me through a lot of difficulties - among which were a fire and two hurricanes.

I will never forget a lesson my mother taught me early in my marriage. I was despairing of the effort of decorating the little place I was about to move into and she laughed. Now, I don't care much for being laughed at when I whine, so it took me a few moments to care enough about the reason for her laughter to ask why. But when I finally did, she told me that after WWII housing was very scarce. She, being a young military bride, was not able to get base housing. After searching for quite a while, they realized that the only housing they would be able to get was from a man who had converted old chicken coops into apartments. The ceiling was so low that my father could not stand up straight. The rooms were so small that they had to leave most of their things in storage. However, the comment she made was this: "You'd be amazed at how cute you can fix up a chicken coop with a little love and ingenuity." Her message rang loud and clear - you don't have to have a lot of things to have a home.

There is a novel that compares the attitudes of two oriental women who lived near one another. Both had an earthen pot that was cracked. One of the women cast the pot into the trash heap and nagged her husband for another, even though she knew he could ill afford such a thing. The other took her cracked pot and mixed a little clay and water - patched the crack and set the pot in her oven to dry. She did the very best she could with the materials she had on hand instead of constantly whining about what she did not have.

In our last lesson we mentioned that your attitude will set the attitude for the home. This is true in the matter of care for the physical things within the house as well. If you do not care about your home, your family will not care either. That does not mean that if you do care, they will automatically pick up after themselves and put the dishes in the sink - but they will be more careful if they see that it is important to you. If, on the other hand, you vocalize how much you hate to clean house and how much you dislike this about your home or that about your home, you are sowing discontentment and you will reap an uncaring attitude in your family. There are a couple of things that will greatly discourage a husband. These are working all day for a woman who lays around eating the bread of idleness, prattling her time away on the telephone, playing video games or soaking in soap (operas) while the house falls down around their ears. She then throws a frozen pizza in the oven when he comes home. Another would be working for one who continuously complains about what she does not have (making him feel as if he were not measuring up as a man.) It will be very difficult for a man who has a woman like this to continue to be faithful in his work - what's he working for?

Let your conversation be without covetousness; and be content with such things as ye have: for he hath said, I will never leave thee, nor forsake thee. Hebrews 13:5

Not that I speak in respect of want: for I have learned, in whatsoever state I am, therewith to be content. Philippians 4:11

But godliness with contentment is great gain. For we brought nothing into this world, and it is certain we can carry nothing out. And having food and raiment let us be therewith content.
1 Timothy 6:6-8

Do all things without murmurings and disputings: Philippians 2:14

#2 – Verse 14 says: She is like the merchant's ships. She bringeth her food from afar. I never look at this verse without thinking of my own mother. My mother began every spring to watch the fields on the roadside. As soon as she saw ripe berries she gathered us kids and a sack lunch and headed out. We picked blackberries, blueberries, plums and peaches which she made into jams and jellies or froze for pies and toppings. Then as soon as the vegetables became ripe she headed with us for the fields to u-pick or glean. She gathered every fresh vegetable she could get her hands on and canned or froze them. She always shopped for bargains on meats and purchased them in quantity whenever she could for better prices. Then she worked for hours dividing and packaging them up to freeze in the right portion sizes for our family. She always made homemade cookies, cakes and pies, sometimes freezing these as well. We lived on the coast and she made her way to the docks to purchase her seafood fresh from the boats or sometimes caught it herself. What am I trying to say? She brought her food from afar. She put a great deal of effort into feeding her family with the very best that she could afford in money, in time and in energy. She did not simply go to the store and throw minute steaks and canned peas on the stove. You may not have fields and docks at your disposal and you may not need to go to the lengths that my mother did to do the best for your family. But you can, in effect, do the same thing. You can do the best you can with what you've got. You can give your family the best you can afford in money, in time and in energy. You CAN look for the best value for your money, you can learn to cook some things the old fashioned way to give your family the benefit of the nutrition and flavor of food that has not been processed to death. You can also use some wisdom and planning in your dealings with food.

#3 She riseth also while it is yet night and giveth meat to her household and a portion to her maidens. I have a whole list of Scriptures here that refer to slothfulness. Please take the time now to look them up.

Proverbs 6:6-11; 10:26; 13:4; 18:9; 19:15 & 24; 21:25; 22:13; 24:30-34; 26:14-16; Romans 12:11

Unnecessary poverty, decay, waste, bad testimony and ungodliness are direct results of laziness. There are those who are natural sleepyheads and as much as our flesh would like to be excused here, I can't find a single Scripture that says it's okay to lay abed when there is work to be done. The only comfort I have to offer a sleepyhead here is that practice makes perfect. You have to condition yourself by constantly crucifying the flesh and just doing it. After a while, it really does become easier to do. It is a proven fact that, unless there is another medical reason for it (and there are some legitimate medical reasons) the more sleep a person gets, the more they want. It is the deceitfulness of the flesh that does this. Left on its own this flesh will develop self-destructing habits left and right and this is one of them. I have known people who sleep almost around the clock - excusing their laziness with all kinds of ailments, medical or emotional, when the truth of the matter is they don't have enough control over their flesh to train it to stay awake and work.

Notice that she rose while it was yet night, her reason was to feed her family. There are two things that should be noted here. The first is that if your family needs breakfast in the morning before work or school, you should be willing to provide it. If your husband wants a "real" breakfast you should not let your desire to sleep-in interfere with him getting it. I've heard rebellious wives say, "I'm not getting up to fix breakfast for him, his arms aren't broken - or - he can eat cereal or buy himself something to eat." For many years my husband didn't want breakfast in the morning. Now things have changed and because of his health he has to eat breakfast. If your husband is okay with a bowl of cereal in the morning or a muffin, don't feel like you have to serve him biscuits and eggs. It's your family, you must meet their needs in the way that is best for them. However, if you are denying them so that you can sleep, you are not in line with the Scripture.

The second thing to note is that we see again that the maintenance of the household is the woman's responsibility. She's seeing to the welfare of the household. It is never once mentioned in the Bible that a man took care of the household. His responsibility from the beginning was to provide for his family by his labor. The woman's job has been to keep the home. Any time that a man and wife step out of this role for another, it creates a stressful situation on the home life. This does not mean, at all, that if your husband chooses to be helpful that your home is out of order. Praise God for his understanding heart and willing hands! (And be willing, in return, to lend a hand when he needs one with his duties.) It does mean that you should never make the mistake of feeling that the care of the home is in any way your husband's responsibility. Biblically, it's yours.

That they may teach the young women to be sober, to love their husbands, to love their children, to be discreet, chaste, keepers at home, good, obedient to their own husbands, that the word of God be not blasphemed. Titus 2:4-5

In our last lesson we saw that a woman who is not in submission to her husband could cause the Word of God to be blasphemed. This time, notice that it can also be caused by not being a keeper at home.

Webster's 1828 defines a "keeper" as one who has the care, custody or superintendence of any thing. Such as a gate-keeper, a lighthouse keeper, a grounds keeper.

Many times this passage is used to say that a woman, basically, should not be allowed out of the house. (She should be barefoot, pregnant, and in the kitchen.) It doesn't refer to staying in the home, but rather keeping the home. Maintaining it, caring for it. Now, granted, a woman who is never home cannot keep it very well. There is a Scriptural precedent for spending your time there, minding your business. Referring back to the woman in Proverbs 7:11 it says that the ungodly woman is "loud and stubborn, her feet abide not in her house." There is a balance in everything that is godly and this is no exception. It is out of balance on one side to say a woman should be under lock and key, yet out of balance on the other side for a woman to feel free to roam and ignore her home and responsibilities.

What about holding down a job? I see nowhere in Scripture that God designed for a woman to work outside the home. Before you throw things at me, listen carefully - we're interested in God's opinion, right? Women in the workforce has been one of the great downfalls of our nation. Not only has it made a political mess out of our nation in the matter of equal rights but it has made a mess out of our homes. Sometimes our society and the pressures it puts upon us have made it necessary for a woman to work. It is still an unfortunate situation and causes things to be stressful at home. It is between you and your husband if you must step into that role (submission to your OWN husband.) Many, many times it can be avoided, even when people don't think so. It's a matter of priorities. Is it more important for you to live in a fancy, high dollar home and have a wardrobe of new clothes than for you to live according to the mandates of God's Word? Or would a lower-income home and shopping at the thrift store be worth the sacrifice for the blessing of God on your home? This is magnified if there are children in the home. I would beg a woman with young children not to work if there is any way at all that she can get out of it.

The rod and reproof give wisdom: but a child left to himself bringeth his mother to shame. Proverbs 29:15

Notice that it doesn't say that it brings his father to shame, but his mother. Why? Because it is his mother that is supposed to be at home with him. Very few mothers stay at home any more. Many times women are driven into the work force by the love of money, the lust after the things of the world or sometimes just out of envy. She makes the choice to work because she feels that the man has the preferred position. He's not stuck at home with the pots and pans and diapers. The life of a housewife is not glamorous at best and is often the most unrewarded, unappreciated office in the world. If you cannot be contented in this role, ask God to make you contented. Then try to take pleasure in the job that you do. He can and will work a miracle in your heart and make you contented in the sphere He planned for you, if you really want Him to.

Notice also that this woman had servants - "And a portion to her maidens." She was obviously wealthy. Yet she did not lay around and play 'queen of the roost' and let them do all the work. She was keeping her home. Dealing fairly and righteously with her family and her servants. And wisely working, willingly with her hands. Can you submit to God to work? To avoid laziness, and sloth? To work willingly, not putting your work off on others but taking your responsibility, "as to the Lord?" To work wisely? To put some time, effort, attention and godly attitude into your labor?

Lesson Four Review

1) Write the Scripture memory portion for this lesson:

_____

_____

_____

_____

2) The three W's in the lesson are _____,
_____, and _____.

3) Our three ladies in this lesson are: _____, who was full of
almsdeeds _____, who worked willingly, and our
_____, who worked wisely.

4) Another name for Tabitha was _____.

5) One camel is capable of drinking _____ of
water.

6) Everything that we do for God should be done with the right
_____.

7) What we do is not for ourselves, or even primarily for our families it is
_____

8) The first thing that showed the wisdom of the Proverbs 31 lady is that
she was looking for _____ for her
labor.

9) List 3 things about instant foods: _____

_____

_____

10) This was not a _____ woman.

11) Laziness is a _____.

51

12) Define Slothfulness

_____

_____

_____

13) Define Diligence

_____

_____

14) A man who does not work does not deserve to _____ by the same token a woman who will not work will have a

_____.

15) _____ and _____ do not necessarily go hand in hand.

16) Attitude is _____.

17) If you do not care about your home

_____.

18) If you complain about your home and housework you will sow _____ and reap _____

19) You can do the best you can with what you've got - give your family the best that you can in _____ in _____ and _____.

20) _____, _____, _____, _____, and _____ are direct results of laziness.

21) The more _____ a person gets the more they _____.

22) It is never mentioned in the Bible that a man took care of the _____.

23) Not only can the word of God be blasphemed by a woman who is not in submission to her husband, but by one who will not be

_____

_____

24) Define "keeper"

_____

_____

25) Why does the Scripture say "a child left to himself bringeth his mother to shame?

_____ _____

26) Many times women are driven into the work force by
_____, _____, or
_____.

27) God can work a _____ in our hearts and make us _____ to be _____ in the role He has designed for us if we _____ want Him to.

A Woman Among all Those
Lessons in Christian Womanhood

Lesson 5

Scripture Memory for this lesson: She considereth a field, and buyeth it: with the fruit of her hands she planteth a vineyard. She perceiveth that her merchandise is good, her candle goeth not out by night. Proverbs 31:16&18

And being in Bethany in the house of Simon the Leper, as he sat at meat, there came a woman having an alabaster box of ointment of spikenard very precious; and she brake the box, and poured it on his head. Mark 14:3

In this lesson we're going to touch on material possessions and how to use them. Notice in our list of trusts we see that we should be able to be trusted with our husband's money and possessions. In our memory passage for this week we see two things. First - she considereth a field and buyeth it. Obviously, it is not a bad thing in God's sight for this woman to be making a major financial decision. That statement would probably get me stoned in some circles but before I'm hooted down, show me otherwise from the Scripture. God called her virtuous - above all others and He praised her for making this purchase. I am sure, all things being in balance, that her husband was very aware of what she was doing and in approval. But he trusted her judgment. SHE considered the field. And SHE bought it. A wise man will know that if his wife has business sense and abilities it does not harm his manhood or his position as leader in the home to make use of those abilities for the good of the household.

Notice what she did with this field. With the fruit of HER hands she planteth a vineyard. Not with the labor of her hands, her servants more than likely did the digging - with the FRUIT of her hands. The fruit of something in the Word of God is the results of it, the outcome of it. So she did so with the results or outcome of her hands. In other words, she was using money for which she had labored to finance the planting of this vineyard. Looking farther in the passage we will see what she did to earn money. But she used her wisdom, prudence and discretion to choose the field, and then her money to make something out of the field that would benefit not just herself but her whole family. Once again we are seeing that she was not selfish with her possessions. She, with planning and care, was doing the best she could with what she had for the good of her entire family. What did she have? Financial wisdom that she could use for the betterment of her family and money at her disposal to finish the project once she started it.

The next thing we see is: She perceiveth that her merchandise is good, her candle goeth not out by night. She was wise in her purchases. She made sure that the things that she bought for her family were of the best quality she could afford. She bought things that endured and lasted.

Don't make the mistake of thinking that price means quality. Sometimes it does but sometimes the only thing a high price means is popularity. Brand names are not always the best bargains. Sometimes they are, because some brand name items are of more enduring quality. Sometimes they are just a name. Seek to be wise in your purchases. Perceive that your merchandise is good. Pray about what you buy. Let the Lord lead you, especially in major purchases. (And ladies, never make a major purchase without consulting your husband and without his approval. It is wrong to take the household finances and spend until you are in debt on things that you could very well do without. It is wrong for a woman to run up credit card bills that they expect their husbands to work to pay off. It is wrong to demand "the best of everything, the fanciest of everything, and the most of everything." And also wrong to then criticize and find fault with a man who can't provide those things for you. It is wrong to spend until your household is so financially strapped that you have no choice but step out into the work world at the expense of your home and children.)

Once, when my children were small, I had all 5 of them in the car which decided to break down on me about a mile from our destination (This was in an age before cell phones - I know, I know, I'm a dinosaur!) My oldest daughter, at the time about 9 years old, looked at me in a panic and said, "Mama, what are we going to do now?" I responded, like I always did to that question, with: "We're going to do the best we can with what we've got." She looked at me, with a child's honest simplicity and said, "What have we got?" I told her, "Feet - let's walk."

My question to you tonight is: "What have you got?" I want you to take 3 or 4 minutes and write down anywhere between 3 and 5 things that you have in the way of material possessions - and tell how you feel they are being used now or could best be used for the glory of God. Then we'll look at some women who used their possessions for wise or foolish things and we'll see what we can learn from them.

Joshua 15:16-19 Caleb's daughter desired of her father a field with water – The field was her inheritance according to the ruling of the Lord in the matter of the daughters of Zelophehad in Numbers 27:1-11 and 36:1-12. Both they and she were concerned that they use their inheritance for the best profit of their families. When Caleb's daughter realized that the land he had given her did not have springs of water she knew that it would not be a profitable land for raising herds and flocks. So she, in the interest of the income of her family went back to her father and asked him to add some land that had water. She could have shrugged it off as her husband's responsibility and expected him to dig wells - but she sought what was best, not just for herself, but for her family. What did she have? An inheritance.

Do you have possessions of your own aside from things you and your husband have obtained together? Are you willing to use what you have for your family -or do you in selfishness consider, "this is mine."

Let nothing be done through strife or vainglory; but in lowliness of mind let each esteem other better than themselves. Look not every man on his own things, but every man also on the things of others. Philippians 2:3-4

Withhold not good from them to whom it is due, when it is in the power of thine hand to do it. Say not unto thy neighbour, Go, and come again, and tomorrow I will give; when thou hast it by thee. Proverbs 3:27-28

If God commands that we do good to others in our possessions outside our home, why should we think the command is not in effect inside our homes? Yet there are so many who do! I could not count you the women I have known that take the attitude "what's yours is mine, and what's mine is mine."

Selfishness in a home dishonors God, and does nothing to promote unity. If you treat your husband and your children with selfishness they will respond in the same way. It never ceases to amaze me, even though it is becoming more and more prevalent, to see families where "he has his possessions and she has hers – and he does his thing and she does hers." It's hard to really call that a marriage or a family. I've seen whole families who were grasping and stingy with each other. Some even stealing from each other, not able to trust one another enough to leave their money and possessions in the open, but having to hide them from one another.

[A side note: We should teach our children from the very start to respect the personal property of others. The other household phrase that my children could quote to you is: "If it's not yours, don't touch it." My son once came to the dinner table and said, "I am so thankful to live in a family where I do not have to hide my things to keep them from being stolen; where I can leave my money out on the table, assured that no one will touch it." He had been speaking to a friend, who had to keep everything he had hidden away from his own brothers to keep it from being stolen. (Yes, this is a "Christian" family.) I have taught children who think that it is okay to go and take what they want from a sibling's lunch box or locker because "it's only my sister or brother." When that pattern of behavior leads to bigger thefts later in life, (yes, it's theft, we need to learn to call it what it is, and not excuse the sin because it's a child) these parents wonder, "what in the world ever happened to Johnny - I don't understand why he would steal." He steals because he was never taught to respect the possessions of others.]

Stealing is a result of selfishness also. Whether in the home or out of it. Our attitude should reflect Jesus' command:

Therefore all things whatsoever ye would that men should do to you, do ye even so to them: for this is the law and the prophets. Matthew 7:12

If we do not want our family to treat us with selfishness and do not want our children to be selfish with each other, we have to learn not to be selfish with them. At the same time we need to teach them that they are not entitled to the property of others.

The woman who anointed the feet of Jesus had an alabaster box of precious ointment worth a year's wage. What did she do with what she had? She poured it out in sacrifice to the Lord. Mark 14:3-6

Here again this woman had something that belonged to her. This time something she had probably saved for years to obtain - it may have been an inheritance or she may have been wealthy- but regardless, the Bible says that it was very costly, and precious.

A missionary friend called me one day as she was preparing to leave for the field. She, with tears, told me that of all of the things that she had to sell, give away or dispose of in her preparation, the hardest to part with was a set of china that had been her mother's. I responded, "That sounds like treasures in heaven to me." She later told me that was exactly what she needed to hear. It was finally okay with her to give up that possession when she turned it over to God.

I once had a similar situation in my own life. I had a couple of teapots, one of which was given to me by my mother, who died about 4 years before. Now, if you've been to my house, you know my "teapot thing". I have collected them for years. I have them everywhere. Almost all of these teapots have been gifts from various people and have a lot of sentimental value to me. These particular ones however, were decorated in figures that are not according to the convictions in my home. Yet I was keeping them because of the sentiment. The Lord convicted me about it and I really struggled with getting rid of them. He finally won and I wondered why it had been such a struggle. When you give yourself to Him fully, He makes the surrender so sweet that you will always wonder why it was so hard. Earthly possessions are never as important as total surrender to the will and way of God.

Lay not up for yourselves treasures upon earth, where moth and rust doth corrupt, and where thieves break through and steal: But lay up for yourselves treasures in heaven, where neither moth nor rust doth corrupt, and where thieves do not break through nor steal: For where your treasure is, there will your heart be also. Matthew 6:19-21

What do you have in material possessions? Are you willing to give what you have to the Lord if He requires it? Or are your possessions too dear for you to let go of them? If God were to call your husband to the mission field - could you go? Or do your possessions have such a hold on you that you could not turn them loose?

Judges 17:1-18:31 tells the story of a man named Micah and his mother. She saved back 1,100 shekels of silver. He stole it from her, but then returned it. She in return took 200 shekels of it and made a molten image and gave it to her son. That one act of direct disobedience to the command of God caused a great deal of trouble for her house. Micah then hired a Levite. (Who was not supposed to be hired for money but was to live by the offerings of the children of Israel in the cities that God had given them.) This man was to be a priest for Micah's household, worshiping that idol. The mess got bigger when an army from the tribe of Dan decided that their land wasn't big enough to suit them. They came by with the intentions of taking over a city of people who were dwelling peaceably, not bothering anyone. Again, this was against the command of God in Deuteronomy 20:10-15. They came by Micah's house, found the idol and the priest and stole them both. The priest told them what they wanted to hear - which was what he was used to doing in Micah's house - and they used his presence for boldness to attack innocent people. All that 'snowball effect' because one woman used her possessions to lead her family into disobedience to the Word of God. What did she have? Money. How did she use it? To throw a stumblingblock in the path of her family.

We never know the effects that our disobedience will have to our family and the others that we have influence over. Do you use the possessions that you have to draw your family closer to God? Or to put a wedge between them and the Lord? Do you allow things into your home that are hurting your family spiritually? Books, magazines, television, etc. How about Satanic or Cultic symbols? There are more "cute little things" that we decorate with that are wicked than we would realize. These things may not be a snare to you but what about your family? What about friends who see those things in your home? What of your testimony? Will they see these things in your home and criticize Christ, or will they see them and think, "If it's okay for them, it's okay for me." Many times I have seen men who would purge things from their homes, but the woman of the house objected because she loved her... this or that... and so he gave in and left an abomination in the household.

The Bible says about Micah's mother, "every man did what was right in their own eyes." She wasn't putting a spiritual snare in front of her family intentionally, but out of ignorance. We do not have to be ignorant. First of all we have the Word of God and secondly we have the Holy Spirit and thirdly we have the availability of Godly counsel. If what you have in your home causes sin in someone else - it becomes a sin for you to have that item.

Neither shalt thou bring an abomination into thine house, lest thou be a cursed thing like it: but thou shalt utterly detest it, and thou shalt utterly abhor it; for it is a cursed thing. Deuteronomy 7:26

But take heed lest by any means this liberty of yours become a stumblingblock to them that are weak. Wherefore, if meat make my brother to offend, I will eat no flesh while the world standeth, lest I make my brother to offend. 1 Corinthians 8:9 & 13

In this passage of Scripture the Corinthians had found a good bargain on meat. The only problem was that the meat was being sold off after being offered to idols. Some of them were even going into the idol's temple for a free meal. Paul explained that an idol is nothing, so the meat was simply a good bargain - except that it would cause a weak brother to sin. Seeing an older Christian in the Lord participating in something that they recognized as a sin from their past would cause them to fall back into idolatry. Even if the first Christian's heart was pure in the matter for himself, it still became a sin in his influence over others.

Some examples that I can think of: I have a friend who collects Indian objects - Dream catchers are part of spirit worship. Another friend had a "family heirloom" given to her that was a Catholic rosary - a symbol of idolatrous worship. A family member participated in the Halloween festivities, dressing their children as werewolves and vampires, also collecting crystals, pyramids, and unicorns. Some have Easter egg hunts. Easter eggs, etc. are symbols of Wiccan worship. There are many things that are used in the celebration of Christmas that are directly taken from pagan worship. Now you might say, "I think you are nit-picking to worry about all that stuff. Deuteronomy 7 is pretty clear about it. We are not to bring an abomination into our house. And even if we have no intention of using that item in a manner contrary to Scripture - how does it affect our testimony and how does it affect the others around us? Remember, there is nothing wrong with meat but if eating meat would cause my brother in Christ to sin, I will eat no meat while the world stands. What items do you have? Will they draw your family closer to God or do you have some things that will cause them to sin?

2 Kings 4:8-11 The Shunamite woman went to her husband for permission to build a room on the side of their home for the prophet to stay in during his travels after repeatedly feeding him on his journey. What did she have? A home and food. How did she use it? To bless the servant of God.

Are you willing to give what you have for God's servants? Are you willing for your husband to support missionaries and give special offerings? Do you have something of your own that you would be willing to offer to the servant of God so that the gospel can be preached and souls can be won? She was a wealthy woman and was willing to use what she had. Most of us are not wealthy but we can still be used of God to bless others. Do you think that you have too little to be of worth? In 1 Kings 17:8-15 The widow of Zaraphath only had a small amount of meal and a little oil but she was willing to give what she had to the prophet of God, believing God would take care of her needs. He most certainly did.

1 Samuel 25:14-42 Abigail the wife of Nabal the Carmelite had the goods of her household at her disposal and used them wisely, unlike her husband, to the saving of her house. A lot of people criticize Abigail for what she did; saying it was not right for her to give David the provisions behind her husband's back and to criticize her husband to David. I really don't know if she was right or wrong. I do know that God blessed her. He did call her a woman of good understanding in verse 3. So, let's take a look at her. When she realized that her household was in jeopardy she took what she had available and did what she could to preserve the life of her husband and servants. He was drunk and could not be reasoned with. Remember that, after the fact, when she knew the details of the danger they had been in and he sobered up, she told her husband the whole story including what she had done. He had a stroke, probably from fear of what could have happened and 10 days later God smote him and he died. David then took Abigail as his wife.

I would never be guilty of encouraging you to disobey your husband even if you feel like you are right and he is wrong. If you ever feel, like Abigail did, that your life is in imminent danger because of the actions of your husband, then by all means seek God personally for what to do and do it. Other than that obey your husband. That is not the issue I want to address here anyway. Notice instead, in verse 18, that Abigail knew exactly what she had available to take to David. In a moment of great distress, not only did she keep a level head but she was able to give directions about just how much of each item to offer from her household provisions. This means she was a good household manager. She did not run around here and there saying, "Oh me! Oh my! What do I do, how much do I take, what do I have?" If you are to do the best that you can with what you have you need to be a wise household manager. Know what you have to work with. Be prudent. What did she have? The goods of her household at her disposal. How did she use them? With good management and care so that she knew what she had available at a moment's notice. When you head for the grocery store do you plan ahead? Or do you walk in and grab what you think will work as you walk down the aisles? Do you use some planning and management in your shopping? Or do you purchase things you don't really need? A wise household manager is not an impulse shopper.

All of these ladies had possessions. Some used them wisely, some foolishly. Now look at the list you made earlier. And I ask you again - What have you got? How are you going to use what you have for the glory of God and the good of your family?

Lesson Five Review

1) Write the Scripture memory portion for this lesson:

_____

_____

_____

_____

_____

2) We should be able to be trusted with his _____ and

_____.

3) It is not a bad thing in God's sight for the woman to be making a

_____

4) We can assume that she had her husband's_____.

5) With the fruit of her hands she planted a vineyard. In the Word of God
the fruit of something is the _____ or

_____of it.

6) She had _____ and _____ to make the choice of field and
_____ at her disposal to finish the project.

7) What did she have? Financial _____ that she
used for the _____ of her family.

8) Next we see that she was _____ in her _____ providing
her family with the best _____ that she could afford.

9) We should _____ about what we buy.

10) Never make a _____ purchase without consulting your
_____.

11) List 4 things that are wrong to do in the matter of household finances:

_____

_____

_____

_____

12) The prudent woman will do the _____ she can with what she's _____.

13) Caleb's daughter had _____.

14) _____ in our home dishonors God and does not promote _____.

15) If we treat our family with _____ they will respond with _____.

16) We should teach our children to _____ the property of others.

17) What did the woman who anointed the feet of Jesus have?

18) What did she do with it?

_____.

19) We should not own anything we are not willing to

_____.

20) What did Micah's mother have? _____.

21) What did she do with it?

_____.

22) Deuteronomy 7 says we should never bring an _____ into our homes.

23) If we keep possessions in our home that causes another person to sin, it also becomes _____ to us.

24) Keeping idolatrous items in our home can damage our
_____ as well as causing a weaker Christian to
_____.

25) What did the Shunnamite woman have?

_____

26) What did she do with it?

_____   _____.

27) We should be willing for our husbands to support
_____ and give special _____ to benefit
God's servants.

28) What did the widow of Zaraphath have?

_____

29) What did she do with it?

_____.

30) Is it necessary to have great possessions to give to God?
_____.

31) What did Abigail have?

_____.

32) What did she do with it?

_____   _____.

33) We should plan _____ and be a good
_____ of our households.

34) A wise household manager is not an _____ shopper.

35) To perceive that our merchandise is good - to be a wise household
manager - and to please God in the ways of our household and decisions
we need to learn to do the best

_____.

A Woman Among all Those

Lessons in Christian Womanhood

Lesson 6

Memory passages: She girdeth her loins with strength and strengtheneth her arms. Proverbs 31:17

A wise man is strong; yea, a man of knowledge increaseth strength. Proverbs 24:5

Gird – to surround, to encircle, to enclose, to encompass

Loins – The space on each side of the vertebrae between the lowest of the false ribs and the upper portion of the osilium or haunch bone, or the lateral portions of the lumbar regions, also called the reins.

Strength – Firmness; solidity or toughness; the quality of bodies by which they sustain the application of force without breaking or yielding.

Strengthen – To make strong or stronger; to add strength to, either physical, legal or moral. To cause to increase in power or security.

This lesson is about strength. We as women seeking godliness should seek to be as strong and healthy as possible. Not just physically, but emotionally and spiritually as well. The Bible mentions several different types of strength. We're going to discuss 3 different aspects of strength over the next couple of lessons. Physical strength, emotional strength and spiritual strength. There were many promises given throughout the Word of God that gave long life and health. There are promises also for emotional health and spiritual health. The answer to every question in life is found in the Word of God.

Know ye not that they which run in a race run all, but one receiveth the prize? So run, that ye may obtain. And every man that striveth for the mastery is temperate in all things. Now they do it to obtain a corruptible crown; but we an incorruptible. I therefore so run, not as uncertainly; so fight I, not as one that beateth the air: But I keep under my body, and bring it into subjection: lest that by any means, when I have preached to others, I myself should be a castaway.   1 Corinthians 9: 24-27

According to my earnest expectation and my hope, that in nothing I shall be ashamed, but that with all boldness, as always, so now also Christ shall be magnified in my body, whether it be by life, or by death. Philippians 1:20

Christ is to be magnified in our body. The dietary law included things that were not observed in Egypt such as the washing of foods and hands. It also included things they were not to eat such as pork and shellfish that need special preserving methods to prevent bacteria, which they did not have at the time. It included abstaining from alcohol which ruins health and morals. The moral law prohibited illicit sex and perverted sex which did away with venereal diseases. The law also provided for proper disposal of waste which protected against plagues and infections. Then there was an additional promise of divine protection from disease and long life in return for obedience to the law such as:

Honour thy father and thy mother: that thy days may be long upon the land which the LORD thy God giveth thee. Exodus 20:12

Strength to the upright is in the way of the Lord. Follow His mandates if you want strength. There are those who say that the law is restrictive. Maybe – in the same way that you restrict your children from things that are harmful for them. God never placed restrictions on His children for the fun of restricting them. He had a reason.

The way of the LORD is strength to the upright: but destruction shall be to the workers of iniquity. Proverbs 10:29

A wise man does not neglect strength, as our memory passage tells us. I believe the Lord would have us look at Sarah as an example of physical strength. It is not simply the fact that Sarah had a son when she was 90 years old. That was clearly a miracle of God as is told to us in Genesis:

Now Abraham and Sarah were old and well stricken in age; and it ceased to be with Sarah after the manner of women.   Genesis 18:11

Sarah had already gone through menopause. What I want to look at is in Genesis 20 verses 1-12. She was at this time around 90 years old. Remember, this was in between the time that God had promised the seed through Isaac, and that Sarah would be the one to bear him, and when she actually conceived the child. Abimelech thought her so beautiful at the age of 90 that he wanted to marry her. Understandably the life expectancies were different then but she was still considered an old woman. And also that we notice in Genesis 23:1 that she lived to be 127 years old.

We could use Rebekah as another example of physical strength. It never ceases to amaze me that she drew gallons upon gallons of water for all those camels and then turned and ran home. I don't believe that I would have had the endurance for that even at the age of sixteen to twenty years old!!

When we think of physical strength in women these two women really say it all. Strength for manual labor and activity, endurance, childbearing, physical appearance and long life.

The Bible does say a few things about physical strength but this passage in Proverbs 31 is the only one that refers to women. Knowing, however, that you cannot have strength without health, we can glean some things from references to health. The starting place is salvation.

That thy way may be known upon earth, thy saving health among all nations. Psalm 67:2

First and foremost, salvation is a healthy thing because it changes your desires from those things which are destructive to your body to those things which honor God. If a person is truly saved and striving to please the Savior, he will not be doing a lot of the things that will drag him down physically. Alcohol, tobacco, drugs, extramarital sex, perverted sex, etc. are things that a Christian who is striving to live according to the Word of God is going to do their very best to stay away from. Notice that I said a Christian who is striving to live according to the Word of God. That does not mean that Christians do not sometimes participate in these sins – they do. And it has been my personal experience that when they do, they suffer the effects of it in the body faster than non-Christians do. When a Christian follows the mandates of the Word of God, and stays away from these destructive sins, not only do they live longer lives, they are healthier, stronger, and more attractive physically.

Bro. Steve Blankenship, who works in the juvenile ministry, has a series of actual police mug shots of a young girl. These were taken beginning at the age of 15 or 16 years old. You can see in the first couple of photos the freshness of youth and beauty on her face. As the time progresses her face becomes hard, haggard and worn. In the last photos she looks 45 or 50 years old when she is, in fact, only in her early 20's. This is the result of a life of sin.

A lot of people want to justify their sin by the lame excuse that God does not specifically list tobacco or drug use as sin in the Word of God as it does the use of alcohol and sexual sins.

1 Corinthians 6:9-20 lists quite a few sins of the body that are destructive to this flesh as well as dishonoring to God. Do not defile the body, it is purchased at an awful cost – the blood of Jesus Christ. Let's look specifically at verse 12.

All things are lawful unto me, but all things are not expedient: all things are lawful for me, but I will not be brought under the power of any. 1 Corinthians 6:12

Expedient means: fit or suitable for the purpose; proper under the circumstances. Many things may be lawful, which are not expedient.

According to this verse anything that you are "brought under the power of," in other words anything that is addictive, is something that you should stay away from. Tobacco and drugs are certainly addictive. Let's look at verse 19 and 20 of the same passage.

What? Know ye not that your body is the temple of the Holy Ghost which is in you, which ye have of God, and ye are not your own? For ye are bought with a price: therefore glorify God in your body, and in your spirit, which are God's. 1 Corinthians 6:19-20

Be not deceived; God is not mocked: for whatsoever a man soweth, that shall he also reap. For he that soweth to his flesh shall of the flesh reap corruption; but he that soweth to the Spirit shall of the Spirit reap life everlasting. Galatians 6:7-8

Some people believe that it is not necessary to glorify God in this physical body – that the heart is the only part of you that interests God. They don't necessarily say it that way but they will say, "It does not matter how I live (talk, act, dress, the places I go or what I do, etc.) God knows my heart." The passage above tells us plainly that we are to glorify God in our body and our spirit.

If you sow to your flesh, notice that you will **of the flesh** reap corruption. We mentioned before that this sinful flesh has a self-destruct tendency. Left on its own it develops habits and cravings that are harmful to it. It desires all of the wrong things and pushes away all of the things that will do it good. This begins very early in life. Give a new born baby a bottle of sugar water and see how much milk they desire. Give a 2 or 3 year old chips and candy and see how much meat and vegetables they desire. Give a 20+ year old woman chocolate, junk food and a T.V. set full of soap operas or a bookshelf full of romance novels and see how much weight she will gain and notice how little housework and Bible study she desires. Give the body alcohol and it will crave alcohol until it kills itself, ditto with drugs and tobacco. Give the body and mind up to sexual sin and it will become vile and base and do things that you would not begin to dream it could lower itself to do.

For if ye live after the flesh, ye shall die: but if ye through the Spirit do mortify the deeds of the body, ye shall live. Romans 8:13

That's pretty blunt but it's Bible truth. This becomes obvious with those who have allowed the flesh to become entangled in addictions. Tobacco causes cancer, strokes, heart disease and lung disease among many other ailments. Alcohol causes cirrhosis of the liver, heart and stomach ailments, not to mention the horrors of poverty, neglected children, etc. Drugs cause wasted lives and a body with a destroyed immune system. Sexual sins cause STDs and like any other addiction lead to worse addictions – pornography and perversion. Overeating or improper eating causes vitamin deficiencies, heart problems, diabetes, back problems, blood pressure problems, sleep apnea, etc. etc. etc.

We are to put down the desires of this flesh. Not only are the desires of the flesh destructive to our spiritual well-being, they are destructive to the flesh itself, making us less effective as a servant of God.

Be not wise in thine own eyes: fear the LORD, and depart from evil. It shall be health to thy navel, and marrow to thy bones.   Proverbs 3:7-8

Here's the question: Have we really seen the thing that is destructive to our flesh as **EVIL**? So what can we do for physical strength? First – Obey the Word of God.

My son, attend to my words; incline thine ear unto my sayings. Let them not depart from thine eyes; keep them in the midst of thine heart. For they are life unto those that find them, and health to all their flesh. Proverbs 4:20-22

Obedience to the Word and will of God is a healthy thing. This will cause us to avoid sinful practices that will tear down the flesh. We will have to put the desires of the flesh down in order to do this. Next, some commonly known things: Get a balance in your life. Eat right, exercise and sleep right. Nutrition is the first element of physical strength. Eating right involves more than the issue of overeating but that is the first thing we think about when we say to eat right, so we'll approach it first. Excessive overeating is gluttony. Gluttony is a sin.

Ecclesiastes 6:7 shows the power of the appetite: All the labour of man is for his mouth, and yet the appetite is not filled.

Proverbs 23:21 puts gluttony in the same category with drunkenness: For the drunkard and the glutton shall come to poverty: and drowsiness shall clothe a man with rags.

Many overweight people eat like birds. My mother-in-law was overweight until the day she died and yet ate so little you would wonder how she lived on it. I could quote you several other examples as well. So just because a person is overweight does not make them a glutton. However, an overweight person will have problems in the flesh that will slow down their service to God and their family. We should seek to be as active and as healthy as we can be for the glory of God. We cannot be at our full potential if we are carrying unnecessary weight.

Here's a word of caution to all of you "skinny girls" when it comes to this subject: The purpose behind this study is for us to examine ourselves not our neighbors. I can tell you from my own experience that you will never help an overweight person to lose weight by belittling them or by pointing out to them that it is a sin to overeat. They already know that. An overweight person has a mountain of frustration that they are dealing with that you do not understand if you don't have a weight problem yourself. Don't try to approach the subject with them – you do not understand. Do pray for them. If you are trying to 'talk to them' about it, and you have not prayed for them about it, you are approaching the problem like a Pharisee.

Matthew 7:3 comes into effect here. And why beholdest thou the mote that is in thy brother's eye, but considerest not the beam that is in thine own eye?

Just as destructive as the glutton is the person who under-eats. I've known very few of these but there are some. More than any other problem are the ones who eat all the wrong things. They fill up on junk and won't eat the right things. Then they wonder why they have so little energy and are sick so easily. It's funny how we want our children to eat right but we won't eat right – with the same excuses, many times, that they use for it.

Another factor is water. Water is the basic element in life. Our bodies are made up of approximately 70% water. Every sensible diet plan that exists says to drink 6-8 glasses of water a day. The reason for this is simple. Water is necessary to keep your digestive system in working order. The less water you drink the more tied up your digestive system will be and the less fat and impurities you can flush from your system. You will lessen your chances for urinary infections, kidney stones, colon cancer and other colon disorders, edema, and many other problems just by drinking water. Also, if water is not a part of your everyday diet, and you are overweight, you can lose 10-20 pounds within a few months just by adding 6-8 glasses of water to your diet every day.

The last thing about diet that we will look at is vitamins. If you eat a properly balanced diet, you receive most of the nutrients that you need from the foods you eat. The problem is that most of us do not eat a properly balanced diet. In woman's health there are several major deficiencies that are problems. One is calcium. If you do not like dairy products, I would recommend a calcium supplement. You can get a good calcium boost just from taking an antacid tablet that contains calcium. Calcium deficiencies cause brittle bones, dull lifeless hair and weak, peeling fingernails and toenails. Older women who have not had proper calcium intake through their lives have a higher chance of developing osteoporosis, which is a disease that causes the bones to develop tiny holes all through them, kind of like Swiss cheese.

The next deficiency that women can sometimes face is iron. Many times women prefer to get their extra iron by increasing the amount of iron rich foods they eat because of the side effects iron supplements can sometimes have. Iron rich foods include leafy green vegetables, meat and fish. If you have a serious iron deficiency you will probably know it. It causes dizzy spells, weakness and tiredness. It will also cause the gums and lining of the eye sockets to fade to a pale pink color.

The last deficiency we will talk about is a Vitamin B deficiency. Vitamin B complex deficiencies cause a whole list of health problems. A deficiency in Vitamin B will cause you to have mood swings, depression and difficulty during your menstrual cycle. In older women it can cause worse hot flashes and again, mood swings. Different B vitamins come from different natural sources such as: potatoes, bananas, lentils, chili peppers, liver oil, liver, turkey, tuna, nutritional yeast (or brewer's yeast) and molasses.

The next thing we will look at in regard to health and strength is exercise. The only thing we have in the Word of God to help us here is:

But refuse profane and old wives' fables, and exercise thyself rather unto godliness. For bodily exercise profiteth little: but godliness is profitable unto all things, having promise of the life that now is, and of that which is to come. 1 Timothy 4:7-8

Bodily exercise profiteth little. If exercise of the body is all you do, you will still be unhealthy. Remember the comparison here – if you are exercising the body and not exercising godliness in your life it won't do you any good at all. It's not telling you not to exercise. We all know that without exercise of some kind, the body is not healthy. You cannot be strong without doing something to gain that strength. Exercise benefits the body in circulation, in digestion, in respiration, in using up calories so you can keep off excess weight, in muscle tone and in increasing strength and endurance.

I'm not suggesting that you become a body builder. YUK! That is not in the least bit feminine. I never knew a man who really thought that was attractive. Balance is the word here. Balance in nutrition and balance in exercise. We can use all kinds of excuses not to exercise. It doesn't have to be complicated. Take a walk around the block or do some simple exercises at home. The truth usually amounts to, "I really don't want to."

Know ye not that they which run in a race run all, but one receiveth the prize? So run that ye may obtain. And every man that striveth for the mastery is temperate in all things. Now they do it to obtain a corruptible crown; but we an incorruptible. I therefore so run, not as uncertainly; so fight I, not as one that beateth the air: But I keep under my body, and bring it into subjection: lest that by any means, when I have preached to others, I myself should be a castaway.   1 Corinthians 9:24-27

The last thing we will look at in this lesson is getting the proper amount of sleep. Sleep in proper amounts is necessary for health. This is something else that should be kept in balance. Teenagers have a tendency to sleep too much. Young adults have a tendency to go, go, go and sleep too little and older adults go back to sleeping too much. To keep the body in functioning order we need about 8 hours of sleep each night. Notice that I said, "night." A medical study once stated that one hour of sleep before midnight was worth two hours after midnight. Benjamin Franklin knew what he was talking about when he said, "Early to bed and early to rise makes a man healthy, wealthy and wise." You can condition your body to go to bed early and rise early. I know it can be done from personal experience.

In summary: For physical strength the virtuous woman should eat right, exercise and get the proper amount of sleep. We've heard all this before. Why should we bother? Why should we care? Because it is a part of bringing our bodies into subjection to the will of God. Because a strong, healthy woman is a good testimony for the Savior and is better able to be the servant He has called her to be.

Lesson Six Review

1) Write the Scripture memory portion for this lesson:

_____

_____

_____

2) Proverbs 24:5 says that a man of knowledge will increase

_____

3) Define Gird:

_____

_____

4) Define loins:

_____

_____

5) Define Strength:

_____

_____

6) Define Strengthen:

_____

_____

7) Define Expedient:

_____

_____

8) The three aspects of strength we will learn about are _____ strength, _____ strength and _____strength.

9) The dietary law provided for:

_____

_____

10) The moral law prohibited:

_____

_____

_____

11) List several ways that Sarah and Rebekah give examples of strength:

_____

_____

_____

12) First and foremost _____ is a healthy thing.

13) When a Christian follows the mandates of the Word of God and stays away from destructive sins, not only do they live _____ lives, they are _____ and more _____ physically.

14) List some examples of these destructive sins:

_____

_____

_____

_____

15) Where will a person who sows to the flesh reap corruption?

_____

_____

16) We are not to be brought under the power of anything. Therefore anything that is _____ is a sin of the flesh.

17) Gluttony is a _____.

18) Water is the basic _____ of life.

19) We should drink _____ of water a day.
20) List the three vitamin deficiencies common in women.

_____

21) List some ways in which exercise benefits the body.

_____

_____

_____

22) _____ in proper amounts is necessary for health.

23) A _____ woman is a good _____ for the Savior and is better able to be the _____ He has called her to be.

A Woman Among all Those

Lessons in Christian Womanhood

Lesson 7

Memory passages: She girdeth her loins with strength and strengtheneth her arms. Proverbs 31:17

Peace I leave with you, my peace I give unto you: not as the world giveth, give I unto you. Let not your heart be troubled, neither let it be afraid. John 14:27

Remember that the definition of strength is: Firmness; solidity or toughness; the quality of bodies by which they sustain the application of force without breaking or yielding. (Tough enough to stand some stuff.)

To strengthen is to make strong or stronger. So we are to gird – surround – ourselves with the quality of being tough enough to withstand some things, and make ourselves stronger as we go.
In our last lesson we talked about physical strength. This lesson will cover emotional strength.

The definition of emotion is: A moving of the mind or soul. Hence, any agitation of mind or excitement of sensibility.

Let's take a look at the example of Job's wife:

So went Satan forth from the presence of the LORD, and smote Job with sore boils from the sole of his foot unto his crown. And he took him a potsherd to scrape himself withal; and he sat down among the ashes. Then said his wife unto him, Dost thou still retain thine integrity? Curse God, and die. But he said unto her, Thou speakest as one of the foolish women speaketh. What? Shall we receive good at the hand of God, and shall we not receive evil? In all this did not Job sin with his lips. Job 2:7-10

78

We are quick to blame Job's wife. She certainly was no help to her husband in his greatest hour of need. But remember the loss that she had sustained, herself. Not only had she lost all of her wealth and possessions and the secure future she had been relying on, but all 10 of her children in the same moment of time. In the crushing loss of all this, her husband breaks out with boils from tip to toe. It was obvious to all that he was under severe judgment. So in her mind, he was clearly to blame for all of the trouble. This was a woman with a legitimate complaint and a serious emotional battle. Her whole world was torn to shreds. If you back up and read the whole story and then consider what she lost, you might even say that she had a reason to react the way that she did. She suffered a whole lot more than any of us can probably imagine. Am I excusing her? No. She was wrong. But do I think I would behave better in her shoes? No, probably not.

How do **we** react when our husband does something that brings chastisement on our family? How do we react when he makes a bad decision that we or our children have to suffer for? Or when we *think* his decision is bad, even before we know the outcome? How do we react in life's crushing moments? Do we fall apart and become an emotional wreck? Or do we show some emotional strength? Life can deal some bitter blows that are very real. How you react to those things can mean the difference between girding your emotional loins with strength and strengthening your emotional arms or not doing so.

Emotional health directly affects physical health. Someone who is emotionally weak is sure to suffer physically as well. The inverse is also true. Someone who suffers physically also suffers emotionally. God has some helps for emotional health as well as those for physical health. Notice that not only is salvation physically healthy, it is emotionally healthy as well.

The way of the LORD is strength to the upright: but destruction shall be to the workers of iniquity. Proverbs 10:29

Let's look at some emotional problems that people suffer, and get some practical help for those things from the Word of God. There are some emotional disorders that are linked to physical problems. There are chemical imbalances in some people's bodies that affect their mind and emotions. There are also the effects of demon possession that cause serious emotional and mental problems. I'm not dealing with these things here. I'm dealing with children of God who know and walk with God on a day to day basis. I gave you that preliminary statement because the next statement I'm about to make is pretty bold in our society today. There is never a reason for a dedicated Christian to seek the counsel or advice of a "mental health professional" for common emotional problems. The reason for this is in our memory passage above. Jesus said that He was leaving us with peace that the world cannot give. And then followed it up with "let not your heart be troubled, neither let it be afraid." This is a promise of peace from the Savior Himself. Remember also that He was telling this to people who were about to face torture and death for what they believed. Also, understand that most mental health professionals deny the power of God and they use philosophy that is directly opposite to the Scripture. No man can serve two masters – by the same token no one can follow the advice of two physicians who are prescribing opposite treatment. So will it be the Great Physician or the mental health professional?

The first thing most people think of when they think of emotional problems is depression. Closely linked to depression would be despondence and dejection. These are so closely related to one another that we will look at them together. Job's wife sure could have been facing all three.

Depression is defined as: a sadness, want of courage or animation, the literal sense of the word is 'to press down.' A person who is depressed feels weighted down with care. They feel overwhelmed by and unable to get the best of their circumstances.

Despondence means: to lose all courage, spirit or resolution or to sink by loss of hope. A despondent person wants to give up.

Dejection means: cast down, grieved or discouraged. A dejected person is easily saddened and discouraged.
There can be many, many reasons that will created depression, despondence or dejection in a person's life. In the case of Job's wife it was the death of her children and the loss of her possessions.

Two weeks after the death of my mother, I had an appointment with my doctor. He had also been my mother's doctor and is a very compassionate man. As I entered the hospital, the last few months of caring for my mother were vivid in my mind. Every step I took through the halls where I had almost lived those last months of caring for her brought more and more memories of what we had been through. By the time I reached the doctor's office I was on the verge of tears. When the doctor greeted me with, "I am so sorry about your mom," they overflowed. I cried, which made me angry with myself, so I cried some more. He sat there sympathetically and wrote me a prescription for an anti-depressant. I left with that prescription in my hand and confusion in my heart. "Do I need this?" "Isn't there a difference between grief and depression?" I filled prescription on the way home and stared at it some more. Then I turned to prayer and the Lord let me know that it was okay to sorrow and okay to cry. John 11:35

The doctor was doing what he could to dry up my tears but pills were the best he could offer. Jesus offered real healing. The pills went down the drain and God gave that healing. Not overnight, but little by little – the way real healing happens. I needed that lesson because it would not get easier. One month later I was scraping all of my belongings out of my sodden home and piling them on the street after Hurricane Ivan. Shortly after that we faced one of the hardest trials of our lives. I won't give details about that but understand that sometimes in this Christian walk the lowest blows you will ever receive come from those who are supposed to be fellow laborers. Did I react always with calmness of temper and ease of mind? No, not hardly. But I did react by turning to God again and again for the need of my heart and mind. And God gave healing – in His time. In the process of turning it over to Him, He turned the worst of circumstances into the best of blessings as He always does. Because I am some Spiritual and emotional giant? Again, not even close. Because we have a wonderful God who is true to His promises. He loves you just as much.

Some side effects of depression, despondence and dejection are: change of appetite, change of sleep habits, loss of interest in daily activity, apathy, a feeling of hopelessness or being overwhelmed, mood swings, outbursts of temper and crying for no apparent reason.

Is it real? Of course it is. You're really not going crazy. It comes as no surprise to the Lord that we are emotional beings. He created us. So, first of all, realize that you are not a horrible creature for being emotional. The issue is: are you going to allow those emotions to control your life or are you going to allow the Lord to heal you?

First, determine the cause and face it squarely. Is it temporary or permanent? Can you, personally, do anything at all to correct the problem? If you can, do so. If you can't, then the only recourse you have is to work your way through it emotionally.

Problems from the past.
1) Guilt: Many people live with a guilt complex. They cannot forgive themselves for their sin, even though they have confessed it to God and received His divine forgiveness.

Our language degenerates every day and words that meant one thing 20 years ago – or sometimes less time than that – now mean something totally different. The word guilt actually means to be criminally liable for wrong doing. The word which has the original meaning that we now associate with "feeling guilt" is compunction.

The word compunction means: a pricking of heart; poignant (i.e. severe, piercing, very painful) grief or remorse proceeding from a consciousness of guilt or sorrow for having offended God.

A person who suffers depression from guilt, or compunction, usually struggles with assurance of their salvation. Or they may have such a sense of unworthiness in service to God that every time they fail Him they want to give up rather than repeat the necessary steps of #1 get up - #2 confess up - #3 and go on.

First: Examine your salvation. Study the book of 1John. This book gives a whole list of 'knows' about your salvation. If you still have questions, go to your pastor or another Christian that you trust to give you straightforward answers. Your eternity is not something to play with and there is no shame in making sure that you know beyond any doubt.

Examine yourselves, whether ye be in the faith; prove your own selves, Know ye not your own selves, how that Jesus Christ is in you, except ye be reprobates? 2 Corinthians 13:5

When you are assured of your salvation, ask God to give you a verse of Scripture that you can turn back to whenever doubts may arise again. Underline that Scripture in your Bible and memorize it.

Second: Remember that we serve a God who is completely trustworthy. He does not change and His mercy endures forever.
If we confess our sins, he is faithful and just to forgive us our sins, and to cleanse us from all unrighteousness. 1 John 1:9

To doubt His forgiveness is to doubt His love and mercy and to challenge His faithfulness. To doubt His forgiveness denies the truth of His Word. "But I do the same things over and over again," you may say. Welcome to the club. Would the Lord require something of you He was not willing to do Himself? He told His disciples that they needed to forgive, forgive and keep on forgiving. Will He not be willing to do the same?

Then came Peter to him, and said, Lord, how oft shall my brother sin against me, and I forgive him? Till seven times? Jesus saith unto him, I say not unto thee, Until seven times: but Until seventy times seven. Matthew 18:21-22

Third: Forget it. - - Confess it, repent of it, (true repentance means, "I never intend to do this again.") forget it and go on.

Brethren, I count not myself to have apprehended: but this one thing I do, forgetting those things which are behind, and reaching forth unto those things which are before, I press toward the mark for the prize of the high calling of God in Christ Jesus.   Philippians 3:13-14

Fourth: Understand that, yes, we are unworthy in God's service. But understand also, that God has chosen to use us. He knows our unworthiness and although He does not excuse our sin, it comes as no surprise to Him that we sin and in His matchless, infinite mercy He provided that those sins could be forgiven – and His mercy endureth forever!

My little children, these things write I unto you, that ye sin not. And if any man sin, we have an advocate with the Father, Jesus Christ the righteous: and he is the propitiation for our sins: and not for ours only, but also for the sins of the whole world. 1 John 2:1-2

The apostle Paul considered himself as the chiefest of sinners and unworthy to be called an apostle. He said:
"O wretched man that I am! who shall deliver me from the body of this death?" Romans 7:24

This reminds me of a lady in our church, Mrs. Mac and her interest in collecting old rusty cans. She finds value in something that is cast off by others. Others look and say, "Of what use is that ugly old can?" but she enjoys them and finds value in them. Christ finds value in us in spite of our worthlessness – amazing!

2) Injury from others:

First: Turn it over to God. Sometimes this is the only step we need take. His awesome power and sweet Spirit can bring healing to things we never would have thought possible.

Casting all your care upon Him; for he careth for you. 1 Peter 5:7

Second: Forgive as much as you can and ask God for help with complete forgiveness. Some things are impossible for us to forgive in the flesh. Nothing is impossible with the help of God.

I can do all things through Christ which strengtheneth me.
Philippians 4:13

Understand one of the difficult truths of the Word of God. If we do not forgive, God will withhold forgiveness from us.

For if ye forgive men their trespasses, your heavenly Father will also forgive you: But if ye forgive not men their trespasses, neither will your Father forgive your trespasses. Matthew 6:14-15

There have been times in my life that I thought, "That's horrible, because that's impossible – I cannot forgive THAT." But yes, with the help of God we can forgive. If there is something in your life that you find impossible to forgive, go to God and ask for His help.

Third: Sometimes (not always, maybe not even most times) it may help to face the person with the hurt they have caused, let them know that God is granting you healing from the situation and that you are making an attempt to forgive.

Take heed to yourselves: If thy brother trespass against thee, rebuke him: and if he repent, forgive him. And if he trespass against thee seven times in a day, and seven times in a day turn again to thee, saying, I repent; thou shalt forgive him. Luke 17:3-4

Notice that in verse 5 the disciples responded to this by saying, "Lord, increase our faith."

Fourth: Forget it. Other than turning it over to God, this is the most important step in overcoming depression from an injury in your past. Forget it and go on.

Brethren, I count not myself to have apprehended: but this one thing I do, forgetting those things which are behind, and reaching forth unto those things which are before, I press toward the mark for the prize of the high calling of God in Christ Jesus.   Philippians 3:13-14

At a crucial time in my life an evangelist preached a message from 2 Samuel 20. He told the horrible story of how Joab murdered Amasa in cold blood, using the heat of the battle to cover his deed. As Amasa lay in the path dying, the men of the army stood stock still in horror at the sight. One man realized that there was still a battle going on and there was no time and no judgment available to deal with the thing right then. So he covered Amasa with a cloth and pulled him aside until the matter could be dealt with properly. Then the battle could go on and the army would not lose. The point is this: there are some things in our life that we will not be able to deal with. There are some things that can only be sorted out at the Judgment Seat of Christ. We cannot let depression stop us in our service for God. We've got to trust Him with our past injuries and go on.

3 Unexplained depression: Sometimes we may become depressed and don't really know why. Sometimes this is simply boredom. Someone who does not have enough to do many times becomes depressed or even has mood swings. The answer to this is quite obvious – get busy. Find something to do. Force some activity out of yourself. Get more involved in the church, volunteer some time at the hospital or nursing home. Visit some shut-ins. Volunteer at the Christian school. Find a partner and do some door to door visitation. Come out of yourself and learn to serve others. A sure fire cure for unexplained depression is to find someone to serve.

There is also a promise in Scripture that our hearts and minds will be kept in peace.

And the peace of God, which passeth all understanding, shall keep your hearts and minds through Christ Jesus. Philippians 4:7

There are conditions to that peace being available, however.

Rejoice in the Lord always: and again I say, Rejoice.   Philippians 4:4

The first condition to peace of mind and heart is to rejoice in the Lord. Another good cure for depression – if you know the cause or not – is to worship. I mean really worship. Don't come to church and sit like a spectator. Take the Word of God and look up passages concerning worship and praise and you might find some very surprising things. God does not expect us to come into His house and sit like dignified bumps on a log. We will get further into what real worship is when we talk about spiritual strength but for now, realize that real worship is a tremendous emotional release. It is far better than any pill that can be prescribed. The next condition is:

Let your moderation be known unto all men. The Lord is at hand. Philippians 4:5

Strive to live a life that is pleasing to God and a good testimony to those around you. It is emotionally as well as spiritually healthy to live a godly life. There is freedom from guilt that comes from living right. The last conditions are:

Be careful for nothing, but in every thing by prayer and supplication with thanksgiving let your requests be made known unto God. Philippians 4:6

Take everything – EVERYTHING – to God in prayer. And do it with thanksgiving. Giving thanks and praise to God is a wonderful emotional release.

Problems coping with the present: Anger and mood swings.

Mood swings, very often, are physical not emotional problems. We noted in our last lesson that a lot of times vitamin deficiencies and the woman's hormone cycles can create mood swings. This is not excusing bad behavior. When the mood swing strikes, we have to make every effort to control the flesh for the glory of God, for the benefit of our families and for our own spiritual and emotional well-being. A moody woman is not a virtuous woman.

A continual dropping in a very rainy day and a contentious woman are alike. Whosoever hideth her hideth the wind, and the ointment of his right hand which bewrayeth itself. Proverbs 27:15-16

It is better to dwell in the wilderness, than with a contentious and an angry woman. Proverbs 21:19

Proverbs 21:9 and Proverbs 25:24 both say the same thing: It is better to dwell in the corner of the housetop, than with a brawling woman in a wide house.

So how do we control those mood swings? The first part of the battle is to recognize a mood swing for what it is. Many women are controlled by their moods simply because they do not notice what is happening. The Bible says that if we are going to be prudent we need to look well to our goings. We need to foresee the evil and hide from it. If it is a physical problem such as a vitamin deficiency seek to correct it. Many times, when a mood swing is recognized for what it is, just the knowledge that the problem is yourself and not the things or people with which you are becoming irritable, is enough to take the starch out of the mood. The next thing to do is to pray. "Lord, my emotions are getting out of control and I don't want to dishonor you. Please, help me." He will. The next thing to do is to separate yourself from the irritant. If your children or your husband are irritating you, go somewhere by yourself for a few minutes until you get yourself under control. Then take stock of the situation. Are you hungry? Tired? Pressured? Get the situation at hand under control as much as you can. Then, when all else fails, use the 1 Peter 3:4 and 1 Thessalonians 4:11 rule – zip up. It is better to be abnormally quiet than to be abominably mouthy.

Then there is temper. If you have an ugly temper, you are going to have to really do some fighting with the flesh. I've heard some people – even women – brag about their bad temper like it was something good to have. It isn't. The Bible tells us quite a few things about someone who has an uncontrolled temper.

He that is soon angry dealeth foolishly: and a man of wicked devices is hated. Proverbs 14:17

Be not hasty in thy spirit to be angry: for anger resteth in the bosom of fools. Ecclesiastes 7:9

Wherefore my beloved brethren, let every man be swift to hear, slow to speak, slow to wrath: For the wrath of man worketh not the righteousness of God. James 1:19-20

Proverbs 22:24-25 tells us not to even make friends with someone who has a bad temper. "Make no friendship with an angry man; and with a furious man thou shalt not go: Lest thou learn his ways, and get a snare to thy soul."

If temper is your problem you need to confess that as a sin in your life and do your best to control it every time it raises its ugly head. If you fly off the handle at the slightest provocation you will not work the righteousness of God. You will be a bad testimony and have an unhappy household. Again, this is a matter for prayer. Ask God to help you control your temper and then every time you lose your temper, repent. It sometimes takes years of hard work at submitting yourself to the will of God to learn to control a temper that has been unmanaged for most of your life. But it is well worth the work and effort to bring your temper under God's control.

Problems coping with the future: Anxiety and Worry

Anxiety and worry stem from a lack of trust.

Trust in the LORD with all thine heart; and lean not unto thine own understanding. In all thy ways acknowledge him, and he shall direct thy paths. Proverbs 3:5-6

The fear of man bringeth a snare: but whoso putteth his trust in the LORD shall be safe. Proverbs 29:25

Every word of God is pure: he is a shield unto them that put their trust in him. Proverbs 30:5

Thou wilt keep him in perfect peace, whose mind is stayed on thee: because he trusteth in thee. Trust ye in the LORD forever: for in the LORD JEHOVAH is everlasting strength: Isaiah 26:3-4

There are more Scriptures concerning trusting the Lord than we have time to go over, but you get the idea. Now the question is: how do I apply that to myself when I am worrying over something and anxiety has set in? Again, stop and consider what you are worrying over. Is it something that you can do anything about? If so, do so. If not – you cannot help the situation by worrying about it.
Trust in the Lord. Pray and ask Him to take control of the matter and then leave it with Him. You may have to go back again and again and leave it with Him – but that's okay. Do it anyway. It will improve your prayer life.

In conclusion, we can have perfect peace – freedom from emotional battles and troubles. It will take some effort in controlling our emotions and ruling our spirit. The devil loves to make an emotional wreck of God's children because he can use it as an attempt to black God's eye in the sight of the world. "If they can't trust in their God to take care of them, why should I trust in Him with my eternity," they say.

He that hath no rule over his own spirit is like a city that is broken down, and without walls. Proverbs 25:28

And a city broken down and without walls is an easy takeover for the enemy. If we are seeking to be God's woman we must gird our loins with strength and rule our spirits.

Lesson Seven Review

1) Write this lesson's Scripture memory passage

_____

_____

2) The definition of strength is:

_____

_____

_____

3) To strengthen is to:

_____

_____

_____

4) We are to gird – surround ourselves – with: _____

5) Job's wife lost all of her _____ and

_____

6) It was obvious to all that Job was under _____

7) Emotional health directly affects _____

8) Someone who is emotionally weak is sure to:

_____

_____

_____

9) Not only is salvation _____ healthy, it is
_____ healthy as well.

10) There is never a reason for a _____ to seek the
counsel or advice of a _____ for
_____

11) Depression is defined as:

_____
_____
_____

12) Despondence means:

_____
_____
_____

13) Dejection means:

_____
_____
_____

14) Some side effects of depression, despondence and dejection are:

_____
_____
_____
_____

15) Compunction means:

_____
_____
_____

16) The four steps for dealing with guilt are:

a) _____

b) _____

c) _____

d) _____

17) The four steps for dealing with injury from others are:
a) _____

b) _____

c) _____

d) _____

18) Many times unexplained depression is the result of

_____

19) A sure fire cure for unexplained depression is to:

_____

20) The first part of the battle in controlling mood swings is:

_____

21) Anxiety and worry stem from:

_____

22) The devil loves to

_____

23) We can have victory over emotional battles if we will learn to trust
_____ and have rule over our _____.

A Woman Among all Those

Lessons in Christian Womanhood

Lesson 8

Memory passages: She girdeth her loins with strength and strengtheneth her arms. Proverbs 31:17

Why art thou cast down, O my soul? And why art thou disquieted within me? Hope thou in God: for I shall yet praise him, who is the health of my countenance, and my God. Psalm 42:11

Remember strength means: Firmness; solidity or toughness; the quality of bodies by which they sustain the application of force without breaking or yielding. (Tough enough to stand some stuff.)

We've talked about physical and emotional strength. We need to look now at Spiritual strength.

The word Spiritual means: Pertaining to the renewed nature of man: as spiritual life.

So to gird our spiritual loins with strength means that we are going to be strong enough in our spiritual life that we will not break or give in or fall apart when the tough times come.

Our example this week is Deborah. Judges 4:4-10 Deborah is one of the most controversial women in the Bible. She is certainly out of her realm. Here is a woman in the place of prominence in the country. She has the position here of president or almost of queen. We can clearly see from Scripture that this is not God's plan for a woman or a nation. However, remember that the theme of the book of Judges is: "Every man did that which was right in his own eyes." There are a lot of 'goings on' in the book of Judges that were simply not right and not in accordance with God's plan. Yet God used the men and women in the book of Judges - once again revealing to us that He is God and in control of each situation in our lives, whether or not we are right and in accordance with His will. Deborah was certainly used of God in spite of her strange situation.

What I see here in, Deborah, is that she was doing the best she could with what she had. And what she had was a nation of wimpy men who would not lead. She tried her best to get Barak to lead that army. He was willing enough to fight but not to lead. The reason that Deborah was judge here was that she knew the Word of God and God spoke to her. Was there not a man in all of Israel to take that position? Obviously not or God would have used him. It is never correct for a woman to take the spiritual leadership in the home unless the man refuses to do so. If your husband is lost, or if he refuses to carry the burden for the spiritual leadership in the home, you need to IN MEEKNESS pick up the burden and bear it. But don't get so comfortable with it that you are not willing to turn it over to him should he get saved or right with God. Remember that Deborah tried to hand the torch to Barak - he wouldn't take it.

If it must be that you are the one to have devotions and prayer time with your children - do so. If it must be you who carries your children to church so that they can learn about God - do so. And be as faithful to all of the services as you can, especially if your children have worldly influences pulling them in the other direction. If it must be you who sets the standard of righteous living and separation in the home, do so to the best of your ability. At the same time you've got to remember that you are not released from the commandment to be submissive to your husband. In fact, it is possibly more necessary for you to be submissive- it may be that submissive spirit that will lead your husband to Christ or to obedience to the will of God.

Likewise, ye wives, be in subjection to your own husbands; that, if any obey not the word, they also may without the word be won by the conversation of the wives; While they behold your chaste conversation coupled with fear. 1 Peter 3:1-2

I do not envy you if you are in this situation. Your task of self-control is not an easy one.

What did Deborah do that we can draw from in our lives to make us spiritually stronger? Verse 4 says she was a prophetess.

A prophet is defined as: A person illuminated, inspired or instructed by God to announce future events.

Therefore she knew the Lord on a personal basis. She spent time in prayer and in the Word of God. She allowed God to speak to her and through her. We are told to abide in Christ.

Abide in me, and I in you. As the branch cannot bear fruit of itself, except it abide in the vine; no more can ye, except ye abide in me. John 15:4. Vs 7 says: "If ye abide in me, and my words abide in you, ye shall ask what ye will, and it shall be done unto you."

(Remember here that the key is abiding in Christ. You are not going to ask for something that is contrary to the will of God if you are truly abiding in Christ. If you are unsure, you will be seeking for and contented with the will of God as your primary goal in prayer.) A consistent fervent prayer life is the first necessary ingredient to spiritual strength.

The sacrifice of the wicked is an abomination unto the LORD: but the prayer of the upright is his delight. Proverbs 15:8

God delights in our prayer. He desires for us to spend time with Him. Considering the awesome price that He paid for our souls, how humbling it ought to be for us to realize that our Holy, Almighty, Matchless Savior wants to spend time with us! Prayer is one of the simplest, easiest and most neglected parts of our Christian life. I've never met a Christian who spends too much time in prayer. Let's take a look at some simple basics of prayer from the Word of God.

Be careful for nothing; but in every thing by prayer and supplication with thanksgiving let your requests be made known unto God. Philippians 4:6

So we are to pray about everything. Even the smallest things.

Praying always with all prayer and supplication in the Spirit, and watching thereunto with all perseverance and supplication for all saints; Ephesians 6:18

So we should pray not only for our own needs but the needs of others and to be ready at any moment to pray and not to quit praying.

Pray without ceasing. 1 Thessalonians 5:17

Continue in prayer, and watch in the same with thanksgiving.
Colossians 4:2

Giving thanks to God should be an important element in our prayer life.
Romans 12 is the checklist for becoming a living sacrifice, which is not an
extraordinary feat but our reasonable service. In verse 12 it says:
Rejoicing in hope; patient in tribulation; continuing instant in prayer; The
word instant means: Pressing; urgent; importunate; earnest.
Our prayer should be urgent, earnest, seeking God's face with all our
energy. It should be fervent and should be direct and real.

Confess your faults one to another, and pray one for another, that ye may
be healed. The effectual fervent prayer of a righteous man availeth much.
James 5:16

A lot of people hesitate to pray in public, and sometimes don't pray much
at all, because they feel like they don't know how. If you study the prayer
life of the heroes of the faith, both in the Bible and in Church history, you
will find that the men and women who were real prayer warriors and able
to get in touch with God in an awesome way were those who were just
themselves. They did not try to toss out flashy words and fancy phrases.
They just talked to God. If you are worried that you might have an
inappropriate approach to prayer (and God is certainly worthy of the
greatest respect) ask Him to help you to pray in a way that is pleasing to
Him.

Let us therefore come boldly unto the throne of grace, that we may obtain
mercy, and find grace to help in time of need. Hebrews 4:16

The biggest key to real prayer is just to be honest with God. By the way,
he already knows who you are! So spiritual strength begins with a
consistent, fervent prayer life. You will never be strong as a Christian
woman without spending time in prayer.

Vs 4. She judged Israel, so she knew the commandments of God. The
children of Israel came to her - she didn't go to them - for judgment. The
next element for spiritual strength is knowing the Word of God.

Study to shew thyself approved unto God, a workman that needeth not to be ashamed, rightly dividing the word of truth.   2 Timothy 2:15

Till I come, give attendance to reading, to exhortation, to doctrine.
1 Timothy 4:13

And these words, which I command thee this day, shall be in thine heart: And thou shalt teach them diligently unto thy children, and shalt talk of them when thou sittest in thine house, and when thou walkest by the way, and when thou liest down, and when thou risest up. And thou shalt bind them for a sign upon thine hand, and they shall be as frontlets between thine eyes. And thou shalt write them upon the posts of thy house, and on thy gates.
Deuteronomy 6:6-9

I will worship toward thy holy temple, and praise thy name for thy lovingkindness and for thy truth: for thou hast magnified thy word above all thy name. Psalm 138:2

The third commandment is "Thou shalt not take the name of the LORD thy God in vain; for the LORD will not hold him guiltless that taketh his name in vain."
Exodus 20:7

If the LORD requires that we hold His name as holy and honor it, yet He has magnified His Word above all His name - How should we respect, love, read and study the Word of God!

Psalm 119:72 The law of thy mouth is better unto me than thousands of gold and silver.
vs 97 O how love I thy law! it is my meditation all the day.
vs 103 How sweet are thy words unto my taste! yea, sweeter than honey to my mouth!
vs 127 Therefore I love thy commandments above gold; yea, above fine gold.
vs 129-130 Thy testimonies are wonderful: therefore doth my soul keep them.

The entrance of thy words giveth light; it giveth understanding unto the simple.
vs 140 Thy word is very pure: therefore thy servant loveth it.
vs 143 Trouble and anguish have taken hold on me: yet thy commandments are my delights.

The second easiest element of spiritual strength is to read and study the Word of God, it is also the second most neglected part of our Christian life. It is so sad that we, in this country, who have the Word of God in our hands -- any number of copies of it in our homes and around our churches -- neglect the Word of God to a shameful degree. It would not at all surprise me if we do not find ourselves in this country wishing and longing for a copy of God's Word one day the way they long for it now in China and Russia. It truly would be what we deserve, considering the way that we neglect to know His Word when it is so readily available to us.

There is another factor here, however. It is not enough to read and study God's Word. You must take heed to what it says and obey it. I have known people who feel that the Word of God is an interesting thing to study but have no more intention of obeying it than if it were a catalog. Further down in the same passage that we read in Deuteronomy it says:

Ye shall diligently keep the commandments of the LORD your God, and his testimonies, and his statutes, which he hath commanded thee.
Deuteronomy 6:17

Looking back on our definitions we know that to do something diligently is: Steady application in business of any kind; constant effort to accomplish what is undertaken; exertion of body or mind without unnecessary delay or sloth; - doing the job with a faithful attitude, without having to be prodded, and without putting it off.

So if we are to apply that to our Bible study we can see that to obey the command in Deuteronomy 6 we are to steadily apply ourselves to obedience of the Word of God, make a constant effort to live as He would have us to live, exert ourselves without delay or sloth in the matter of obeying His Word. Obey the Word of God with a faithful attitude without having to be prodded, without putting it off.

To apply this practically to our devotional life: We need to come before God in prayer boldly, seeking His face and asking Him to meet our needs. We need to confess our sins and make things right with Him. Unconfessed sin will hinder your prayer life.

Behold the LORD's hand is not shortened, that it cannot save; neither his ear heavy, that it cannot hear: But your iniquities have separated between you and your God, and your sins have hid his face from you, that he will not hear. Isaiah 59:1-2

Next, we need to spend some time in thanksgiving and praise –

Enter into his gates with thanksgiving, and into his courts with praise: be thankful unto him, and bless his name. Psalm 100: 4

Then spend time asking for our needs, the needs of others and for strength for the day ahead. Then we need to ask Him to open His Word to us. Understand that the Word of God is a spiritual Book. You cannot understand it without His help.

Which things also we speak, not in the words which man's wisdom teacheth, but which the Holy Ghost teacheth; comparing spiritual things with spiritual. But the natural man receiveth not the things of the Spirit of God: for they are foolishness unto him: neither can he know them, because they are spiritually discerned.
1 Corinthians 2:13-14

But the Comforter, which is the Holy Ghost, whom the Father will send in my name, he shall teach you all things, and bring all things to your remembrance, whatsoever I have said unto you.   John 14:26

Then read the Word of God. It is helpful to have a reading schedule or plan to follow. It makes you more accountable for getting your reading done. Do not expect that you will automatically understand everything you read. Those of us who have been saved any length of time can tell you that God's Word is an awesome book - every time you read it, He will reveal something new. Many times you will read and the Holy Spirit will give you a little something from the passage and you say, "I can't count how many times I've read that - but I never saw that in it before!" If you do not understand, that's okay - read anyway. The Lord will reward your faithfulness and will begin to open it to you more and more each day. We also need to search His Word with a prayerful and repentant attitude; willing to make the changes that He brings into focus and desiring to have Him mold our lives to His will and way. Being faithful to church will help you understand the Word more because the Lord will speak to you through the preaching and teaching. I know all of this may sound basic to some but this is the basis of spiritual strength. I've known many who long for spiritual strength but neglect the Word, church attendance and their prayer life. When you tell them this is the key they think, "It can't be that simple - I was looking for some big mysterious answer." It IS that simple. Pray + Read and obey your Bible and the preaching of His Word + Worship the Lord faithfully in His house and at home + time for Him to work in your life = spiritual strength.

In Judges 5:1-2 we see the next thing that Deborah did that will help us learn spiritual strength.

Then sang Deborah and Barak the son of Abinoam on that day, saying, Praise ye the LORD for the avenging of Israel, when the people willingly offered themselves. Judges 5:1-2

She wholeheartedly worshiped the Lord. There are several purposes for regular church attendance.

Not forsaking the assembling of ourselves together, as the manner of some is; but exhorting one another: and so much the more, as ye see the day approaching. Hebrews 10:25

Here are two things we should notice. One of the reasons for gathering together is so that we can exhort one another.

To exhort means: to excite or to give strength, spirit or courage.

God planned for us to be together, to help one another. We need one another. No one, on his own, can be as strong spiritually as when we are worshiping and working and fellowshipping together. We have the responsibility to build one another up, to look out for one another's spiritual well-being. When we spend too much time alone, fighting against the world, the devil has more opportunity to tear us down.

Secondly notice that it says "and so much the more as ye see the day approaching." We are not to go to church less and less as the time gets closer to the Lord's return but more and more. The more wicked this world becomes the more we need the strength of each other and the preaching and teaching of the Word of God.

But be ye doers of the word and not hearers only, deceiving your own selves. James 1:22

It does no good to come to church if the purpose is to tear down instead of edifying one another. It also does no good to listen to the preaching of the Word of God and walk out and ignore it and not apply it to our lives. It also does no good to come to church and sit like a spectator. Church is not a spectator sport. It is a place to learn and to serve. I once had a lady ask me for help who said that she was ready to drop out of church because she did not ever get anything out of it. My reply was: "How much do you put into it?" If you never get involved, you will eventually get out. Couch potato Christianity does not honor God. After a time it becomes so hum drum that you cannot stick with it.

There is a time for growth. When a person is first saved they need to come to church as much as they can, so they can learn as much as they can. Then there is a time to begin to serve; working at the labor level. Get involved in serving in some way, learning as you go. This is the apprenticeship stage. Latch on to a godly, laboring Christian and learn from them. (Notice that I said a godly Christian! Don't make the mistake of building close friendships and learning from carnal Christians!) Then there comes a time to teach. What level you get involved at depends upon your own spiritual growth, the needs of your church and the desires of your pastor - but you cannot be spiritually strong unless you exercise your faith in serving God actively.

If any man serve me, let him follow me; and where I am, there shall also my servant be: if any man serve me, him will my Father honour. John 12:26

If we were asked, "What is the main reason for going to church?" most of us would reply, "To worship God." And it is. But do we really worship

Him? We said last week that worship was a healthy thing, a wonderful emotional strength builder. It also builds your spiritual strength. The problem is that so few people really know how to worship. In the process of being so careful to not get caught up in the foolishness and demonic activity of the Charismatic movement, we have jumped all the way to the other extreme. We have become so dead in our attempts to worship that we have almost begun to feel like if we give any outward show of love toward our God that it is a sin. Nothing could be more opposite to the truth!! In studying the Word of God we find some fascinating things about worship.

Worship means: To adore; to pay divine honors to; to reverence with supreme respect and veneration.

It is very difficult to really come into the presence of someone you *adore* and sit still, quiet and solemn. How did Jesus say we were to worship Him?

God is a Spirit: and they that worship him must worship him in spirit and in truth. John 4:24

We are given some guidelines to go by in worshiping God. It's funny that in our Baptist churches, where the truth of the Word of God is so very important to us, so many don't pay any attention to these guidelines. Psalm 100 tells how we should come into the Lord's presence. Joyful, singing, with thanksgiving and praise.

Give unto the LORD the glory due unto his name: bring an offering, and come before him: worship the LORD in the beauty of holiness.
1 Chronicles 16:29

So part of worship is to bring an offering.

Give unto the LORD the glory due unto his name; worship the LORD in the beauty of holiness. Psalm 29:2

The beauty of holiness that is talked about here is not the Lord's - it's ours. We are to offer Him worship in the beauty of a holy life.

Exalt the LORD our God, and worship at his holy hill; for the LORD our God is holy. Psalm 99:9

Exalt means: To elevate in estimation and praise; to magnify; to praise; to extol.

Praise ye the LORD. Sing unto the LORD a new song, and his praise in the congregation of saints. Psalm 149:1

Singing is worship – privately and in the congregation of saints, together.

Make a joyful noise unto the LORD, all the earth: make a loud noise, and rejoice, and sing praise. Sing unto the LORD with the harp; with the harp, and the voice of a psalm. With trumpets and sound of cornet make a joyful noise before the LORD, the King. Psalm 98:4-6 (A loud noise??)

Rejoice in the LORD, O ye righteous: for praise is comely for the upright. Praise the LORD with harp: sing unto him with the psaltery and an instrument of ten strings. Sing unto him a new song; play skilfully with a loud noise. Psalm 33:1-3

Oh, there it is again - you mean it's okay to be loud? Not just okay, we're *told* to be loud. Why? Because timidity in worship makes people think you don't really believe in what you're worshiping. There is no more beautiful sound and sight than a group of worshipers of the Lord God Almighty who are singing with all of their might and heart with the love of God radiating from their faces... and the Spirit of God responds with His sweet presence and touches the heart.

We will go into his tabernacles: we will worship at his footstool. Arise, O LORD, into thy rest; thou, and the ark of thy strength. Let thy priests be clothed with righteousness; and let thy saints shout for joy. Psalm 132:7-9

Notice that this shouting for joy is taking place in the church.

Be glad in the LORD, and rejoice, ye righteous: and shout for joy, all ye that are upright in heart. Psalm 32:11

Mrs. Mary, you don't really expect me to shout, do you? No, not necessarily. But don't be unnerved if others do and do be completely real in your worship of the Lord. He's desiring your honest worship - and you can't honestly worship if you are so caught up in the ritual or so worried about what others think that you can't really even think about God, Himself.

O Clap your hands, all ye people; shout unto God with the voice of triumph. Psalm 47:1

It's okay to clap your hands in church? Yes, that too. In praise to God....not in applauding (exalting) the singing group or other "performers."

Let us lift up our heart with our hands unto God in the Heavens. Lamentations 3:41

Raising hands? That too.

Isaiah 12; Psalm 134; Psalm 150 - In his sanctuary: Praise with instruments of music, with the timbrel and dance. A serious note of caution here!! We don't know what kind of dance they used - we do know that it was not the flesh satisfying junk that goes on today. A lot of people want to say it was leaping for joy before the Lord like the man who was healed at the temple.

And he leaping up stood, and walked, and entered with them into the temple, walking, and leaping and praising God. Acts 3:8

Now, we really could learn something from him, because he was excited about what the Lord had done for him. The Bible did not say he was dancing. It does say that David danced before the Lord in 2 Samuel 6: 14-16 and in this passage it uses leaping and dancing in the same context. It also, in several passages, mentions that the women of Israel went out together and danced during certain festivities. This dancing was in praise to the Lord. Exodus 15:20, Judges 21:19-21.

Since we are ignorant of how to properly praise the Lord this way it is best that we stay away from it. It would be far easier to fall into a sinful show of the flesh here than to really worship. However, you can see that it is obvious that praise and worship of the Lord is a much more active thing than sitting on a pew in your Sunday morning starch and singing

"Bringing in the Sheaves" in a monotone. Ezra 3:11-13 gives a picture of a worship service - it was very noisy and emotional. Am I saying that you have to shout and leap and clap your hands and cry in order to worship God? No, not necessarily. And please don't do those things if you can't do them from the heart! But those things are not, in God's eyes, unacceptable parts of worshiping Him. It is only the pride of man that has made those things unacceptable. Too many times we go to church and spend the entire service concerning ourselves with what the other people around us are thinking and barely focusing ourselves on the fact that we are there in the name of God. If you go back to the passage in John Chapter 4 you will see that He told the woman at the well that God seeks for those who will worship Him in spirit and in truth. In spirit - with your heart and your emotions. In truth - learning and obeying the Word of God. If you study the picture God gives us of His throne room in Heaven in Revelation 4 you will find that it is very noisy and joyful. I had a pastor who said, "you need to get used to some shouting and praising God here because if you don't you won't want to go to Heaven, it's a noisy place." This is a much different picture than our typical Baptist church services.

What are we really saying here? Get real. Worship God with the real you. If you are prone to cry - go ahead and cry. Sing out with your heart and soul. If you are prone to be excited at ball games and family outings and sit like a piece of furniture in church then I would guess that you are not really worshiping.

Remember that the Bible says that all things should be done decently and in order. He is not the author of confusion and should the church service become out of order and in confusion it's wrong. That, among other things (such as major doctrinal error,) is what is wrong with the Charismatic movement. But by the same token deadness does not honor God and **honest adoration** does honor Him. Where do you strike the balance? With the authority of your pastor, who is the REAL "praise and worship leader" in your church.

Spiritual strength: Pray, Read your Bible, Apply God's Word practically to your life and obey it, Go to church every opportunity that you have and really Worship God. You will be amazed at the strength you receive. And then be ready for the task ahead.

Lesson Eight Review

1) Strength means:

_____

_____

2) Spiritual means:

_____

_____

3) Deborah is one of the most _____ women in the Bible.

4) She has the position here of _____, or almost of

_____.

5) The theme of the book of Judges is:

_____

_____

6) Deborah was that she was doing the best she could with what she had. And what she had was

_____

_____

7) If your husband is lost, or if he refuses to carry the burden for the spiritual leadership in the home, you need to

_____

_____

8) Deborah was a _____, this meant that she knew God in a personal way.

9) Define prophet:

_____

_____

10) The first necessary ingredient to Spiritual strength is

_____

_____

11) God _____ in our prayer, He _____ for us to spend time with Him. Prayer is one of the _____, and _____ parts of our Christian life.

12) We are to pray about _____.

13) _____ should be an important element in our prayer life.

14) The word instant means

_____

_____

15) Our prayer should be _____, _____, seeking _____ with _____

16) The third commandments is

_____

_____

17) The LORD requires that we hold His name as holy and honor it, yet

_____

18) The second easiest element of spiritual strength is _____ and it is the second _____ of our Christian life.

19) The biggest key to real prayer is _____

20) It is not enough to _____ God's Word. You must _____

21) To do something diligently is:

_____

22) Unconfessed sin will _____

23) The formula for Spiritual strength is _____ +
_____ and_____ your _____ and
_____+ _____ faithfully +
_____ = spiritual strength.

24) Worship means:

_____

25) List 5 things that the Bible tells us are a part of true worship.

_____

_____

_____

_____

_____

A Woman Among all Those
Lessons in Christian Womanhood

Lesson 9

Scripture memory for this lesson: She layeth her hands to the spindle, and her hands hold the distaff. Proverbs 31:19

And whatsoever ye do, do it heartily, as to the Lord, and not unto men; Colossians 3:23

The dictionary defines Spindle as: The pin used in spinning wheels for twisting the thread, and on which the thread when twisted, is wound.

Distaff: The staff of a spinning wheel to which a bunch of flax or tow is tied, and from which the thread is drawn.

I always pictured a woman sitting down to the spinning wheel when I read this verse. However, in the Wikipedia, I found that spinning wheels were not invented until around 500 A.D. Until that time (which means during Bible times) the spindle and distaff were hand-held objects and the spinning done by twirling the spindle. This made spinning thread a very time consuming matter and a skill not easily attained. That is why clothing was prized so highly - especially well made clothing. Good clothes were of such value that they were taken as spoil in war. Joshua 7:21. They were used as collateral for debts. Exodus 22:26-27. When Jesus, and others who were condemned to death, were crucified, they stripped the prisoner and divided his clothing up amongst the soldiers. John 19:23-24.

So spinning was a much needed skill and one that every woman needed in that day to properly clothe her family. The virtuous woman's skill was evidently great in this area. We see that she took the raw materials that she sought for in verse 13 and made it into thread. Then in verse 21 she made clothing for her household from that thread and in 22 clothing for herself. In verse 24 she used it for income to help her household. In verse 16 she took money, wisely saved from the sale of her labor, and invested it back into her family.

109

The Bible mentions in Acts 16:14 that Lydia was a seller of purple - more than likely this was thread that she had spun and dyed and was selling to make, or improve, her income. Purple, blue, scarlet and fine linen were the threads, and the cloth made from them, that were most prized in that day. They were usually worn by the higher class. The common people wore wool, spun goats hair and a lower grade of linen, in their natural colors, or dyed with less expensive materials. In Exodus is the only other mention of spinning in the Bible.

And all the women that were wise hearted did spin with their hands, and brought that which they had spun, both of blue, and of purple, and of scarlet, and of fine linen. And all the women whose heart stirred them up in wisdom spun goats' hair. Exodus 35:25-26

In this passage we find that the women who were doing the spinning were wise hearted. What they were doing was to use the skills that they had for the service of the Lord.

Our example this week is Priscilla.

After these things Paul departed from Athens, and came to Corinth; and found a certain Jew named Aquila, born in Pontus, lately come from Italy, with his wife Priscilla (because that Claudius had commanded all Jews to depart from Rome:) and came unto them. and because he was of the same craft, he abode with them, and wrought: for by their occupation they were tentmakers. Acts 18:1-3

My guess is that Priscilla was involved in making the cloth for the tents. Perhaps in spinning the thread and/or weaving the cloth. And that Aquila and Paul put the tents together and sold them at market. This is supposition. We don't know exactly what her role was - but she was a help to her husband and to the man of God.

Other mentions of Priscilla are in Vs. 18 – 19. Paul took them with him when he left Corinth. He left them in Ephesus. Then in Vs. 24-26 Aquila and Priscilla led Apollos to the Lord. In Romans 16:3 Paul sends them a greeting. In 1 Corinthians 16:19 He sends the church at Corinth their greeting, making mention that there is now a church established in their house.

There are several things about Priscilla that stand out to me. One is that wherever you read of her she is with her husband. And wherever you read of her husband she is there. They obviously had a good relationship and obviously worked and cooperated well with one another.

The next thing you see about her is that she was a helper to her husband in his tent-making business. They were tent-makers. The antecedent of the pronoun 'they' is Aquila and Priscilla. Then you see that they used their tent-making skills as a ministry to God's man. It was certainly a great help to the Apostle Paul to be able to stay with someone and join in the family business for a time. Next you see her willing to pull up roots and go her husband as he followed the man of God when he left there, seeking God's will. Also, she was willing to be left in Ephesus to carry on the ministry there; witnessing in the synagogue; beginning a church in their house. All of it was a joint effort. She is a perfect picture to me of a missionary's wife and a picture, too, of how God in His infinite wisdom uses us for His work. He begins with the minor tasks and slowly moves us upward in knowledge, skills, and abilities as we are submissive to His will and able to handle it. She went from being faithful to the simple basic tasks of menial work, learned and grew as she went along, until she was a pastor's wife, laboring in a church side by side with her husband.

Do you have a skill or talent? Can you give that talent as an offering to the Lord? Notice that the women in Exodus are mentioned as wise hearted. Both those who spun the expensive materials and those that spun the goats' hair. Are you willing to be of use to the Lord? You may think that your talent is not worthy of His notice but nothing could be further from the truth! 1 Corinthians 12:12-27 talks about using our gifts and talents for the Lord. God gives us gifts and abilities to use for His glory. The things that He gives, He expects us to use for Himself and for each other.

The difference between a gift and an ability?

Gifts: Anything given without price, anything bestowed by the creator.

Abilities: Physical powers, whether bodily or mental; natural or acquired; force of understanding; skill in arts or science.

So we see that a gift is given by God and an ability is something we learn to do.

For example: some have a musical gift, some have an ability - both of which God wishes to use for His glory.

Jesus gave the parable of the talents in Matthew 25:14-30. In each case of the servants that He praised, He said: "Well done, thou good and faithful servant: thou has been faithful over a few things, I will make thee ruler over many things: enter thou into the joy of thy lord."

The one who was only given one talent was called wicked and slothful for not using what he had been given, even in the smallest way. The lord told him that even if he could not have been wise hearted enough to use it the way the other men did, he could have made some use of it for profit for the lord.

Many times a person yearns to do great things for God but they are not faithful in the small things that they are given to do - not realizing that this is the testing ground God gives them.

He that is faithful in that which is least is faithful also in much: and he that is unjust in the least is unjust also in much. Luke 16:10

If God gives you small things to do, Praise His name, for ".....For unto whomsoever much is given, of him shall be much required:." Luke 12:48

If you are given small things - be faithful in those small things and you will answer for your faithfulness to Him. If He gives you greater things you must give an account for those larger responsibilities. Be faithful in the thing that He has given you and use it for His honor and glory. You will find that when you have been judged faithful in the small things that He gives you to do, He will give you larger things. He will build your responsibility as you prove yourself faithful. Why? Because He does not know what you will do? Not at all. Our God is omniscient - that means that He knows everything. He uses this to prove us to ourselves and He sets this as a pattern we are to follow in our lives.

 As we train our children, we should not heap responsibilities on them that they are too tender to handle. They need to build up to it. Nor should we neglect to give them responsibilities as they can handle them. Otherwise, they will never learn to accept responsibility. In the church as we train people to walk with God, it is the same way. We should not heap responsibilities on young Christians that they are not ready to handle. Neither should we fail to give them responsibilities as they grow ready for them. [One of the most horrible mistakes that some pastors make today is in not using their young people in the service of the Lord. Instead they give them all play and no responsibility. Then they expect them, all in a year's time, as soon as they turn about 20 years old, to know how to accept responsibility in the church. Then they are surprised when they get out of church or still expect to be entertained, rather than accepting a position of leadership.]

So how do I use my talents for the Lord? First of all determine what your talents are. Can you sing? Play an instrument? Arrange flowers? Clean? Decorate? Teach? Sew? Knit? Crochet? Quilt? Do handcrafts? Cook? Bake? Tend to and grow pretty flowers? Do you work well with small children? Or older ones? Do you relate well to the elderly and infirm? Do you have the gift and ability to talk to people? Do you like to write letters and correspond with people? Do you have computer or filing or typing skills? Any and all of these things, and more, can be of use right here in the church - and the church is usually in great need of these things. Some of the simplest things that you may not think are of any worth are the biggest blessings in the church when someone will take it upon themselves to make it their ministry.

I have been in a church where one of the ladies could not do anything else because of physical problems but she had her husband purchase a bunch of mixed cards and stamps. She got a list of all the birthdays and anniversaries of the members of the church and the missionaries of the church. She sent out cards to them on birthdays and holidays as well as cards when they were sick.

I have seen ladies of the church use their ladies' fellowship time to make Sunday school materials for missionaries, to fold, staple, stamp and label flyers going out for meetings of the church. I have known ladies in the church who had time to visit shut-ins on a regular basis and just sit and chat with them, or take them some goodies from the kitchen.

It is an awesome blessing to the pastor's family to have someone willing to clean the church and care for the grounds. I could go on and on but you get the idea. Take what you have and give it to the Lord. Turn your abilities, no matter how great or small, into a service for God by serving others. So where do we begin? By giving ourselves to God. Not dictating to Him how we want to serve Him but by willingly turning ourselves over to Him as a vessel for His use.

But in a great house there are not only vessels of gold and of silver, but also of wood and of earth; and some to honour, and some to dishonour. If a man therefore purge himself from these, he shall be a vessel unto honour, sanctified, and meet for the master's use, and prepared unto every good work. 2 Timothy 2:20-21

Romans chapter 12 is an outline given to us on how to present ourselves as a living sacrifice to God. If you will study it you will see that there is enough in that one chapter to keep us busy the rest of our lives. We're going to take a look at it verse by verse during this lesson and the next. It will show us what God requires of a living sacrifice, a gift of ourselves to Him. We can't possibly do it justice in the space and time that we have but we can take a glance.

Vs. 1 "I beseech you therefore brethren, by the mercies of God, that ye present your bodies a living sacrifice, holy, acceptable unto God, which is your reasonable service."

Understand that it's not some great thing you are doing more than anyone else has ever done. It is only reasonable that you give **all** of your heart and life to God.

What? know ye not that your body is the temple of the Holy Ghost which is in you, which ye have of God, and ye are not your own? for ye are bought with a price: therefore glorify God in your body, and in your spirit, which are God's. 1 Corinthians 6:19-20

There is a huge gap in Christianity today - and this is it. Christians are not dedicated to the Saviour. They are wrapped up in the world and themselves. They give the Lord their spare time. A friend of mine repeatedly said, "God does not want your spare time, He wants your precious time."

Jesus said unto him, Thou shalt love the Lord thy God with all thy heart, and with all thy soul, and with all thy mind. Matthew 22:37

All your heart - all your soul - all your mind. That is the first and great commandment. He wasn't making a suggestion. The gap I see in Christianity is that Jesus is not Lord. They are willing enough to have a Saviour but not a Lord. Willing enough for God to do for them what they need done but unwilling for the Lord to disrupt their plans and their lives. Many of them are not really saved. They've caught the easy-believism bandwagon as it went by and they are on a one way slide to Hell, all the time calling out, "I'm saved, saved, saved." Others truly have repented and believed the Saviour but they don't understand a thing about true Christianity and sold out dedication to God. It's not a great thing - it's only reasonable. He gave Himself for us - we give ourselves to Him.

Vs 2 "And be not conformed to this world: but be ye transformed by the renewing of your mind, that ye may prove what is that good, and acceptable, and perfect, will of God."

The world's ideas and philosophies do not line up with the Word of God. We should not talk like, walk like, dress like, act like the world.

Love not the world, neither the things that are in the world. if any man love the world, the love of the Father is not in him. 1 John 2:15

Ye adulterers and adulteresses, know ye not that the friendship of the world is enmity with God? Whosoever therefore will be a friend of the world is the enemy of God. James 4:4

God likens a Christian who embraces the world to a woman who steps out of her marriage bonds. I don't know about you but I do not want to stand at the judgment seat of Christ and have my Saviour tell me that I was His enemy because I embraced the code of conduct of the world. I don't want the world's ideas, their entertainment, their language, their dress - none of it. And to risk walking as close to the edge of worldliness as you can is to risk walking over the edge of being considered, by the Saviour, as the enemy of God.

Wherefore come out from among them, and be ye separate, saith the Lord, and touch not the unclean thing; and I will receive you, 2 Corinthians 6:17

The renewing of your mind.

That ye put off concerning the former conversation the old man which is corrupt according to the deceitful lusts; And be renewed in the spirit of your mind; And that ye put on the new man, which after God is created in righteousness and true holiness.   Ephesians 4:22-24

Set your mind on Christ. When you do you will be amazed at the contentment and fulfillment you will receive.

We'll skip down to Vs 6-8, "Having then gifts differing according to the grace that is given to us, whether prophecy, let us prophesy according to the proportion of faith; Or ministry, let us wait on our ministering: or he that teacheth, on teaching; Or he that exhorteth, on exhortation: he that giveth, let him do it with simplicity; he that ruleth, with diligence; he that sheweth mercy, with cheerfulness."

What is this saying? Give to the use of the church what you have been given by God: the talents, abilities, skills that you have. And give with a right heart. A heart overflowing with gratitude for what God has done for you.

And whatsoever ye do, do it heartily, as to the Lord, and not unto men; Colossians 3:23

Vs 11 "Not slothful in business; fervent in spirit; serving the Lord;"

Get the job done, faithfully. Don't put it off until the last minute and don't do a half-job. When you have a job to do for the Lord, it should be done as if your whole life depends upon it. Serving the Lord - THE LORD - don't lose track of whom you are serving. That will help with the central part of the verse, fervent in spirit. With energy, enthusiasm, dedication and drive.

Vs 21 "Be not overcome of evil, but overcome evil with good."

This is the summary verse for the chapter. We have the ability to overcome evil with good. If we will back up and take a good long look at what this chapter is telling us to do and apply it to our lives we CAN overcome evil with good, step by step as a child of God. But it takes dedication. It takes self-sacrifice. We've got to be willing to give it our time and attention.

And let us not be weary in well doing: for in due season we shall reap, if we faint not. Galatians 6:9

But ye, brethren, be not weary in well doing. 2 Thessalonians 3:13

Many times this verse is used in connection with soul winning. It is true there also, it takes dedication and time going out faithfully, sometimes without seeing any real results. But God rewards our faithfulness. He does not expect US to get results. He expects us to be faithful and He will take care of providing the results. But look at the context of both chapters and you will see that it is connected with overcoming evil, separating ourselves from it, and fighting against sin in our own lives and in the lives of our brothers and sisters in Christ. We shall reap, if we faint not. We can overcome evil with good in our own lives if we will learn to dedicate ourselves as a living sacrifice to God. It begins with the little things. Just like spinning the thread.

Are you wise hearted like the women in Exodus and our virtuous woman? Will you begin by giving the Lord the little things in your life and let Him build a faithful servant - a usable vessel - out of you? It will happen step by step, as it did in Priscilla's life, as you give yourself daily as a living sacrifice to God.

Lesson Nine Review

1) Define Spindle

_____

_____

_____

2) Define Distaff

_____

_____

_____

3) Spinning wheels were not invented until _____

4) Why was clothing prized so highly?

_____

_____

5) List 3 things that show us that clothing was considered very valuable in Bible times.

_____

_____

_____

6) God said the women in Exodus were _____ both those who spun _____ and those who spun

_____

7) Priscilla and Aquila had a family business making _____

8) They began their ministry by being a _____ to the _____ of _____.

9) Wherever you read of Priscilla she is

_____.

10) Outline the steps of Aquila and Priscilla's ministry.
A) First they were _____
B) then they _____
C) then they _____
D) then they _____

11) A gift is _____

12) An ability is: _____

13) Many times a person yearns to do great things for God, but
_____

14) When we are faithful in the _____ things that God gives us
to do then He will give us _____ things to do.

15) Our God is _____ that means that
He _____

16) Some of the _____ things are the _____ when
someone will take it upon themselves to make it their
_____.

17) We begin by _____ ourselves to God.
Not _____ to Him how we want to serve Him, but by
willingly _____ as a _____ for
His use.

18) It is only _____ that you give all of your heart and life to
God.

19) The gap in Christianity today is that
_____.

20) What does God compare a Christian who embraces the world with?
_____

21) To risk walking as close to the edge of worldliness as you can is to risk:_____

_____

22) Letting Christ build a faithful servant - a useable vessel out of us will happen _____ as it did in Priscilla's life as you give yourself daily as a _____.

23) Write the Scripture memory passage for this lesson:

_____

_____

_____

_____

A Woman Among all Those
Lessons in Christian Womanhood

Lesson 10

Scripture Memory: She stretcheth out her hand to the poor; yea, she reacheth forth her hands to the needy. Proverbs 31:20

Pure religion and undefiled before God and the Father is this, to visit the fatherless and widows in their affliction, and to keep himself unspotted from the world. James 1:27

This passage deals with our relationships and our attitude toward others. The virtuous woman is a compassionate woman. Compassion has some sisters. One of these is meekness and the other is mercy. All three of these things are a requirement for a God-fearing Christian.

Our Bible example this week is Esther. Esther, to me, is a picture of meekness, compassion and loyal devotion. Vashti, the queen, disobeyed the command of Ahasuerus to come before him and as a result was banished and removed from being queen. A new queen was sought here in Esther 2:5-23.

Notice several points of meekness in Esther's life - first that she was in obedience to Mordecai, even after becoming queen (vs. 20). Second, notice that she made no demands on the king's chamberlain. Every young woman was given the opportunity to "shine" in her own style with all the clothes, jewels, makeup, etc. that she could ever hope for. Esther let someone else choose for her. Realizing, perhaps, that the king's chamberlain knew far better than she what would please the king. The result was that she received the crown – which was all in God's plan. Then notice that when the plot on Ahasuerus' life was discovered she was quick to give credit where it was due. She did not seek to make herself more attractive in the king's eyes by getting the glory for herself. Instead, she told the king that Mordecai had found out the matter.

All of these things spell out meekness. She was obedient, undemanding and willing to concede to one who had more knowledge and experience in the matter at hand than she did. She was not seeking glory for herself.

In the matter of compassion, we look at Esther Chapter 4 when the great crisis came. Her love for Mordecai drove her to seek every means to relieve his distress. She could not bear to see him weeping, dressed in sackcloth. Her natural response when he told her what he wanted her to do was to recoil from the idea - 'you're asking me to risk my life!' The king's temperament was well known. He could have gotten rid of her just as easily as he did Vashti. But when she realized that she was the only hope the Jewish nation had, she put her very life on the line to seek their safety. That's the biggest picture of compassion one could ever hope for.

Greater love hath no man than this, that a man lay down his life for his friends. John 15:13

When she had received the king's favor for herself and for her loved ones, she did not stop there. Her compassion extended as far as her influence with the king would let it go.

And Esther spake yet again before the king, and fell down at his feet, and besought him with tears to put away the mischief of Haman the Agagite, and his device that he had devised against the Jews. Esther 8:3

Compassion means: A suffering with another; painful sympathy; a sensation of sorrow excited by the distress or misfortunes of another; pity; commiseration.

Compassion is a mixed passion, compounded of love and sorrow; at least some portion of love generally attends the pain or regret, or is excited by it. There are 3 areas in the Word of God where we are told specifically to have compassion - one is on a poor brother:

But whoso hath this world's good, and seeth his brother have need, and shutteth up his bowels of compassion from him, how dwelleth the love of God in him? 1 John 3:17
The Bible has a great deal to say about helping the poor and needy.

Defend the poor and fatherless: do justice to the afflicted and needy. Psalm 82:3

Here it specifically mentions orphaned children as those requiring compassion. Remember that we are given the definition of true religion.

Pure religion and undefiled before God and the Father is this, to visit the fatherless and widows in their affliction, and to keep himself unspotted from the world. James 1:27

The phrase "to visit in their affliction" doesn't mean go by and tell them hello. It means to give them what they need.

Blessed is he that considereth the poor: the LORD will deliver him in time of trouble. Psalm 41:1

He that hath pity upon the poor lendeth unto the LORD; and that which he hath given will he pay him again. Proverbs 19:17

Not only does God promise blessings on those who give to the poor, but He is seriously displeased when we do not.

If there be among you a poor man of one of thy brethren within any of thy gates in thy land which the LORD thy God giveth thee, thou shalt not harden thine heart, nor shut thine hand from thy poor brother. Deuteronomy 15:7

Whoso stoppeth his ears at the cry of the poor, he also shall cry himself, but shall not be heard. Proverbs 21:13

We are not to see a brother in Christ do without something they sincerely need if we have the power to do something about it. However, there are some guidelines that we should go by in helping the poor.

First: Our help should be directed first toward the Church.

As we have therefore opportunity, let us do good unto all men, especially unto them who are of the household of faith.   Galatians 6:10

In our last lesson we went over some passages in Romans 12 - our guideline for being a living sacrifice. A lot of the verses in Romans 12 fit into this lesson as well.

Distributing to the necessity of saints; given to hospitality. Romans 12:13

We are to be giving people, welcoming each other into our homes and lives. Notice here that it says the necessity of *saints*. Saints are defined by the Bible as the children of God, born again by His spirit. (Not some elite group elected by a church counsel after they are dead - - otherwise how could they have any necessity we could distribute to?) Also, 1 John 3:17 and Deuteronomy 15 that we mentioned above are referring to brethren.

For as we have many members in one body, and all members have not the same office: So we, being many, are one body in Christ, and every one members one of another. Romans 12: 4-5

We need each other. We are fellow-labourers. We are commanded to edify one another, help one another, pray for one another, love one another, exhort one another, to care for each other as family.

Be kindly affectioned one to another with brotherly love; in honour preferring one another; Romans 12:10

To prefer means to regard above others. To honor or esteem above another. We are to prefer to be with the children of God above all others in this world. That is not really hard for a real Christian to do. It does not take us very long in this walk with God to realize that other Christians are really the only ones that understand us and that we understand. But that's okay, because God told us to prefer each other. We should not wish for each other to do without any more than we would wish for our brother or sister in the flesh to do without.
Why? Shouldn't we care for all men? Yes, to a certain extent. However, God understands the hearts of wicked mankind
much better than we do and He knows that this world is full of scam artists who like nothing better than to use the compassion of the church for their own devices. There are people who make a profession out of going from church to church begging money. They make a good living

out of it too. This is NOT what God meant when He told us to give to the poor. He meant the honestly poor. God also does not intend for us to aid and abet those who are too lazy to work. He also does not want the church to be burdened with trying to support those who have other means of taking care of themselves. Even when the Bible speaks of the widows who were dependent upon the church for their support and upkeep they were told not to accept them as "widows indeed" unless there was no other way for their support to be earned. A widow indeed was one who had no family.

If any man or woman that believeth have widows, let them relieve them, and let not the church be charged; that it may relieve them that are widows indeed. 1 Timothy 5:16

If the Lord gave that guideline for widows who were members of the church then it is a given thing that he does not expect the church to support able bodied men and women in order for them to be lazy.

Secondly: We are not to give with the idea of getting anything back again.

And if ye lend to them of whom ye hope to receive, what thank have ye? For sinners also lend to sinners, to receive as much again. But love ye your enemies, and do good, and lend, hoping for nothing again; and your reward shall be great, and ye shall be the children of the Highest: for he is kind unto the unthankful and to the evil. Be ye therefore merciful, as your Father also is merciful.   Luke 6:34-36

Notice here that we are not even to expect thanks for what we do. That's a hard one! But if you will give, and you truly do not expect a return from the gift, you will have a much better attitude about the gift in the first place. You will be doing it as a service to the Lord and pride will have no place. Also, when you see a true need that you are able to meet, it should not matter what your personal feelings are toward that person.

Therefore if thine enemy hunger, feed him; if he thirst, give him drink: for in so doing thou shalt heap coals of fire on his head.
Romans 12:20

This is the attitude that God wants us to have toward our enemies at all times.

We're told to pray for them, bless them and do good to them. Not to seek after vengeance. Understand when it comes to deciding whether it is right for you to meet a need that it is not the person themselves or their personality that determines their eligibility. It is whether or not the **need** is legitimate and whether or not the person is able to meet the need for themselves. God expects a person to bear their own burden if they are able.

For every man shall bear his own burden. Galatians 6:5

If they are not able to meet the need, and we are, then we have an obligation before God to meet that need without considering our personal opinion of the person and without seeking any return.

Thirdly: We are to give as much as possible in total secret – not seeking glory for the gift in any way.

Take heed that ye do not your alms before men, to be seen of them: otherwise ye have no reward of your Father which is in heaven. Therefore when thou doest thine alms, do not sound a trumpet before thee, as the hypocrites do in the synagogues and in the streets, that they may have glory of men. Verily I say unto you, They have their reward. But when thou doest alms, let not thy left hand know what thy right hand doeth: That thine alms may be in secret: and thy Father which seeth in secret himself shall reward thee openly. Matthew 6:1-4

Some of the best fun I have ever had is when we knew of a need and we had the chance to meet that need without it being known. To slip in and give and slip out without being detected and then sit back and listen happily to the one who received it bubble over with excitement and listen to them thank God for their blessing! Get your kids in on it. They love being God's private "blessing squad." It's kind of like cat burglary in reverse!! If you know someone is struggling and God sets them on your heart - slip some money in their Bible or their purse at church. Send them a sealed envelope through the hands of a mediator or slip it onto their pew at church, in their mailbox, on the dash of their car. Set a sack of groceries on their doorstep. Then ring the doorbell and hide! Set the groceries in their car during church. Hang a gasoline gift card on a string around their rear view mirror. Send them a gift card in the mail with no return address. There are lots of ways you can meet a need and do it "without letting your left hand know what your right hand is doing."

Fourth: We are to give cheerfully with a willing heart and to give bountifully.

But this I say, He which soweth sparingly shall reap also sparingly; and he which soweth bountifully shall reap also bountifully. Every man according as he purposeth in his heart, so let him give; not grudgingly, or of necessity: for God loveth a cheerful giver.   2 Corinthians 9: 6-7

(A lot of times this passage is used in reference to giving to the church, sometime by people who want to excuse themselves for not tithing, but that's not what it's talking about. If you read the context of the chapter, it's talking about giving to the poor.)

The word alms means: Anything given gratuitously to relieve the poor, as money, food, or clothing, otherwise called charity.

Fifth: We are to give when the need is seen, without unnecessary delay.

Withhold not good from them to whom it is due, when it is in the power of thine hand to do it. Say not unto thy neighbour, Go, and come again, and to morrow I will give; when thou hast it by thee. Proverbs 3:27-28

If you were in their place, you would not want someone to be so short of compassion as to see your need, have what you needed, intend for you to have it, then just keep putting it off and let you do without.

Sixth: We are not to give with the results of encouraging sinful sloth or laziness.

This is where it becomes necessary for you to make the judgment of whether or not this is an honest need. If you give to someone who takes the money and spends it on sin you have aided and abetted them in sin. If you give to someone who is lazy and will not work when they are able you have violated Scripture - we are specifically told not to do so.

Therefore the judgment in this area is not only acceptable, it is commanded by God.

For even when we were with you, this we commanded you, that if any would not work, neither should he eat. For we hear that there are some which walk among you disorderly, working not at all, but are busybodies. Now them that are such we command and exhort by our Lord Jesus Christ, that with quietness they work, and eat their own bread. But ye, brethren, be not weary in well doing. And if any man obey not our word by this epistle, note that man, and have no company with him, that he may be ashamed. yet count him not as an enemy, but admonish him as a brother.
2 Thessalonians 3:10-15

This is a pretty hard saying. But it's Bible. The Lord has nothing good to say about laziness and slothfulness and does not intend for His children to be that way. And if they choose to be that way He does not intend for them to be comfortable in that role. It is **not** being compassionate to continue to give to a person who will not work when they are able. It is simply encouraging them in sin that will eventually bring the judgment of God on their lives. It is far more compassionate to let them find out as early as possible that the church is not there for a free ride for those who don't want to work or who foolishly spend their substance.

Prayer is the essential when it comes to compassionate giving. If you will allow the Holy Spirit to lead you in the matter then all will be well. If you see a need, and you feel God is nudging you to meet the need, then pray and ask Him for wisdom. One of the sweetest promises in the Bible is:

If any of you lack wisdom, let him ask of God, that giveth to all men liberally, and upbraideth not; and it shall be given him. James 1:5

Remember also, that submission to your husband dictates that he is the primary decision maker in whether or not you meet a financial need.

Another area where we are told to have compassion is the relationship between husband and wife - we are told to have compassion on one another.

Finally, be ye all of one mind, having compassion one of another, love as brethren, be pitiful, be courteous: 1 Peter 3:8

Look back at verses 1-7 and you will realize that the context of this passage is the husband and wife relationship. At first glance it would seem unnecessary for the Lord to tell us to have compassion on our marriage partner, to love as brethren(?) to be pitiful and to be courteous. But when you look at most marriages these things are sorely lacking. Sometimes a husband or wife will be much quicker to have compassion on, or be courteous toward, someone outside their home and to treat their husband or wife like an old shoe. The old phrase that the world uses is "familiarity breeds contempt." The Lord intends for us to treat our spouse with the same consideration that He expects out of us toward other brothers and sisters in Christ. (If they are saved they *are* your brother in Christ as well as your husband, and they are entitled to all of the love, respect and benefits that other brothers in Christ are entitled to - **plus** the reverence of a wife toward her husband.) That's why He told us "love as brethren." Looking back at the definition of compassion we see that it has a lot to do with walking in the other person's shoes - considering their feelings as if they were your own. Once again, do you approach your marriage with the idea of "What's in it for me?" Or do you approach it with the idea of "How can I be the very best I can be for my husband's good?" Are you expecting him to live for you or are you doing everything in your power to live for him?

When my middle son was a baby he came down with pneumonia and was hospitalized. He was placed in a semi-private room. The mother of the baby in the other crib was a young woman, about 21 or so. My husband was with me every moment he could be, during visiting hours, and I stayed around the clock, as did this other mother. I did not know she was paying any attention to us until one night she approached as I stood at the window and asked a question that seemed to come from out of the blue. "How long have you been married?" "10 years," was my reply at the time. "That's incredible," she said. "You are so sweet to each other, you act like newly-weds." "Well," I answered, "We're having a hard time with this, we need each other right now very much." Her answer was a trembling lip and a glance at her baby. "I'm having a hard time with this, too." Her unspoken comment was that her husband spent very little time in the hospital room. However, I had already noticed that the time he did spend there was spent in argument. Each blamed the other for the baby's sickness, along with everything they could remember that the other had ever done wrong. They made no attempt to hide the argument from any who might overhear.

When hard times come, do not lash out at each other. Love as brethren. Consider one another. Show some of the same kindness and understanding that should be shown to brothers and sisters in Christ. Don't get so familiar with one another that you forget that he has feelings. Have compassion. Treat him as you would wish to be treated.

The last requirement is to have compassion on the lost

And of some have compassion, making a difference: And others save with fear, pulling them out of the fire; hating even the garment spotted by the flesh. Jude 22-23

Compassion toward the lost is sometimes a difficult thing. Sometimes it's really hard to have compassion with them. They're ornery and hard to get along with. They lie. They cheat, They steal. They debate and argue. They cuss and drink and fight and live immorally. But remember that they are our responsibility. We sometimes get so wrapped up in the new life that Christ has given us that we forget where we came from. Don't make the mistake of expecting lost people to act saved. Why does a dog act like a dog? - - Because he's a dog. And lost people act like lost people because they are lost people. (It really is much better that they DO act lost. One of the great tragedies of our church age is that we have tares among the wheat. Lost people who have learned to look like, act like and smell like Christians and so they think they *are* Christians.) We need to be compassionate - their end is Hell. Their life here is misery. We have the only hope available to them. Sure, they don't see it. They're blinded by the devil to the truth, so they think they don't want it. They lash out at you for trying to show them the way - but we still must be compassionate. We cannot harden our hearts toward them because to do so is to doom them eternally.

Now don't think that I am trying to tell you to appease them, pat them on the back and gush over them. That's not compassion, that's flattery, and that's a sin. The Bible says the fear of the Lord is to hate evil. We are never told to excuse sin. God does not excuse it and they need to know that He does not. He forgives it but He does not excuse it. True compassion means tell them the truth but don't harden your heart toward them. I didn't say it was easy.

So as our virtuous woman is stretching out her hands to the poor, she's doing it compassionately. She's honestly feeling the pain of the one she is helping. If that help is in this world's goods, she is helping according to the will and Word of God. Biblical principle is her guide. She's not demanding anything in return, not seeking glory for herself, obtaining the permission of her husband and giving with simplicity (Romans 12:8.)

If that help is in the husband/wife relationship, she is still reaching out her hands to meet the needs of her husband in compassion. Compassion leaves no room for selfishness. The biggest poison a marriage can have is selfishness. Approach your marriage relationship with the idea that "He is going to meet my needs," and you are pretty much doomed to disappointment. Approach your marriage relationship as a ministry and ask the Lord for a compassionate, servant's heart - and you will be amazed at the joy and fulfillment you will receive.

If that help is in reaching out hands to this lost world, remember compassion is the key ingredient. I have seen people who call themselves witnessing who badger and argue and insult the people to whom they are witnessing. There is no compassion in that. There is none of the love of Christ in that. This is just a person with an attitude problem or they're too dumb or too lazy to really witness. They seem to think they can bully someone to Christ. They can't. They are not truly seeking that person's soul. They are seeking to pat their own selves on the back and say what a good job they did. I've actually heard them brag about how many people they made mad while they were "witnessing." A witness for Christ should be bold and up front - with no apology for the message and no corners cut - but it should be compassionate. If someone gets angry with the message when it is delivered clearly and compassionately, that is unavoidable and sad. However, we should not go out seeking to make people angry with the Gospel. You can't find anyone in the Word of God who witnessed, seeking to make someone angry.

I have also seen people who call themselves witnessing who want to slide people under the gate with a quick prayer and no repentance. They do not address the subject of sin, just "Do you believe, of course you do, repeat after me…" I have even seen them in a children's church setting address a whole room of children and ask them "How many want to go to heaven? Raise your hand, hold it up now while we count how many there are....now bow your head and pray this prayer with me... Wow! We had 52 saved in children's church this morning." That is wicked!! They do not care about the person's soul any more than the first one did because they are not really leading them to the Lord. They're giving them an easy way out excuse that will land them straight in Hell. And they're doing it for another number to notch on their "gospel gun." Giving a report of "numbers saved" is more important to them than the person's never dying soul! There is no compassion in either of these. Compassion sees a soul - a real person - headed for a real Hell. Compassion understands that that person won't really understand the message fully because compassion remembers that "I was once a sinner on my way to hell also." And compassion takes the time to really meet the need.

Let love be without dissimulation. Abhor that which is evil; cleave to that which is good. Romans 12:9

Dissimulation is defined as: The act of dissembling; a hiding under a false appearance; a feigning; false pretension; hypocrisy.

In other words - don't pretend that you love them - really love them. Now, we have discussed before that love does not accept their wrongdoing and pat them on the back for it. True love corrects as much as it encourages. It rebukes as well as praises. But for the right reasons. Not in hateful criticism but with a desire to see growth in the life of the one corrected. We are, in the same verse, told to abhor evil and to cleave to that which is good. We need to surround ourselves with, and love, the things that are good and hate the evil.

She stretcheth out her hand to the poor, and reacheth forth her hands to the needy. It goes a lot further than we may think.

Lesson Ten Review

1) Write today's memory portion:

_____

_____

_____

2) Define Compassion:

_____

_____

_____

3) Define Saint:

_____

_____

4) A saint is not _____

How do we know this? _____.

5) What does it mean to prefer each other?

_____

_____

6) The word "alms" means

_____

_____

7) Define dissimulation:

_____

_____

8) Compassion's two sisters are _____ and

_____

133

9) Esther's life showed meekness in 4 areas: She was
_____, _____, and willing to
_____. She did not seek
_____ for herself.

10) The greatest picture of compassion is to be willing to
_____

11) List the 3 areas where we are commanded to have compassion:
A)_____

B)_____

C)_____

12) List the six guidelines for helping the poor:

_____

_____

_____

_____

_____

_____

13) _____ is the essential when it comes to compassionate
giving.

14) Sometimes a husband or wife will be much quicker to have
compassion on or be courteous toward _____, and to treat
their husband or wife like _____The old phrase that
the world uses is _____

15) A dog acts like a dog because: _____
 and a lost person acts like a lost person because: _____

16) God does not _____ sin. He _____ it.

17) We should not go out _____ to make people _____ with the Gospel.

18) It is not compassionate to be _____ when delivering the gospel message, nor to try to _____

19) We need to _____ ourselves with and love the things that are _____, and hate the _____.

A Woman Among all Those

Lessons in Christian Womanhood

Lesson 11

Scripture Memory for this lesson: She stretcheth out her hand to the poor; yea, she reacheth forth her hands to the needy.
Proverbs 31:20

But let it be the hidden man of the heart, in that which is not corruptible, even the ornament of a meek and quiet spirit, which is in the sight of God of great price. 1 Peter 3:4

This lesson will continue our study about our relationships and our attitudes toward others. In our last lesson we studied compassion. Remember the definition of compassion:

A suffering with another; painful sympathy; a sensation of sorrow excited by the distress or misfortunes of another; pity; commiseration. Compassion is a mixed passion, compounded of love and sorrow; at least some portion of love generally attends the pain or regret, or is excited by it.

Mercy and compassion are closely related but are not the same thing. In fact the dictionary made a note that there is no other word in the English language that is a perfect synonym for the word mercy.

Mercy means: That benevolence, mildness or tenderness of heart which disposes a person to overlook injuries, or to treat an offender better than he deserves; It implies benevolence, tenderness, mildness, pity or compassion, and clemency, but exercised only towards offenders.

The difference here between compassion and mercy is that compassion may be deserved. Mercy on the other hand is given to one who is not deserving of it. So we can extend compassion sometimes much more easily than mercy.

Mercy is withholding yourself from giving someone what they deserve for their wrongdoing. Mercy is not giving them a "piece of you mind" when they earn one. Mercy is overlooking their failings… again. Mercy is giving them another chance at a responsibility in which they have proved unfaithful. Mercy is accepting their apology, their repentance, at face value and not pronouncing the deserved judgment for whatever they have done. Forgiving and forgetting an offense is sometimes the hardest thing that we have to do. It is no big deal to say that you are merciful - until the mercy needs to be extended when someone has done you harm. Then it's not always so easy to do. But it is a command of God that we be merciful.

Be ye therefore merciful, as your Father also is merciful. Luke 6:36

Let not mercy and truth forsake thee: bind them about thy neck; write them upon the table of thine heart: Proverbs 3:3

The merciful man doeth good to his own soul: but he that is cruel troubleth his own flesh. Proverbs 11:17

He hath shewed thee, O man, what is good; and what doth the LORD require of thee, but to do justly, and to love mercy, and to walk humbly with thy God? Micah 6:8

The best example that I can give of a woman who showed mercy and the mercy that God gave in return is Rahab. Joshua 2:1-21; 6:22-25; Matthew 1:5. Rahab had no real reason to hide the 2 spies from the Israelite army. She would have been a hero in her community if she had turned them over to the authorities. But she looked ahead and believed in God. She provided them with a hiding place and helped them down over the wall to get away. In return she received her life and the life of all her family and household in the fall of Jericho, which was what she was after. But in addition she received far, far more. She married an Israelite man and was in the lineage of King David and of Christ. She's a perfect example of one of God's basic laws:

Blessed are the merciful: for they shall obtain mercy. Matthew 5:7

The opposite of mercy is an unforgiving spirit - bitterness.

And be ye kind one to another, tenderhearted, forgiving one another, even as God for Christ's sake hath forgiven you.
Ephesians 4:32

Forbearing one another, and forgiving one another, if any man have a quarrel against any: even as Christ forgave you, so also do ye. Colossians 3:13

Bitterness is like a cancer. It eats away at what is good and leaves only behind that which is destructive. Don't make the mistake of harboring bitterness. It is not only damaging to you but also to those around you.

Looking diligently lest any man fail of the grace of God; lest any root of bitterness springing up trouble you, and thereby many be defiled; Hebrews 12:15

But if ye have bitter envying and strife in your hearts, glory not, and lie not against the truth. This wisdom descendeth not from above, but is earthly, sensual, devilish. For where envying and strife is, there is confusion and every evil work. James 3:14-16

Harboring bitterness will destroy you spiritually, harm the church and defile those around you. There is only one way to get rid of it once it takes firm root in your being. Go to God with an honest heart, and some fervent prayer, and ask God to take the bitterness from you. Ask Him to help you to love the person involved with His love.

How far do we go with this mercy? Isn't there a limit? As Christ forgave. The only limits Christ puts on the mercy that He provides is that it is sought for by us with an honest heart.

Then came Peter to him, and said, Lord, how oft shall my brother sin against me, and I forgive him? till seven times? Jesus saith unto him, I say not unto thee, Until seven times: but, Until seventy times seven. Matthew 18:21-22

We can look again at our passage on being a living sacrifice, Romans 12, to teach us more about mercy, compassion and meekness.

Bless them which persecute you: bless, and curse not.   Romans 12:14

Oh, me! Again. We never have an excuse to be hateful. Not even when persecuted. If you have never done so, I would recommend that you read "The Hiding Place" by Corrie Ten Boom. This is the greatest personal account (excepting only the account of our Savior's love) that I have ever read of someone overcoming bitterness and showing mercy.

Vs 15 Rejoice with them that do rejoice, and weep with them that weep.

Feel honestly for one another, draw close to each other, care for one another. If you say, "I just can't feel close to that person," back up to verse 11. Spend some fervent time in prayer for them. God will help you to get the right perspective on how you should treat them. It is much easier to be merciful and compassionate toward someone for which you are praying earnestly.

Vs 16 Be of the same mind one toward another. Mind not high things, but condescend to men of low estate. Be not wise in your own conceits.

Part of the problem when we find ourselves unable to forgive and unable to show mercy is that we feel that this person does not deserve our mercy. That's not really supposed to be an issue. Do we deserve God's mercy? The very definition of mercy means that it is not deserved. If we got what we deserved, we would all be in Hell. Unforgiveness is pride. We feel like we deserve better treatment than what we got and feel we have a right to hold a grudge against the one who offended us. Yet, when we sin against someone and they will not forgive we cannot understand how they could be so unmerciful. Pride is an abomination in the sight of God. We must treat others in the same manner that we would wish to be treated.

Vs 17-19 Recompense to no man evil for evil. Provide things honest in the sight of all men. If it be possible, as much as lieth in you, live peaceably with all men. Dearly beloved, avenge not yourselves, but rather give place unto wrath: for it is written, Vengeance is mine; I will repay, saith the Lord.

If it be possible - as much as lieth in you. God does understand that there are some people that it will be impossible to get along with. But you can live peaceably even in that situation. Sometimes the only way to get along with someone is to distance yourself from them - in as Godly a manner as you possibly can. It is also to recognize that the problem may be yourself as much as the other person. Some personalities just clash but that does not mean we have to seek harm for the other person. To seek to "get back at" someone or to hold a grudge against someone for their wrongdoing is simply not Christian. We need to turn those things over to the one who is the righteous judge and let Him handle it. There are two issues to consider here. One is that God knows the whole situation. He sees the past, the present and the future in the situation which we cannot see. He knows the motives and the hearts of each person involved and He judges in complete righteousness. Why do we try to take matters in our own hands?

Compassion will lead to mercy. The two walk hand in hand. And it is much easier to have the compassion and mercy in our lives that is required of us, when we have a spirit of meekness.

Meekness means: Softness of temper; mildness; gentleness; forbearance under injuries and provocations. In an evangelical sense, humility; resignation; submission to the divine will, without murmuring or peevishness. Opposed to pride, arrogance and refractoriness.

For I say, through the grace given unto me, to every man that is among you, not to think of himself more highly than he ought to think: but to think soberly, according as God hath dealt to every man the measure of faith. Romans 12:3

Understand who you are and who God is. We have no reason to think ourselves above anyone else. We may have gained some knowledge but only through the grace of God and because of His love. And we are told to share that knowledge with any who will receive it. We may have talents and abilities or even have come a long way toward a holy life. But again, only because it is the gift of God through the sacrifice of Jesus, not because we are anything in ourselves. Those talents and abilities are **not** ours to do with as we please, they are given to us to use for the benefit of the body of Christ and the winning of souls. If we will take a look at the one who bought us, oh, how humbled we should be!! If we would take a look at the unmatchable holiness of our Almighty God. How could we lift our heads in pride?

For my thoughts are not your thoughts, neither are your ways my ways, saith the LORD. For as the heavens are higher than the earth, so are my ways higher than your ways, and my thoughts than your thoughts. Isaiah 55:8-9

Meekness is an attribute that we are told to develop in our lives. Meekness does not mean timidity. It does not mean a denial of your own abilities. I have seen people who think they are being meek by refusing to step up and take any responsibility in the church. Often shyness is mistaken for meekness. It's not the same thing, either. A refusal to speak in public, a backwardness about meeting people, reluctance to take any responsibility that will cause one to be open to the "public eye" is shyness or timidity. It is not meekness. Meekness is often mistaken for a lack of courage or backbone. You know that meekness cannot mean weakness - because God would not have told you to be strong, then to be weak. Look what the Word of God has to say about Moses:

(Now the man Moses was very meek, above all the men which were upon the face of the earth.) Numbers 12:3

Moses was, at the time, leading 5 million cranky Jews across the wilderness. He was certainly no weakling. He simply understood where his strength really came from, and acted accordingly.

Have you ever heard of Phebe? (Has anyone ever heard of Phebe?) The Bible only mentions her in one place - but look what it says:

I commend unto you Phebe our sister, which is a servant of the church which is at Cenchrea: That ye receive her in the Lord, as becometh saints, and that ye assist her in whatsoever business she hath need of you: for she hath been a succourer of many, and of myself also. Romans 16:1-2

Then we are given this note at the end of the chapter:

To God only wise, be glory through Jesus Christ for ever. Amen. Written to the Romans from Corinthus, and sent by Phebe servant of the church at Cenchrea. Romans 16:27

The Bible probably does not say any more about her than this because this was all that needed to be said. She was a servant of the church! Could meekness be spelled out any better than that? We are told to seek meekness.

Seek ye the LORD, all ye meek of the earth, which have wrought his judgment; seek righteousness, seek meekness: it may be ye shall be hid in the day of the LORD's anger. Zephaniah 2:3

Put on therefore, as the elect of God, holy and beloved, bowels of mercies, kindness, humbleness of mind, meekness, longsuffering; Colossians 3:12

So if we are told to seek it, we really need a clear understanding of what it is.

The meek shall eat and be satisfied: they shall praise the LORD that seek him: your heart shall live for ever Psalm 22:26

The context in vs. 23-27 is praise and acknowledging the power of God. As Moses did, we should acknowledge that any ability or wisdom that we have comes from God. We should acknowledge our weakness to God and seek His help daily for the tasks He has given us to do. A woman with a meek spirit understands that she needs God in every aspect of her life, during every moment of her life. We step away from meekness when we try to surge ahead and tackle God's work without seeking God's help.

The meek will he guide in judgment: and the meek will he teach his way. Psalm 25:9

The context in vs. 8-10 is being teachable. A meek woman is teachable. Someone once said, "It is what you learn after you know it all that really matters." This entire life and walk with God is a learning process. You will never "arrive" until you reach the streets of Glory. The more teachable you are, the more usable you will be for God. You can learn something from anyone if you will have a teachable heart. A meek spirit will never display itself in a 'know it all' attitude. Even if you know a great deal about the subject at hand, you should never lift your nose in the air and assume that the person teaching has nothing to offer you - you might be surprised to find out that you really don't know it ALL if you would just be teachable. If nothing else, as you seek the right way from God's Word, you can learn from those who set a bad example or teach a false lesson not to be that way. The book of Proverbs is the book of God's wisdom and it says, in one way or another, in almost every chapter, that we should listen to instruction. It says we should pay attention to teaching and counsel and have a teachable spirit. The opposite of a teachable spirit is a stubborn and rebellious spirit.

For rebellion is as the sin of witchcraft, and stubbornness is as iniquity and idolatry. Because thou hast rejected the word of the LORD, he hath also rejected thee from being king. 1 Samuel 15:23

But the meek shall inherit the earth; and shall delight themselves in the abundance of peace. Psalm 37:11

The context of Psalm 37 in vs. 1-11 is trusting and resting in the guidance of God. A meek person is a peaceful person and delights in peace. A meek person is not going to stir up strife and trouble.

Blessed are the meek: for they shall inherit the earth. Matthew 5:5

Take my yoke upon you, and learn of me; for I am meek and lowly in heart: and ye shall find rest unto your souls. Matthew 11:29

We see that Jesus was meek - He is our pattern. He said He was lowly in heart. The Bible says that He made Himself of no reputation and took upon Him the form of a servant and was made in the likeness of men. To learn of Him in this manner means that we do not always have to have the high place of prominence even if that is the place that we feel rightly belongs to us. Be always willing to serve. Be reluctant to push yourself to the front in order to be seen or applauded. Don't be so quick to make sure that everyone recognizes your talents and abilities. Look closely at this passage:

Whose adorning let it not be that outward adorning of plaiting the hair, and of wearing of gold, or of putting on of apparel; But let it be the hidden man of the heart, in that which is not corruptible, even the ornament of a meek and quiet spirit, which is in the sight of God of great price. For after this manner in the old time the holy women also, who trusted in God, adorned themselves, being I subjection unto their own husbands; 1 Peter 3:3-5

We see here that meekness is not loud, brassy or showy. It is an ornament to holy women. Meekness has a lot to do with being in willing subjection to God given authority. It is part of the fruit of the Spirit.

But the fruit of the Spirit is love, joy, peace, longsuffering, gentleness, goodness, faith, Meekness, temperance: against such there is no law. Galatians 5:22-23

I therefore, the prisoner of the Lord, beseech you that ye walk worthy of the vocation wherewith ye are called, With all lowliness and meekness, with longsuffering, forbearing one another in love; Endeavouring to keep the unity of the Spirit in the bond of peace. Ephesians 4:1-3

Meekness is necessary for unity in the church. We cannot have a grasping, self-serving, push-ahead-of-one-another attitude and have a church that is in harmony and unity.

But thou, O man of God, flee these things; and follow after righteousness, godliness, faith, love, patience, meekness.   1 Timothy 6:11

We are told to put it on, to seek it, to learn it from Christ, to adorn ourselves with it, to follow after it. We are told what it is not: It is not weakness, or timidity. Not pushing yourself to the forefront, not loud or showy, not demanding. We are told some things that it is: It is an ornament, quiet, peaceable, understanding that we have no power of our own, acknowledging and openly praising the power of God in and with our lives. It is lowliness of heart, willingness to take a servant's place. It is being teachable. It is subjection to authority. It is seeking unity. Then we are told how to use it once we get it: To instruct in meekness - referring to witnessing. Remember that in our last lesson we went over those who witness with arrogance and hatefulness. That's a direct violation of this Scripture.

In meekness instructing those that oppose themselves; if God peradventure will give them repentance to the acknowledging of the truth; 2 Timothy 2:25

This also can teach us the attitude with which we should approach teaching the Word of God in any matter. Haughtiness and pride has no place in the presentation of God's Word.

Put them in mind to be subject to principalities and powers, to obey magistrates, to be ready to every good work, To speak evil of no man, to be no brawlers, but gentle, shewing all meekness unto all men. Titus 3:1-2

We are to display meekness in our dealings with the world as well.

Who is a wise man and endued with knowledge among you? let him shew out of a good conversation his works with meekness of wisdom. James 3:13

Let your light shine and your words will mean more. A person who is truly meek does not talk the talk without walking the walk. Moses was meek in that he knew the power and authority rested in God and not in himself. Esther displayed meekness in placing herself under Mordecai's authority and in not making demands on the king's chamberlain. She displayed meekness in not following her own ideas but realizing someone else knew more of the situation than she did. She displayed meekness in not seeking glory for herself but giving credit where it was due.

And if any man think that he knoweth any thing, he knoweth nothing yet as he ought to know. But if any man love God, the same is known of him. 1 Corinthians 8:2-3

You don't have to run around telling everyone how much you love God – your life will tell it for you.

Not that we are sufficient of ourselves to think any thing as of ourselves; but our sufficiency is of God; 2 Corinthians 3:5

When you understand and acknowledge that your power comes from God and not from any abilities or talents that you have on your own, you've taken a step toward meekness.

For if a man think himself to be something, when he is nothing, he deceiveth himself. Galatians 6:3

Wherefore let him that thinketh he standeth take heed lest he fall.
1 Corinthians 10:12

A meek woman allows her husband to take the lead. She allows God to be in control. She's not bossy, yet can handle responsibility when given to her. She's not showy and show-offy (if that's a word.) Yet, she's well groomed and ladylike. She does not try to take a man's position.

Let your women keep silence in the churches: for it is not permitted unto them to speak; but they are commanded to be under obedience, as also saith the law. And if they will learn any thing, let them ask their husbands at home; for it is a shame for women to speak in the church. 1 Corinthians 14:34-35

If you want a picture of women out of order in the church, First Corinthians is the place to look. This church was in total confusion. Sin was openly flaunted. They were grasping, selfish and self-serving. They were pushing each other to the side, lording over one another and trying to claim a rightful spot as being better than one another. The context of this chapter is women who are speaking in tongues, prophesying and trying to assume a man's responsibility in running the church. This does not mean that women should not praise God or testify or sing in church. It does mean that they should be quiet and not speak up in matters of business or do anything that speaks of trying to control the services of the church. A woman should not attempt to teach men nor interfere in the running of the church. It is the men's responsibility to handle the running of the church. The example is given by the husband's role in leadership of the home.

Let the woman learn in silence with all subjection. But I suffer not a woman to teach, nor to usurp authority over the man, but to be in silence. 1 Timothy 2:11-12

This is not timidity. It does not deny God given ability and talents. It's not an excuse to shirk responsibility, hospitality or witness. We have a balanced God who seeks balance in our lives. However, a domineering, controlling, bossy woman with aspirations of power and ambitions of leadership that do not belong to her is an abomination to God and a shame to her husband. This behavior has no place in the house of God.

So where is the balance? How do we know how to act in a given situation? How do we balance meekness with responsibility? The answer has a lot to do with motive and method. Take a little test to determine if your motive is Godly and your method is holy.

#1 The first major factor is to always stay within the bounds of submission to your husband. Ask him about the things you wish to do, seek his counsel and guidance. If he says no - then accept no as your answer. If someone wants you to take on a responsibility, go to your husband first and ask him.

#2 Is what you are seeking to do within the boundaries of the Biblical role of a woman? Your relationship with God is primary and you should never let the flattery of being in a position of leadership overshadow or push aside your obedience to God's Word.

#3 Have you taken your situation to your husband? And is what you are deciding to do under the Biblical authority of your husband and pastor? Or will you be accepting a role of leadership that takes you to a place of independence that is unsubmissive?

#4 Can you be ladylike and a womanly example in it? Will you be displaying yourself in a showy, immodest or unfeminine way?

#5 Would you want to teach your daughters or granddaughters to be just like you in this situation, and if you would, would that draw them closer to God?

#6 Can God receive the glory for what you are doing - or will you be receiving the glory?

If you are out of bounds Biblically, out from under your God given authority, unladylike or glory seeking in the situation - then you are not within the bounds of meekness.

Compassion, Mercy and Meekness. You will need all three to stretch out your hands to the poor, to reach forth your hands to the needy. In each step of our Christian lives, and each individual situation, compassion, mercy and meekness are things that we will have to work on, learn about and grow in for the rest of our Christian lives.

Lesson Eleven Review

1) Write the Scripture memory passage for this lesson:

_____

_____

_____

_____

2) The definition of compassion is:

_____

_____

_____

3) The definition of mercy is:

_____

_____

_____

4) The definition of meekness is:

_____

_____

_____

5) The difference between mercy and compassion is that compassion may be _____ But mercy

_____

6) In return for showing mercy to the spies from Israel Rahab received_____

_____

7) Rahab was in the lineage of _____ and

_____.

8) Bitterness is like a _____. It is not only damaging to _____ but also to _____.

9) We are to forgive as _____.

10) We never have an excuse to be _____. Not even when _____.

11) It is much easier to be merciful and compassionate toward someone that you are _____

12) Sometimes the only way to get along with someone is to:

_____

13) God judges in: _____.

14) Our talents and abilities are given to us to:

_____

_____

15) List 4 things that meekness is not:

_____

_____

_____

_____

16) A woman with a meek spirit understands:

_____

_____

17) A meek woman is _____.

18) The opposite of a teachable spirit is a _____, which is a _____

19) A meek person is a _____ person. A meek person is not going to _____.

20) Be always willing to _____. Be reluctant to _____

21) The Bible says that Moses was the _____ man in all the earth, yet he was able to be the leader of the nation of Israel - that is because he realized that his _____ came from God and not himself.

22) Phebe is mentioned as a _____ of the church.

23) List 4 things that meekness is:

_____
_____
_____
_____

24) List the steps in testing your motives for meekness:

_____
_____
_____
_____
_____
_____

A Woman Among all Those
Lessons in Christian Womanhood

Lesson 12

Scripture Memory for this lesson: She is not afraid of the snow for her household: for all her household are clothed with scarlet.
Proverbs 31:21

That they may teach the young women to be sober, to love their husbands, to love their children, Titus 2:4

This verse in Proverbs speaks of two things. One is the virtuous woman's priority and the other is her foresight. She is to diligently care for her family's needs. We live in an age where the independence of women has caused the home to fall to pieces. The Bible does not even consider the possibility of what our society now deems the norm: a woman who "stands on her own two feet, independent and capable." What happens when a woman takes the worldly attitude that she is independent of her family is that she develops a selfishness that destroys the structure of the family.

I know this is archaic thinking and perhaps I should catch up with the times. (By the way, I was **not** raised in a Christian home and I **was** raised with the idea that I should be an independent, liberated woman with my own career, and my own ideas - God taught me better.) What the Bible does teach is that a young woman should stay under the care of her parents until she is under the care of her husband and at that point the labor of her life should be her Lord, her husband, her children and her home.

I have seen first-hand, in teaching children for many years, the pitiful sight of more neglected children - yes, in the church - than I could possibly relate. Children run around unbathed in dirty, tattered, unmatched, ill-fitting clothing when the family has the ability to do better with a little effort. Children are fed whatever they can find or junky meals loaded with sugar. Then they are allowed to feed their minds on equally junky things like television and video games. The result? The mother throws her hands up in despair when they have behavior problems and "just can't understand it." We have mothers of three and four year old children complaining that they can't handle the child - - and the problem is that they can't! They, many times, don't have the training themselves to sort out the problem.

Equally, in the home where children are that neglected, the husband is often neglected as well. He's neglected in the care of his clothing, in properly provided meals and in the companionship of his wife that is his rightful due. Along with that he has the added burden that his children are unmanageable and unhappy. The woman seeks her independence (usually a career, a social group, or her own hobbies and interests) and the family suffers. She feels she's got to have "her space." It is no wonder that the divorce rate is so high. Ladies, let's face it - womankind is a lot to blame for it. She does not deserve all of the blame but does deserve a healthy portion of it.

Notice, first of all, that the virtuous woman's first priority is her family. The entire chapter shows that her family is first and foremost in her mind and labor. She labors for them in food, clothing, care and concern. Notice particularly verses 21 and 22. Her family's clothing needs come first, then her own. And God honors it. It is a miserable shame for a woman to dress to the teeth, with the excuse that she has to 'look right for her job,' when her children look shabby and unkempt. I'm not saying that you have to purchase expensive clothing and dress your kids in the best of everything - far from it. And I'm certainly not recommending that you dress them in the latest style and designer fashions - that is frivolity and vanity at best and worldliness and ungodliness at worst. It's perfectly okay to shop yard sales and thrift stores, in fact I highly recommend it. It's wonderful to have sewing skills and to be able to make your children's clothes. What I am saying is that your children should be dressed with the best you can reasonably afford for them and their clothing should be appropriate for the weather, kept clean and in good repair. I am saying that you should care for your family's needs; your husband's and your children's first. Then care for your own. This is simply a Christian attitude.

I once had a little girl in my classroom, a 9 year old, whose mother worked. This little girl got herself and her younger brother ready for school every morning. She fixed their breakfast and they walked to school together. One morning she walked in wearing a pair of sandals. Not so unusual, except that there was a foot of snow on the ground. Her feet were nearly frozen. This was only one incident but there were many others. Children suffer when there is no continuous parental guidance in their lives. Too many parents take the attitude, as this one did, that the child should know better. They know better when they are taught better. They can't be taught unless someone is there to teach them.

Next, notice the virtuous woman's foresight. She knew that cold weather was coming on and she prepared for it ahead of time.

Go to the ant, thou sluggard; consider her ways, and be wise: Which having no guide, overseer, or ruler. Provideth her meat in the summer, and gathereth her food in the harvest. How long wilt thou sleep, O sluggard? when wilt thou arise out of thy sleep? Yet a little sleep, a little slumber, a little folding of the hands to sleep: So shall thy poverty come as one that traveleth, and thy want as an armed man. Proverbs 6:6-11.

Open your eyes to your family's needs and seek, well in advance, as much as possible, to meet them. This is not restricted to just their physical needs, it also holds true for their spiritual needs and their emotional needs.

We're going to take a look, in this lesson, at one of the wickedest women in the Bible, Athaliah. 2 Chronicles 22:1-4; 10-12. Take a look at her priority: herself and her desires for power. Take a look at her "foresight" - all she looked at was what she wanted and what it would take to get it. Even her dealings with her son were evil before she ever got to the state of deprivation that she would murder her grandchildren. She was setting her son up for his own ruin by training him to do the opposite of God's commands. It was total selfishness with no regard for anyone else. It's really horrible to think that a woman would have so little natural affection, and be so power hungry, that she would destroy her own grandchildren to get what she wanted. How cruel to be so wicked that she would train her son in her wickedness, to his own destruction. Yet, how cruel to care so little for the children in one's own home that a woman would see them do without basic needs, without training in manners and obedience and without proper spiritual training. How cruel to neglect their training to the point of seeing them lost and going to hell. All because she has her own interests to pursue.

Another Biblical example of a woman who used her child for her own devices is Herodias. Mark 6:17-28. She had a beautiful daughter and she had the kingdom at her disposal. She had resources for training her daughter that most people do not have. What did she train her daughter to do? To dance for drunken men. And then she used her daughter's ability to please those drunken men to carry out her own evil vengeance against John the Baptist. Her priority was obviously not in seeking her daughter's good. Instead she taught her daughter to use her attractions to manipulate the will of men.

Now the contrast: Look at Exodus 2:1-4. This is Jochebed. Imagine the love and care that went into that little ark! Well sure, you might say, his life was in danger! Notice something though; she was the only one of the Hebrew women who did this! She very carefully, tightly wove that little basket and waterproofed it with love and care. Then she set Miriam to watch him. His life was important to her. I can see her in my mind's eye as she went to work at her slave-labor that day and how constantly her mind was on that little spot in the river where her baby boy was floating. Then I see her that same night with her son in her arms, holding him without fear of losing him because he was now legally the "son of Pharaoh's daughter." She taught him the ways of God; probably in desperation, because she knew that her time was short and he would be called into the palace to take his place among the princes of Egypt. He would be trained in all their ways. Can you imagine the prayer of that mother as she turned him back over to Pharaoh's daughter? In committing him to God, praying for him and teaching him while she had him, she was giving him something that God could use in his life, to mold him into the man of God that he eventually became. This was a mother who thought more of her son's needs than her own wants.

Children have some very basic needs that we are going to cover in this lesson. Your children are grown? All the more reason to learn some of the basics over again. Our memory passage this week says that it is our responsibility as older women to teach the younger to love their husbands and children. He more than likely gave us this responsibility because we can look back at some of the tragic mistakes that we have made in the rearing of our own children and warn those that are bringing up little ones of the pitfalls ahead. Young women – please listen and avoid some of the mistakes that your elders have made, for the sake of your children. So, what do children need?

#1 They need your love and affection.

Our society today is steeped in selfishness, many women are even choosing not to have children at all because they want to pursue their own interests—because they feel that having children will interfere with their lives. This is not in keeping with the precepts of the Word of God.

As arrows are in the hand of a might man; so are children of the youth. Happy is the man that hath his quiver full of them: they shall not be ashamed, but they shall speak with the enemies in the gate. Psalm 127:4-5

Children's children are the crown of old men; and the glory of children are their fathers. Proverbs 17:6

Then, among those who do choose to have children, it is alarming to see how many women today hold their children at arm's length and do not touch them, cuddle them, play with them or spend time with them. They seem to have this little person that has invaded their world that they really don't know what to do with. Sadly, many women have a house full of children, yet instead of loving them and training them they alternate between yelling at them and ignoring them.

Lo, children are an heritage of the LORD: and the fruit of the womb is his reward. Psalm 127:3

Children are a precious gift from God and an awesome responsibility. Even before a child is born he can pick up on the touch and sounds of his environment. I recommend that you read the Bible and sing hymns to your children before they are born. As soon as they are born, begin to tell them about Jesus. Make sure they are surrounded with sound Gospel music and the Word of God - and add to that plenty of affection and openly demonstrated love. As they grow take the time to play with them and read to them (It is a proven fact that parents who consistently read to their children when they are small, accompanied by a good measure of cuddling, produce children who love to read and learn.) Talk to them, let them talk to you. And really listen to them. This will give them stability of emotions. It will teach them the love of God, it will show them that God is loving. They will relate your affection with the things of God and it will be a pleasant thing to them. They will be more settled in their emotions and their behavior will be easier to control if they are always sure of your love. Insecurity is one of the biggest causes of behavior problems in children. This is one reason why parents need to not only display their affection for their children openly but toward each other as well. Children whose parents are affectionate toward each other are not as likely to be insecure. Notice how sure that Solomon, the wisest man in the world, was of his mother's love.

For I was my father's son, tender and only beloved in the sight of my mother. Proverbs 4:3

Another main cause for insecurity in children is parents who are inconsistent. A child needs to be able to trust his parents. He needs to know that they mean what they say and say what they mean. Never be guilty of promising a child something and neglecting that promise - they will lose their trust in you. Yes, circumstances sometimes get in the way but that should be the rare exception, not the rule. If you do find yourself unable to keep a promise to a child you should carefully explain the circumstance that makes it impossible. This will retain their trust in you and at the same time train them to accept that life sometimes interferes with plans.

Another area of inconsistency is in discipline. A child needs to know that if he oversteps boundaries that the punishment for the offense is sure to follow - every time. If you let them get by, they will always feel that there is a possibility that they will get by again. Then they will continually test and try the limits. Consistency in discipline is extremely hard to maintain but one of the basic necessities of parenting.

Children need to know that their parents are on the same page. If Dad says no, they need to know that they cannot go to Mom and get a yes. If you allow them to play one parent against another, you have completely lost the battle and your child rules the home. Our children knew that if they were caught going to the other parent for a different answer than they had already received, the automatic answer was "no" (along with other repercussions) even if they would have received a "yes" under different circumstances. Children need to know that Mom and Dad are a team working together to rear the children for the Lord.

#2 They need teaching and training.

Train up a child in the way he should go: and when he is old, he will not depart from it. Proverbs 22:6

Notice that there is a difference between teaching and training. Teaching refers more to the use of words, training refers to showing by words and example. It will never be enough for you to tell your children the right way to live if you live something different in front of them. Teach them how to live and then show them how to live. This is not a lecture style class - this is apprenticeship. Unfortunately, this society is full of women who train their children in the very opposite of godliness. If you would have godly children, seek godliness in your own life - then live it as an example for your children. If you do not train your children in the ways of God, mark it down - they WILL be trained in the ways of the world. The world and the devil will make sure that they are.

And these words, which I command thee this day, shall be in thine heart: And thou shalt teach them diligently unto thy children, and shalt talk of them when thou sittest in thine house, and when thou walkest by the way, and when thou liest down, and when thou risest up. And thou shalt bind them for a sign upon thine hand, and they shall be as frontlets between thine eyes. And thou shalt write them upon the posts of thy house, and on thy gates.   Deuteronomy 6:6-9

God gave a command here - to place the Word in your heart and then teach it to your children. Then He gave the method by which they were to be trained - talk of the Word of God when you are sitting in your house, while you are walking by the way, when you go to bed and when you get up. You are to live your Christianity for all to see, constantly keeping the Word of God before yourself and before your children. The Word of God needs to be constantly before your children in every form possible. They cannot get enough of it. Make sure that they are in a good solid church. Make sure that the people that they look up to, spend their time with and who are teaching them are solid in their beliefs and walk in holiness.

I can tell you from experience that you can teach your children diligently in the right path but if you let them rub shoulders with the world you are setting yourself up for heartbreak. You are letting them walk a tightrope over the world. One of the hardest things you will ever have to do is make the decision to protect your children spiritually by removing them from worldly influences. Especially if those worldly influences are close family members or friends that your children really like. I wish with all of my heart that someone had taught me, when my children were small, to get them away from worldly family members. I have seen, in the lives of my own children and in more examples of others than I can count, those families who have labored and prayed and trained their children while letting them associate with worldly family and friends and have lost their children to the world. To do this is to give your children a choice between God and the world. And the devil will make sure that the world glitters before them. Mark it down, if you allow them, all their lives, to associate with worldly family or friends they will eventually be given the following comparison: "Yes, I know your mom and dad teach that those things are wrong but I know plenty of Christians who do those things." And the devil will present them with idea that they can compromise their standards for a "fun lifestyle."

Train them in the Word of God. Teach your children to pray. Pray with them. Read the Bible to them. Tell them Bible stories. Surround them with Gospel music and Bible stories. Fill your home with books, puzzles, games, coloring books, etc. that have to do with the Lord and the Bible. Ask your husband to lead in a family altar time, if he does not already. When they are very young, have a morning "quiet time" with them, as well as one of your own. Then as they get older, encourage them to spend time with God on their own. Don't make the mistake of letting your children ride on your spiritual coattail. They need a relationship of their own with God. But they need for you to show them how to begin and develop that relationship.

I assure you that if they are in public school, you **will** have trouble with them. The philosophy of public schools is completely opposite of the teachings of the Word of God. It is not only evolution and sex education. The very nature of public education teaches children disrespect for authority, denial of morality, worldliness and selfishness. It teaches them to embrace the ideas, terminology and entertainment of the world and to poke fun at Christianity and moral decency. It teaches them "diversity" which means that they are to accept sinful lifestyles as normal and other religions on equal terms with Bible Christianity. Thank God that we still have the privilege of choice in this country in how we educate our children. I pray that God will preserve that freedom of choice.

Home schooling is the ideal. If that is not possible for you in your situation, a solid, local church based (preferably your own local church) Christian school is what I would recommend. I do not recommend your very large community "Christian" schools. Most of them are in it for the money, are not under the Biblical authority of a local church, and are not at all careful about the students they take - - anyone who has the money is welcome. And, they sometimes are not even careful about the type of teachers and workers they hire. If you place your child in a Christian School and if you can at all do so, get yourself involved in that school on a regular basis. Volunteer your time. It will keep you closer to your children and it will give you an inside picture of what is being taught to your child, as well as an inside picture of what your child is really like in the school setting. You will also be a big blessing to the school.

The word nurture means nourishment. So to nurture them in the Lord is to 'feed' them the things that will grow them in God. Surround and saturate your children in the Word of God and the things of God. Again, you cannot give them too much of it.

Admonition means: Gentle reproof, counseling against a fault, instruction in duties, caution, direction.

How can we nourish our children with the Word of God - which teaches separation from worldliness; how can we admonish (counsel against fault, and instruct in duties in service to the Lord) if we just let them make their own choices and choose their own friends? That's like taking a vine and saying you are going to train it by letting it ramble wherever it pleases. Caution them, direct them. Gently reprove them. None of these things is possible if you just let them choose their own way. Letting a child choose his own pastimes and his own friends without your direction is like letting him choose his own diet without any direction. Most people have the sense to know that a child, if left on his own, would not choose healthy food to eat. Yet they think the same child has the sense to choose the right activities and friends without direction.

#3 Children need discipline
When I speak of discipline I am not just speaking of punishment for wrongdoing, although that is part of discipline.

The word discipline means: Education; instruction; cultivation and improvement, comprehending instruction in arts, sciences, correct sentiments, morals and manners, and due subordination to authority. Rule of government; method of regulating principles and practice; Correction; chastisement; punishment intended to correct crimes or errors.

So discipline is not only in correcting the wrong, but in teaching the methods behind how to do right.

He that spareth his rod hateth his son: but he that loveth him chasteneth him betimes. Proverbs 13:24

Chasten thy son while there is hope, and let not thy soul spare for his crying. Proverbs 19:18

Foolishness is bound in the heart of a child; but the rod of correction shall drive it far from him. Proverbs 22:15

Withhold not correction from the child: for if thou beatest him with the rod, he shall not die. Proverbs 23:13

The rod and reproof give wisdom: but a child left to himself bringeth his mother to shame. Proverbs 29:15

Unmannerly, rowdy, rebellious children are unhappy children. Children need limits and rules. The most miserable, angry children you will find are children who rule their parents. In helping with services in the juvenile detention centers I have heard more than one young person tell us that they wish their parents had set firmer rules, had more control and enforced the rules.

Structure your children's life. Not just in setting limits for what they will not do with their time - but for what they WILL do with their time. This is time consuming--that's the reason most parents today fail in this area. They are either too lazy, too apathetic, too untrained themselves (because they were raised by parents with no parenting abilities of their own) or too self-centered to invest the time in their children that it takes to supervise their activities and to structure their time.

Children should have responsibilities as well as privileges. Part of those responsibilities should be keeping up with their schoolwork. Part of it should be proper care of their own belongings and part of it should be contributing in some way to the care of the household. If you choose to give your children an allowance - please set certain chores for them to do to earn that allowance (And please be consistent about withholding that allowance if the required chore or responsibility is neglected.) In addition, please see to it that they have things to do around the house for which they do not get paid. No one is going to pay them to wash the dishes or take out the trash when they are grown and they need to realize that they must participate in keeping the home running smoothly. They need to realize that Mom and Dad are not the only "maintenance people" at home.

I have seen a lot of women who do not train their youngsters to clean, sew, cook or anything else because they feel it is easier to just do those things themselves. Sometimes they do not feel like they have the patience to teach them. Yes, it is easier and yes, children can sometimes try your patience, especially when you are trying to teach them something that they really don't care to learn. But that does not relieve us from the responsibility that we have in teaching them. There should be consequences for failing to carry out their responsibilities or for doing a half-hearted job.

One of my children tried the age old trick, when it was his turn to wash dishes, of doing a half-way job on them so he would get out of it. Instead he found himself doing them over and then over, until he did the job right. Yes, this means that you will have to spend a lot of time with them and checking up on them. That's parenting. The reward in the end will be well worth the time that you have put into them.

#4 They need bodily care.
This ought to go without saying, but it doesn't. It is so important for a mother to train her children in how to present themselves. To dress modestly and properly. Teach them to be clean and wear clean clothing. Teach them what clothing matches and what does not. Train them to care for their grooming. To comb their hair and brush their teeth. Teach them manners. Practice table manners with them and give them a chance to use them when they are around other people. Teach them good manners toward adults, especially the elderly. Teach them to say, "yes, ma'am and

no, ma'am, yes, sir and no, sir." Teach them not to interrupt conversations.

Train your young boys to treat a girl with respect and politeness. To never touch them. To open doors. To give their seat to an older person or a young lady. (Two older ladies in our church, years ago, adored my young sons because I had taught them to open their car doors and the doors of the church and to carry in anything for them that needed carrying. The boys, by the way, loved this task and raced each other to be the first to be available to do it.)

Another thing to teach your boys when they are young (pre-teen) is how to and how not to look at a girl. They need to be taught to keep their eyes on a girl's face and not stare inappropriately at her. I taught my young men early that whenever they were in the presence of a female of any age who was inappropriately dressed that they should, in preservation of their own purity, stare at their own shoes until their eyes could be safely lifted.

Teach your young girls not to flirt, tease and slap at young boys. Teach them how to sit and stand modestly. It's appalling how many mothers are more interested that their young girls know how to apply makeup and dance than how to sit properly in a skirt or how to bake a loaf of bread. Then there are those who think they can begin to teach those things when their children become teenagers - no, no, no!! It doesn't work that way. If you wait to train your children in these areas until they are in their teens, you have lost the opportunity. Teach them while they are young. I was so pleased and encouraged recently to watch my one year old granddaughter as she played. Her little hands automatically reached to straighten her skirt as she sat down. That teaching came from her gentle mama, who gives her the best of attention. Two to four year olds can be taught to pick up after themselves and, with some help, do supervised small chores. Five and six year old boys should be taught to open doors for ladies and girls and to carry out responsibilities at home. Five and six year old little girls should have already begun to learn household chores and cooking. If you do not train your children to have a work ethic, do not be surprised if they grow into lazy adults who expect that the world owes them everything. If you wait until they are teenagers to begin to train them in modesty and propriety, you will have rebellion and inappropriate behavior at every turn.

I remember vividly a young girl that I saw at a meeting in recent years. She was somewhere between fourteen and sixteen years old. She entered the dining room, following a whole group of boys about her same age. I couldn't help but notice her. She spoke in very loud tones, punctuating everything with a boisterous laugh. She leaned on the back of the boys' chairs reaching over them, slapping their arms and such like behavior. She was clearly sending a message and the boys were clearly receiving it. The glances that they made at her, and to each other, plainly showed a lack of respect for her and a knowing ridicule of her lack of appropriate behavior. Where was her mother? She was there, fellowshipping with a group of women, ignoring her daughter's behavior. That mother will be the only one shocked when her daughter turns up pregnant.

What are we, as Christian mothers, trying to train our young people to be? Have some foresight - where is your training going to lead them? Is that where you want them to be? What are your priorities? Are you and your wants on your most important items list? Or is training your children in the nurture and admonition of the Lord the focal point of being a parent? Sadly, too many women wait until their children are grown and then wish they had really been parents to them. The Scriptural principle is - oh, so true - in this area:

Be not deceived, God is not mocked, for whatsoever a man soweth, that shall he also reap. Galatians 6:7

Lesson Twelve Review

1) The definition of nurture is:

_____

2) The definition of admonition is:

_____

_____

3) The definition of discipline is:

_____

_____

_____

_____

4) An attitude of independence and selfishness destroys

_____

5) The Bible teaches that a young woman should stay under the care of her

_____ until she is under the care of _____, and at that point the labor of her life should be

_____

6) The virtuous woman's priorities are to place her family

_____

7) What was Athaliah's priority? _____.

8) What was Athaliah's foresight?:

_____

_____

9) Herodias had the resources of the kingdom at her disposal - what did she train her daughter to do?

_____.

10) How did Herodias use her daughter's ability?

_____

_____

11) Jochebed was the _____ of the Hebrew women who made an ark to save her son's life.

12) The Bible says that it is the _____ of the _____ to teach the younger to: _____

13) List 4 things that children need:

_____

_____

_____

_____

14) _____ is one of the biggest causes of behavior problems in children.

15) Teaching refers more to _____, training refers to showing by _____

16) If you do not train your children in the ways of God, they WILL be

_____

17) One of the hardest things you will ever have to do is make the decision to protect your children spiritually by

_____

_____

18) The very philosophy of public education teaches children:

_____

_____

_____

19) Unmannered, rowdy, rebellious children are _____ children.

20) To structure your children's life means not just in setting limits for _____ but for _____

21) List 3 practical things a mother can teach a young boy:

_____

_____

_____

22) List 3 practical things a mother can teach a young girl:

_____

_____

_____

23) The Scriptural principle in training our children is:

_____

_____

_____

24) Write the Scripture memory portion for this lesson:

_____

_____

_____

_____

_____

_____

A Woman Among all Those
Lessons in Christian Womanhood

Lesson 13

Scripture memory portion for this lesson: She maketh herself coverings of tapestry; her clothing is silk and purple.   Proverbs 31:22

In like manner also, that women adorn themselves in modest apparel, with shamefacedness and sobriety; not with broided hair, or gold, or pearls, or costly array; But (which becometh women professing godliness) with good works. 1 Timothy 2:9-10

I find it very interesting that this lesson fell out in such a way that it is "lesson 13" since thirteen is the number of rebellion in the Word of God!! This week's lesson is the one that is the most difficult among all others to address with Christian women and the one of all others that most easily sparks rebellion from us. It is on godly clothing. Why is it so difficult for us to submit ourselves to God in the area of our clothing? We mentioned before that the two hardest areas of surrender for a woman are in the matter of submission and clothing. Why? Because to give our clothing over to God to choose for us is to give him part of our identity. It requires the crucifixion of the flesh. Aren't we required by Scripture to give our identity over to Christ? And aren't we required to crucify the flesh with its affections and lusts? It is also one of the most basic and necessary steps in becoming a virtuous woman. A woman who desires a standing with God as a virtuous woman and yet will not surrender her wardrobe to Him will **never** reach the goal. It is honestly a shame to the modern Christian woman to read of those ladies in the past who laid their lives on the line for the cause of Christ when women in our country today are not even willing to give over to Christ their desires where their apparel is concerned.

I beseech you therefore brethren, by the mercies of God, that ye present your bodies a living sacrifice, holy, acceptable unto God, which is your reasonable service. And be not conformed to this world: but be ye transformed by the renewing of your mind, that ye may prove what is that good, and acceptable, and perfect, will of God. Romans 12:1-2

Notice that the Bible does not say in this passage to surrender your soul, your spirit, your heart or your conscience - it says your body. A living sacrifice. A sacrifice does not choose for itself. When you look at your clothing are you concerned that it is holy, acceptable unto God? Or are you more concerned that it is fashionable, acceptable unto you?

We will be covering a lot of area in the class on clothing. Because it is such a touchy and controversial subject, yet so important to our Christian walk, we are going to take our time and cover it thoroughly. I am also going to get very pointed and detailed about some areas of clothing that are a sore spot of rebellion amongst Christian women. It does us no good to point our fingers at the world and say, "I wouldn't dress like that." We are not looking to compare ourselves to the world. We are looking to bring ourselves up to Christ's standard of a virtuous woman, in spite of the fact that we have been subjected to the ideology of this wicked world and have watched the Church's standards melt away.

One of the reasons that women balk at allowing the Lord to have control over their clothing choices is because they feel that He will choose something that will make them feel dowdy, unattractive and frumpish. Take a look at the virtuous woman. Her coverings are tapestry, her clothing is silk and purple. Her clothes are well done and beautiful. You do not have to have ugly clothes to have modest clothes. There are modest items of clothing that are very beautiful. In fact, a well-dressed, modest woman is far prettier than one who dresses in skimpy, immodest clothes. The issue here, along with a lot of virtuous womanhood, is attitude. Can you trust God with your eternity? Then how can you **not** trust Him with your present, your day to day living? I have even met women who were headed for the mission field, or for some other ministry, who were not willing to surrender their attitude about their clothing to the Lord. I have also seen God delay their deputation and deal with their attitudes. I have also seen them fail on the mission field, or other ministry, because they were a poor testimony for the Lord and they were not surrendered to His will. Then they gave up, dragging with them a defeated and discouraged man of God. It's a sad, pitiful excuse for a woman who would defeat her husband in the will of God for his life because she wanted to be rebellious in her dress - but it happens. We simply cannot say that we love the Lord and say at the same time that we will dress as we please. With all that He has done for us, how can we let something as paltry as our clothing keep us from full surrender?

Let's take a look at the woman in the Bible who is known more than any other for her wickedness - Jezebel. 2 Kings 9:30-37. This passage never ceases to amaze me. At the time that Jehu came into the city, Jezebel was an older woman. It had been 20 years since the prophet Elijah had given the prophecy concerning her death but she thought that she was something! The new king was coming to take over so she dolled herself up, expecting to make an impression on him!! The only impression she made was on the dogs that ate her (they probably got indigestion.) She was dressing to attract the attention of a man.

Let's refer back to our Proverbs 7 woman and take a look at her dress as well. Verse 10 says: And, behold, there met him a woman with the attire of an harlot, and subtil of heart. So we see there is attire that identifies a woman as having loose morals. This woman was not actually a prostitute. She was, however, an adulteress. She was dressing for the purpose of allurement and her clothing displayed her lewd behavior. The Lord is very pointed in how He feels about a woman who has loose morals. The clothing that we wear sends out a message about the attitude of our heart. If we have a desire to attract the attention of men, our clothing choices are going to reflect that attitude and our reputation will reflect it as well.

Isaiah 3:16-26 - In this passage the daughters of Zion are behaving themselves lewdly - dressing and acting in such a way as to attract men. The word wanton means: deviating from the rules of chastity; lewd; lustful; lascivious.

The word mincing means: To walk with short steps; to walk with affected nicety; to affect delicacy in manner (in other words walking in such a way as to show off.)

The judgment that the Lord pronounces on them is enough to make any woman gasp in horror. He gives the reason for this judgment in verse 16. BECAUSE they are haughty, and walk with stretched forth necks and wanton eyes, walking and mincing as they go, and making a tinkling with their feet. Because they are showing themselves. Chasing men with the way they are dressed and the way they display themselves.

Whose adorning let it not be that outward adorning of plaiting the hair, and of wearing of gold, or of putting on of apparel; But let it be the hidden man of the heart, in that which is not corruptible, even the ornament of a meek and quiet spirit, which is in the sight of God of great price. For after this manner in the old time the holy women also, who trusted in God, adorned themselves, being in subjection unto their own husbands: 1 Peter 3:2-5

Modest apparel speaks of not drawing attention to yourself in an ungodly way. Ladies, there are many ways of drawing ungodly attention to your body that have nothing to do with bikinis and halter tops. The fashions of this world are designed to show off a woman's body and spark sexual interest in the minds of the men around them. The universal motto of fashion designers is (I'm not kidding or making it up) "sex sells." Unfortunately many Christian women play right into the devil's hands in this respect. A woman has a natural instinct to make herself attractive. It is one of the ingrained parts of her nature to fuss with her hair, her face and her figure. Wrong? No, not at all. But, as with all parts of our life, it must be brought into submission to the will of Christ. It is not the character of a godly woman to draw sexual attention from men.

Now the argument comes. "They are going to think that way no matter how I dress." You might be surprised. Even in this age where men have very little respect left for women, if you dress like a Christian lady you will get more respect than you may realize, even from the roughest characters. Of course there are those who are just sleazy in mind and then it would not matter if you were wearing a brick wall. Those are usually the ones who feed their minds on pornography and yes, you cannot do anything about that. But may I ask you this? Is it right for you to dress in a tempting way simply because there are those who will think it anyway even if you don't? What of those poor men who are trying to shield themselves from those type of thoughts. They are bombarded on all sides by the ungodly dress of the women in the world. They deal with such things as advertising photos everywhere of half dressed women, etc. Then they come into the church - our place of refuge from the world – only to find that the women in the church do not dress much better, if at all better, than those outside it?

Is it really our responsibility? Or is it up to them to control their minds? I cannot count the number of times I have heard carnally minded women say, "That's his problem, he should control his eyes." I would like to show you from Scripture that if you dress before him in such a way as to provoke his lust you have your part in the sin as well as he does. I would not be at all surprised to find out that God holds YOU with the major portion of the blame.

Ye have heard that it was said by them of old time, Thou shalt not commit adultery: But I say unto you, That whosoever looketh on a woman to lust after her hath committed adultery with her already in his heart. Matthew 5:27-28.

Notice the word "with." She has her part in this sin. Okay, so you think I'm stretching it? Let's look at another one. Let's take a careful look at 1 Corinthians 8. Some background - The members of the church here have found a way to get some cheap meat. There is nothing wrong with a bargain, right? The difference is that this meat has been used in sacrifice to an idol. Paul makes it clear that an idol is nothing - therefore the meat, in itself, is not bad. What makes the issue become sin is that it has caused a brother in Christ to stumble. It has made him sin. Look particularly at verses 11-13

And through thy knowledge shall the weak brother perish, for whom Christ died? But when ye sin so against the brethren, and wound their weak conscience, ye sin against Christ. Wherefore, if meat make my brother to offend, I will eat no flesh while the world standeth, lest I make my brother to offend. 1 Corinthians 8:11-13

So we see that we have a responsibility toward our brothers in Christ not to put a stumbling block in front of them that would cause them to sin. We also see that if we do wound a weak conscience we have sinned against Christ. We are to a certain extent responsible before God for what we cause others to think about us.

Abstain from all appearance of evil. 1 Thessalonians 5:22

Let us not therefore judge one another any more: but judge this rather, that no man put a stumblingblock or an occasion to fall in his brother's way. Romans 14:13

It is good neither to eat flesh, nor to drink wine, nor any thing whereby thy brother stumbleth, or is offended, or is made weak. Romans 14:21

We then that are strong ought to bear the infirmities of the weak, and not to please ourselves. Let every one of us please his neighbor for his good to edification.

For even Christ pleased not himself; but, as it is written, The reproaches of them that reproached thee fell on me.   Romans 15:1-3

It is our job to see to the spiritual well-being of each other and these passages teach us that our desires should not matter. The spiritual health and growth of one another should be of far more importance to us than what we want to eat, than saving a little money, than our desires as far as our dress or anything else in our lives. The Scripture makes it plain that if we please ourselves at our brother's expense then we are not only dealing in ungodly selfishness, we are partakers of his sin. We should look at this next verse with fear and trembling if our attitude is "that's their problem."

Woe unto the world because of offences! for it must needs be that offences come; but woe to that man by whom the offence cometh! Matthew 18:7

Offense is defined here as: Scandal; cause of stumbling (anything that causes someone to sin or to turn away from the truth.)

Here is the responsibility of all Christians where their thought life is concerned:

Finally, brethren, whatsoever things are true, whatsoever things are honest, whatsoever things are just, whatsoever things are pure, whatsoever things are lovely, whatsoever things are of good report; if there be any virtue, and if there be any praise, think on these things. Philippians 4:8

How can a man follow these guidelines for his thought life with flesh flashed before his eyes continually? Think to yourself how hard it is to keep your own thoughts pure. Think of our responsibility to our brothers in Christ to aid them in NOT sinning – then tell God, if you can, that it doesn't matter how you dress.

What? know ye not that your body is the temple of the Holy Ghost which is in you, which ye have of God, and ye are not your own? For ye are bought with a price: therefore glorify God in your body, and in your spirit, which are God's. 1 Corinthians 6:19-20

We do not belong to ourselves, we belong to the Christ who paid the ultimate price for our unworthy souls - He has a right to tell us how to conduct ourselves. He has a right to tell us how to dress.

Imagine this by way of illustration: Take a small child whom you know has a love for chocolate and a terrible sweet tooth. Place that child in a room just full of every goody you can imagine. Pile the room with chocolate cake, candy and ice cream – then tell that child he is not only **not** allowed to have it - he's not allowed to **want** it. That is what you do to a healthy normal man when you display your body in front of him.

Okay - so now we are convinced, perhaps reluctantly, that we have a responsibility toward our brothers in Christ not to cause them to sin. So just how do we dress in a way that glorifies God? I'm glad you asked. Let's tackle the biggest monster first. Pants. I have several things recommend to you in the way of supplementary material. One is a book I highly recommend called, The Abominable Sin of Cross Dressing by Hal Stultz. The next is a copy of a survey that I will include at the end of this lesson called, "Pants and the Christian Woman." and another booklet called, Christian Modesty and the Public Undressing of America. (If you do not know where to get these booklets and want them, please contact me at my e-mail address: mrs.mary1611@yahoo.com and I will get the information to you or help you obtain a copy of the books.)

This is a lot of reading, I understand, but it is worth the time if you are really seeking God's will in this area. In this material you will find the history of women and pants as well as many well-made points concerning the issue. I will only cover a couple of highlights from the material here. One is that the Scripture expressly forbids us to wear a man's garment - even more so – that which pertaineth to a man.

The woman shall not wear that which pertaineth unto a man, neither shall a man put on a woman's garment: for all that do so are abomination unto the LORD thy God. Deuteronomy 22:5

'I only wear women's pants' is a defense I've heard more than once. In the past I've even used it myself; along with the old classic: 'sometimes pants are more modest than some dresses.' The lame things that we will say when trying to justify ourselves! Let me give you an illustration. If you were to go into a place of business for the first time and look for the restroom, which one would you go into?

Figure 1   Figure 2

Why? Because the first picture **pertains** to a man and the second picture **pertains** to a woman.

The word pertaineth means: belongs to or has a relation to.

The word abominate means: To hate extremely, to abhor, to detest.

I had to come to the point in my Christian life where I realized that an article of clothing was not worth the risk of having my Savior consider me as an abomination. The Lord convicted me in this area many years ago. I bounced back and forth in the decision whether to wear pants or not to wear pants until one day I was walking in the mall with my baby in a stroller and happened to run across an old friend from high school. She came over to see the baby and I stood there - in my jeans - talking to her with my heart crushing in conviction at the poor testimony I was to the change God had made in my life. When I surrendered to the Lord in this area He reinforced it in my life so many times. One incident was a matter of fact statement by my own mother when someone asked me why I never wore pants. Now, my mother was not saved but she rallied to my defense

174

so quickly that I never had to say a word. She turned the conversation by commenting, "When I was a girl, NO woman wore pants. Well, no nice women anyway. The streetwalkers did. Women began to wear pants when they had to take over men's jobs during WWII. After the men came back they decided they liked their independence so much they didn't want to go back to the homemaker's role and they didn't want to go back to dresses and skirts." This was not hearsay on my mother's part - she was a riveter in an airplane factory during WWII. She knew what she was talking about. What kind of example are we following? Where is our heart if the women that we are following in the footsteps of were in such rebellion to the moral principles in which they were brought up?

Another reinforcement God gave to me was during my husband's years in Bible School. At the time I had 3 small children. While waiting to pick him up from work one day the kids got restless. There was a large grassy area nearby, so I got them out of the car and walked with them over to it so they could stretch their legs. My husband was standing in line to punch the time clock on his way out. One of the men in front of him, not realizing he was there, said to another, "That's Cliff's wife over there." "How do you know, have you met her?" the other man asked. "No, but look at the way she's dressed - that's a Christian woman." I don't need to tell you my husband's heart was soaring with joy at the testimony. Now, imagine if I'd shown up in tight jeans and a tank top to pick him up.

Even years later, at my age now, God continues to give me reinforcement of how precious the testimony of modesty is. An employee at Walmart recently approached me and said, "I know you are going to think I am really weird. But I just wanted to say that every time I see you, you are dressed so nice. You are just a lovely lady." (I am far from lovely by any standard - considering my age, weight and health.) What she was really commenting on was the modesty with which I dress.

Another issue is modesty. Look again at our memory portion for this week: 1 Timothy 2:9-10 - we are commanded to dress modestly. It wasn't a suggestion. The argument that I have heard so many times here is that some women's pants are more modest than some skirts that they wear. My response is that if that is so in the light of what we have here to study - those are skirts that don't belong in a godly woman's wardrobe either. You can't make something right because something else is more wrong. I have also heard many times that there are just some things that you do that

175

wearing a skirt would not be modest. I again would argue that perhaps the skirt you are wearing is not long enough, or full enough. I have played sports, ridden a bicycle, ridden horseback, climbed a hillside, played in the snow or in the dirt with small children, run races, etc. etc. in skirts with complete modesty because I choose my skirts for the activity carefully. If an activity cannot be possible with modesty, I don't do it. My testimony is more important to me than my fun.

We're going to use the terminology "focal point" a lot during the rest of this study and the next lesson also. A focal point is the area of your body to which the eyes are naturally drawn at first glance. Why is it important? Because your clothing will send a message to those who look at you. If the focal point of your clothes is drawing the attention of the gaze to a sexual reference point on the body, you will create the beginnings of a lustful thought in the minds of any normal man. If he is a godly man, he will have to turn his gaze away from you and fight for Spirit control in order to keep his thoughts pure.

When teaching these lessons in person, I have held up pictures of girls in pants – both front and back view – and have asked the ladies present to look at them for 10 seconds. Then I have taken the pictures down and said, "Now – I want you to tell me what hair color these girls had. Were they wearing jewelry? What kind? What type of shoes did they have on? Now let's look at it again and in all honesty tell me, where do your eyes first focus? If YOUR eyes focus there, what makes you think that a man's do not when his natural tendency is to be attracted by sight?" As a general rule, none of the ladies could answer the questions in that first glance and most admitted that their first glance carried to the pelvic area or the bottom of the women in the picture. The focal point of a woman in pants is a sexual stimulus.

One of my "adopted sons" recently told me, when I told him I was researching for this class, "Oh, Mrs. Mary, tell them, please! Tell them that when they wear pants it is a horrible fight for a man not to focus his eyes on their private area." Please, now, take the time to read "pants and the Christian Woman." You will find it at the end of this chapter, after the review questions.

I want to challenge you to do two things - first to get on your knees and pray for the mind of Christ in the matter of your dress, personally - just you and God. Next, read carefully over the lesson again and read the supplementary material. If you will do so, I guarantee that you will find that submission to the Lord in this area is not only necessary, it IS possible with the Lord's help and leading. In our next lesson we will get into some specifics for those of us ladies who already have the pants issue under control and see what the Lord requires of us concerning our skirt, blouses and dresses.

Lesson Thirteen Review

1) Write the memory portion for this lesson

_____

_____

_____

_____

2) Why is it so difficult to submit ourselves in the matter of godly clothing?

_____

3) A woman who desires a standing with God as a virtuous woman, yet _____will never reach the goal.

4) According to Romans 12:1-2 we are to _____ our _____ as a _____

5) One of the reasons that women balk at allowing the Lord to have control over their clothing choices is because they feel that He will choose something that _____

_____

6) The virtuous woman's clothing was

_____

_____

7) We simply cannot say that we love the Lord, and say at the same time that we will

_____

8) It had been _____ years since the prophet Elijah had given the prophecy concerning Jezebel's death.

9) The new king was coming to take over, and she

_____

_____

10) There is _____ that identifies a woman as having loose morals.

11) The word wanton means:

_____

_____

12) The word mincing means:

_____

_____

13) List 5 items of clothing that the Lord mentions in Isaiah 3:

_____

14) List 4 Judgments God pronounced upon the women in Isaiah 3:

_____

_____

_____

_____

15) What is the reason for God's judgment on these women?

_____

_____

16) Modest apparel speaks of

_____

_____

17) It is not the character of a godly woman to

_____

_____

18) We have a _____ toward our brothers in Christ not to put a _____ in front of them that would

_____

_____

19) The Scripture makes it plain that if we

_____ then we are

not only dealing in ungodly selfishness, we are

_____.

20) Offense means:

_____

_____

21) The Lord has a right to tell us: _____

22) The Scripture expressly forbids a woman to wear "that which _____ to a man.

23) The word pertaineth means:

_____

_____

24) The word abominate means:

_____

_____

25) We are _____ to dress modestly.

Pants and the Christian Woman

One of the battlegrounds of standards for Christian dress in North America and many other places is the issue of pants on women. I do not believe this is a complex issue. There are two simple Bible reasons why we are convinced that Christian women should not wear pants.

First: The Unisex Issue
First, female pants are a unisex fashion statement and play a central role in the modern unisex movement.

Deuteronomy 22:5 forbids women to wear that which pertains to the man. "The woman shall not wear that which pertaineth unto a man, neither shall a man put on a woman's garment: for all that do so are abomination unto the LORD thy God."

Those who argue that pants are suitable attire on Christian Women often try to discredit the use of this verse by claiming that it is part of the Law that was done away. While we know that the Law of Moses is not the Christian's Law, it does contain lessons for Christian living.

In 1 Corinthians 10 Paul recounts many things from the Pentateuch and concludes, "Now all these things happened unto them for ensamples: and they are written of our admonition, upon whom the ends of the world are come" (1 Corinthians 10:11)

While Deuteronomy 22:5 is a part of the Law of Moses and the New Testament believer is not under that Law and lives by a higher law, the Law of Spirit, it is also true that Deuteronomy 22:5 contains a moral principle that is written for our admonition. That principle is that there is to be a clear distinction between how men and women dress.

Another way that some try to discredit the use of Deuteronomy 22:5 is by saying that if we follow this verse today we must also follow Deuteronomy 22: 9-11, which says: "Thou shalt not sow thy vineyard with divers seeds: lest the fruit of thy seed which thou hast sown, and the fruit of thy vineyard, be defiled. Thou shalt not plow with an ox and an ass together. Thou shalt not wear a garment of divers sorts, as of woolen and linen together." Though we do not obey these commandments in the material realm today, we still must follow the principle that they teach in the spiritual realm. By giving these commands, God was teaching Israel the principle of separation. They were not to mix seed or types of cloth because by so doing they were illustrating in their daily lives the fact that they were to make a distinction between good and evil. Such laws were designed to teach them "that ye may put a difference between holy and unholy, and between unclean and clean." (Leviticus 10:10)

Deuteronomy 22:9-11, then, reminds the New Testament Christian that he is to separate from everything that is evil and wrong before the Lord (Matthew: 24; 2 Corinthians 6:14-17; 1 John 2:15-16 etc.) Commentators of past centuries, who were

181

not prejudiced one way or the other by the debate on modern fashions, held that the teaching of Deuteronomy 22:5 is applicable to the Christian life.

The footnotes in the Geneva Bible (1560) said: "The woman shall not wear that which pertaineth unto a man, neither shall a man put on a woman's garment: for all that do so are abomination unto the LORD thy God. For that alters the order of nature, and shows that you despise God."

Matthew Poole (1624-1679) said: "Now this is forbidden, partly for decency sake, that men might not confound, nor seem to confound, those sexes which God hath distinguished, that all appearance of evil might be avoided, such change of garments carrying a manifest umbrage or sign of softness and effeminacy in the man, of arrogance and impudence in the woman, of lightness and petulancy in both; and partly to cut off all suspicions and occasions of evil, which this practice opens a wide door unto."

Matthew Henry (1662-1714) said: "The distinction of sexes by the apparel is to be kept up, for the preservation of our own and our neighbours's chastity, Deuteronomy 22:5. Nature itself teaches that a difference be made between them in their hair (1 Corinthians 11:14) and by the same rule in their clothes, which therefore ought not to be confounded, either in ordinary wear or occasionally.

John Gill (1697-1771) said: "The woman shall not wear that which pertaineth unto a man," It being very unseemly and impudent, and contrary to the modesty of her sex. Neither shall a man put on a woman's garment; which would betray effeminacy and softness unbecoming men, and would lead the way to many impurities, by giving an opportunity of mixing with women, and so to commit fornication and adultery with them; to prevent which and to preserve chastity this law seems to be made; and since in nature a difference of sexes is made, it is proper and necessary that this should be known by difference of dress, or otherwise many evils might follow; and this precept is agreeable to the law and light of natures."

Adam Clarke (1762-1832) said: "It is, however, a very good general precept understood literally, and applies particularly to those countries where the dress alone distinguishes between the male and the female. The close-shaved gentleman may at any time appear like a woman in the female dress, and the woman appear as a man in the male's attire. Were this to be tolerated in society, it would produce the greatest confusion."

Albert Barnes 1789-1870) wrote: "The distinction between the sexes is natural and divinely established, and cannot be neglected without indecorum and consequent danger to purity. (Compare 1 Corinthians 11:3-15)

Jamieson, Fausset, Brown (1864) said: "They were properly forbidden; for the adoption of the habiliments of the one sex by the other is an outrage on decency, obliterates the distinctions of nature by fostering softness and effeminacy in the man, impudence and boldness in the woman as well as levity and hypocrisy in both; and, in short, it opens the door to an influx of so many evils that all who wear the dress of another sex are pronounced 'an abomination to the Lord.'"

Perhaps you have observed that many of these older commentators crass-referenced the principle of Deuteronomy 22:5 with that of 1 Corinthians 11 where Paul teaches that the woman and the man are to maintain a difference in appearance.

"Doth not even nature itself teach you, that, if a man have long hair, it is a shame unto him? But if a woman have long hair, it is a glory to her, for her hair is given her for a covering." (1 Corinthians 11:14-15.)

Paul says the distinction in appearance should be maintained because of the created order and the different roles that the man and the woman were designed to fill.

"For a man indeed ought not to cover his head, forasmuch as he is the image and glory of God: but the woman is the glory of the man. For the man is not of the woman; but the woman of the man. Neither was the man created for the woman; but the woman for the man." (1 Corinthians 11:7-9)

In the beginning God made the man and woman for different roles on the earth.

"So God created man in his own image, in the image of God created he him; MALE AND FEMALE CREATED HE THEM" (Genesis 1:27)

Thus, both the Old and the New Testaments teach that it is God's will for the man and the woman to dress distinctively. One woman made the following important observation: "People seem to be playing 'pick-n-choose' with Old Testament verses. They want the twenty third Psalm, the hundredth Psalm, and all the OT verses that won't affect their lifestyle, but then they try to explain away any OT verse that would have any effect on how they live. Well, 2 Timothy 3:16 says, "ALL SCRIPTURE is given by inspiration of God, and IS PROFITABLE for doctrine, for reproof, for correction, for instruction in righteousness."
(http://www.momof9splace.com/modesty.html)

The History of Female Pants in Western Society

Since the created order has not changed and God has not changed, it is obvious that the modern unisex movement is an open and wicked rebellion against the almighty and His Word. The Christian should have nothing whatsoever to do with such a movement and such a philosophy. That pants on women is a unisex fashion is obvious when one examines the history of when and why women began to wear pants in Western culture. Pants on women arose from a social revolution in the twentieth century wherein women were fighting for their "rights" and struggling to be equal to men. Their pants are a feminist and a unisex statement. The saying, "Who wears the pants in the family" illustrates the fact that pants were traditionally male attire and the woman who wore them assumed a masculine role. The universal symbols distinguishing the male from the female (a stick man in pants and a stick woman in a dress,) and still used on the doors of public toilets to this day, arose from the fact that pants were traditionally male attire.

The article "Pants for Women" on the secular web site BookRags.com observes that "pants for women emerged" from the "feminist movement." William Nicholson, in the book Clothing, the Universal Language, observed that in the 1920's "wearing slacks to the office or to a park was still out of the question and any female who appeared on a formal occasion in a trouser suit was assumed to be a Bohemian eccentric and probably a lesbian."

It was in the late 1930's prior to World War II that pants on women began to be a fashion statement, and it began in Hollywood, which has always pushed the moral boundaries. Katherine Hepburn and Marlene Dietrich were at the forefront of this. "When diva film star Marlene Dietrich appeared in slacks with flared bottoms in her United States debut film Morocco in 1930, she signaled the emergence of women's pants from sportswear to high fashion. Wearing them both in films and private life, she popularized the pants look."
("Pants for Women," www.bookrags.com)

Pants still were not commonly accepted among women in society at large, though. That did not happen until after World War II. Women's slacks and capris grew in popularity in the 1950's, but it was not until the 1960's that pants on women came into their own through the rock & roll revolution. "The jeans and pants of the 1960's and the 1970's were serious gestures toward total sexual equality." (Nicholson)

Both men and women wore blue jeans, 'hipsters' and close fitting pants with zip fly fronts. The spirit of this latest association of pants with social and sexual liberation can be seen in Alice Walker's novel, The Color Purple (1982), in which the social victory of heroine culminates in her opening of a unisex jeans shop." (Pants for Women)

The Illustrated Encyclopedia of Costume and Fashion makes the same observation on the history of pants on women: "The real pants revolution came in the 1960's with unisex fashions, though even at this time women wearing pants were often refused entry to restaurants and the whole subject was one of heated debate. By the 1970's rules and social attitudes had relaxed and pants of many lengths and styles had become an acceptable part of female dress for both casual and formal attire." This secular book admits that the growth in the popularity of pants of females I Western culture was part and parcel with the sexual revolution and the unisex phenomenon, both of which are an affront to the God of the Bible. Social attitudes had to be changed, and that occurred through the onslaught of the rebellious rock & roll culture.
The modern unisex society knows that there is a major difference between the male and female, of course, but it emphasizes only the physical difference and the result is lust and immorality. One woman wisely observed: "Oh there will always be a difference in gender, because there HAS to be. But now, the emphasis is not on the beauty of a girl's femininity (which brings out the masculinity in a man.) NOW the

emphasis in in the difference in BODY PARTS! There is no longer the striking difference between a beautiful woman in feminine attire, long pretty hair, and a masculine man that practices chivalry. (Put a real feminine woman around a man and see how chivalrous he becomes.) Now the difference is emphasized in her physical body difference, which leads to lust and a degradation of womanhood (and manhood too.) A feminine woman is in her rightful place of an elevated position. But as soon as she steps down off her pedestal to wear pants and be 'equal' to a man, it drags everybody down, which is exactly what Satan wants. The devil is still whispering in Eve's ear to destroy mankind."
(http://www.momof9splace.com/modesty.html)

Why would the godly woman want to be identified with a fashion that is so intimately associated with a movement and philosophy that is in rebellion against God's created order? Many men of God have observed that the popularizing of pants wearing by women in the past 40 years has gone hand-in-hand with a shocking decline in female modesty. One pastor wrote: "I believe it leads to a breakdown of the sexes, causes immorality and contributes to homosexuality. Pants cause a woman to act masculine. Women today do not know how to sit like a lady or to act modestly because of their pants. They have lost the ability to act modestly. They no longer bend at the knees, but they bend at the waist, exposing their chest in even a modest garment.

They do not sit with their knees together and the ankles crossed.

Another wrote: "Are we godlier today than our grandparents' generation? I think not! They were scandalized by women who wore pants and swimsuits and mini-skirts. Today, those things are commonly accepted among believers and even in churches."

Another man said: "I am 68 years old and have been married to a wonderful, modest lady for 49 years. I am appalled at how so many women dress, even in church. My mother is 88 years old and worked in the cotton fields alongside my father back when we did it all by hand. I've never seen my mother or either of my grandmothers in pants or shorts and they all worked in the fields. I have never seen any of the women who raised me in any of the items that you mentioned. I thank God for the example they were to me. By the way, they all washed their clothes by hand and I never saw any women's undergarments hanging out on the clothes line for all that passed by to look at. This proves that their modesty went far deeper than what they put on their bodies. It was in their hearts."

While we cannot turn the clock back to that bygone era, God's people can hold to the old Bible paths and reject the dictates of the shallow, lascivious, and rebellious age.

Second: The Modesty Issue
The second reason why we are convinced the Christian women should not wear pants is that they are not modest. Advertisements for women's jeans leave no doubt about the fact that pants on women are immodest. On what part of the body do these advertisements focus? The focus on the way that men respond lustfully to the way the

jeans accentuate the woman's figure and a most sexually stimulating part of her body. Jeans are portrayed as the party girl fashion, as something that worldly guys love because of what they can see.

In her book, How to Marry the Man of Your Choice by Margaret Kent (New York: Warner Books 1987) this secular author instructs women how to use clothing to "manipulate men." She says, "Don't let the power of clothing pass you by, for it can be a major asset in attracting men, and stir his sexual imagination without satisfying his curiosity about your body." (pp 29, 32) As for pants on women, the author states that "jeans are likely to get a positive response because they are snug and outline the body; they also represent casualness." (p 36)

The Christian female authors of the book, Dress: The Heart of the Matter, give the following testimony: "Should women wear pants? No! In fact, wearing pants accents or draws attention to the pelvic and hip area of the lady, areas only her husband should see. A dress does not draw attention to this area unless it is too tight and formfitting. (Shirley Starr and Lori Waltemyer, Dress: The Heart of the Matter, p. 37)

Cathy Corle, in her book, What in the World Should I Wear? Describes the following enlightening scene: "A friend of mine told me that her decision to restrict her wardrobe to dresses and skirts came as a result of a ladies class. All the arguments and reasons that could be given were unheeded until the lady who was speaking said," Let me just demonstrate something to you." She asked the ladies in the audience to close their eyes momentarily. She held up a large picture of a woman in an attractive, modest, feminine skirt and blouse. She asked the ladies to open their eyes. Then she inquired, "What is the primary focal point of the picture? Where did your eyes first fall naturally?" The audience agreed that their eyes were first drawn to the face of the woman in the picture. She again asked the ladies to close their eyes. When they opened their eyes they were looking at a large poster of a woman in a sport shirt and hip-hugger blue jeans with snaps down the fly. She asked, "Now, be honest with yourselves and tell me where your eyes first fell naturally when you looked at this picture?" Many of the ladies in the crowd were surprised to find that most people's eyes first focused upon the hips and crotch area that were so vividly emphasized before they ever noticed the woman's face. If this happened in a crowd of ladies, how much more would it be true of men? For my friend, Joetta, this was all the evidence that was needed."

One lady wrote to me in response to my quest for testimonies from women who have gotten a conviction against wearing pants and said, "I have never felt comfortable in wearing pants. Anything that brought attention to certain parts of my body bothered me." Another lady wrote, "Pants only attract the wrong attention, and the only way to change your attitude is surrender, to desire to please the Lord more than yourself and the world.

A Woman Among all Those
Lessons in Christian Womanhood

Lesson 14

She maketh herself coverings of tapestry; her clothing is silk and purple. Proverbs 31:22

Whose adorning let it not be that outward adorning of plaiting the hair, and of wearing of gold, or of putting on of apparel; But let it be the hidden man of the heart, in that which is not corruptible, even the ornament of a meek and quiet spirit, which is in the sight of God of great price. 1 Peter 3:3-4

This e-mail came across my husband's computer as I was studying for this lesson - it was an article on Fox News Network published in memory of a fashion designer that had just died and it emphasizes our last lesson so well: First comes to mind a quote from Spurgeon: "London gets their fashions from Paris and Paris gets their fashions straight from Hell."

Next, I'd like to point out a particular quote from the article:

**Also from the 60s came Beatnik chic — a black leather jacket and knit turtleneck with high boots — and sleek pantsuits that underlined Saint Laurent's statement on equality of the sexes. He showed that women could wear "men's clothes," which when tailored to the female form became an emblem of elegant femininity...........
Some of his revolutionary style was met with resistance. There are famous stories of women wearing Saint Laurent pantsuits who were turned away from hotels and restaurants in London and New York."**

Oh, but we Christians think it's okay to wear pants now. Because society has accepted it, therefore Christians accept it. The very DESIGNER of women's pants say he wanted women to be able to wear "men's clothes"!!!!!! What else can we say?

Last week we spent a great deal of time covering our responsibility toward our brothers in Christ and the fact, from the Word of God, that we are responsible to dress modestly before them. If you have taken the challenge that I gave you in our last lesson, to honestly seek God about your clothing, then you are ready for this week's lesson. As my pastor of many years used to say, "Buckle up." It's going to take a heart that really desires the mind of Christ to accept what we have to study in this lesson without rebellion. I'm going to be very pointed and specific – I've been asked, "Why so detailed?" And the answer is, because there are so many women who just don't know!

The handout I have for you today is a survey taken among Bible Believing churches. (You will find it in the back of the lesson, just before the review page.) Most of the responses are from pastors. These are not ungodly men with wandering minds and dirty hearts. They are men who are honestly seeking to keep their lives pure before God. Let's take a look at women's clothing from their perspective. (Please take the time now to prayerfully read the hand-out -- Survey of Christian men on the subject of women's clothing.)

Remember from lesson 13 that we have a responsibility before God to never set a stumbling-block in the path of our brother in Christ. We have a responsibility before God to be pure and holy in our dress.

We're going to spend a lot of time in this lesson studying what fashion designers call 'focal points.' What do I mean by a focal point? As we saw in the last lesson, there is a physical reference point to which your eyes are first drawn when you look at someone. It works that way with other things as well. Interior designers use focal points in decorating to make rooms look larger or smaller or to add or detract from certain features in the room. Photographers are taught to use focal points with their cameras and to point their cameras in a particular way to give the best shot possible, or to draw attention to or detract from certain things in the photo. It is a commonly known fact that, in advertising, focal points are used subliminally to awaken the subconscious. This makes the product they are selling more desired. Fashion designers also use focal points to sell their clothes. As I mentioned last week their motto is "sex sells." They use the lustful eyes of men and the desires of women to make themselves attractive as a selling point for their clothing. Doubt my word? Look at this portion of an article from Teen Magazine:

"Hi! I have a weird Q for you: If your outfit could talk, what would it say about you? Think about it for a sec. We put so much importance on first impressions. And when you're going back to school, meeting new teachers, checking out cute guys, and seeing your friends again after a long summer, it's especially important - you're making impressions on about 150 people a second. Sure, your energy and vibe go a long way toward telling people who you are and what you're about, but your clothes and makeup are an important part of the package. That's why I'm practically obsessed with helping you get your look just right for the first day of school. So when your fourth-period history teacher sees you in class, or when your secret crush (who, BTW, got the best muscles over the summer) asks where the music room is, you'll be saying all the right things - before you even say a word! How's that for an awesome payoff from a day of shopping?"

The further this world goes into sin, the worse the fashions get. Why do advertisers place nearly nude women in front of a vehicle they are trying to sell or on a billboard for tools or insurance? They know that it draws a man's gaze like a magnet. Clothes designers are in the business for one reason - to sell clothes. And the clothes that sell to this wicked world are the clothes that scream sexuality. The focal points that draw a man's gaze and are the opening of a potential for lust are a woman's legs, her hips, behind and pelvic area, her breasts, her shoulders if bare, and in her face, her eyes and lips if they are overdone in makeup. If you do not believe me, take a look through the fashion magazines and advertisements for clothing - remembering the motto "sex sells." Designers focus on those areas of a woman's body that is the most attracting to a man because they know that is what sells. Clothing and makeup that accentuate these areas and make them a focal point of interest is clothing that we, as women seeking modesty and godliness, need to stay away from. I recently picked up a sales circular for a department store. On one page was a sale on men's jeans. The picture showed a stack of men's jeans with the price displayed under it. On the facing page was a sale on "women's jeans" the picture was of a woman from the waist down in a pair of tight jeans with her bottom displayed in a provocative manner. I know you have all seen similar things – have you ever asked yourself why?

We are Christians. And as Christians we need to be very careful that the way that we conduct ourselves and the way we present our bodies is in accordance to the word of God. The trouble is that many women haven't been taught anything about their clothing except what the world wants them to know. Too many preachers and preachers' wives are afraid to broach the subject lest they get a rebellious response from the ladies in their congregation. Let's get really specific. The first focal point that we will be talking about is where the neckline of your blouse should be.

No man, except your husband, needs to see anywhere close to your cleavage! If you are unsure as to the depth of your neckline - ask your husband. (Or girls, ask your mother to ask your father for you.) If your husband is unsure, ask him where the neck of your blouse becomes the most interesting focal point of your attire to him. When in doubt, go a little higher. The rule of thumb that I use is to hold 2 fingers below the hollow at the bottom of the throat. With your neckline at that point, you can move about with freedom and not have to worry that if you bend over you are exposing yourself. You can also wear any shape of neckline with modesty. I have seen many women who attempt to dress modestly but complain if their neckline is too high, "I can't breathe." That's quite an exaggeration. You **can** get used to a higher neckline if you try.

Try this on for an experiment: Stand in front of a full length mirror, hold your arms down and bend over as though you were picking up something from the floor. Then without moving your body, lift your head and look in the mirror. If your top is open in the front - even a few inches - when you bend over everything from your neckline to your waist is exposed to view. I cannot count how many times I have seen godly men have to turn their heads in embarrassment over a woman in a blouse or dress with a lower neckline who has bent over a table or pew and did not realize how vulgarly she had just exposed herself.

Another problem is a blouse that accentuates the bustline. Tight shirts leave little to the imagination. V-neck shirts are usually trouble. They seldom are high enough to keep from looking like an arrow pointing directly between the breasts. Many blouses have gatherings around the bust, open lacework at the bustline, designs that lace up the front like an old fashioned corset. Some have ruffles or frills that circle the bustline. Some of these blouses cover the bare skin high enough to be modest but

190

then destroy modesty and draw the gaze directly to the bosom by the design or pattern of the blouse.

Here's a no brainer: writing on the front of a shirt causes a man's gaze to be focused to the front of your shirt. If he's going to read it, he has to stare at your chest. Large jewelry that hangs down on your bosom, double patch pockets that cover the breasts (particularly if they have patterns on the pockets or if the pockets are a contrasting color to the shirt) and pictures or patterns that outline the breasts are all problems.

Let me give you an example of what I am talking about. I have a watch that I really prize, but I will not wear. It is on a chain that you wear around your neck. It belonged to my mother. She wore it for years rather than a wrist watch because she owned a pet store that specialized in tropical fish and she kept her hands in and out of water all day every day. When she passed away I became the proud owner of this watch, and wore it happily, until I realized what a focal point it created. After talking to a man at church, who was obviously trying to notice the watch without noticing where it was, I questioned my husband. "Yes, it does create that kind of focal point." The watch has stayed in the jewelry box since that time. My desire to wear my keepsake from my mother is not worth immodest behavior. Anything - jewelry, pictures, writing, even some embroidery and designs that draw your attention to that area ought to be avoided. Take a critical look in the mirror and ask yourself, "What is the focal point of this blouse - does it draw the gaze to the breast area or reveal the breast area in an immodest way?"

Recently a Christian sister who is dear to my heart wanted to dress very nicely for an occasion at church. She did. Her clothes were very pretty, her skirt long and flowing, her neckline high. However, the shirt she was wearing was so tight that it outlined her bust so revealingly that every time she moved it drew the eyes like a magnet to her breasts. The shirt was also so short that every time she raised her arms her midsection was exposed. This has become a problem in the fashions available for women in the stores right now. The shirts available are thin, low cut, tight and very short. Women right now seem to wish to wear their skirts slung low on their hips and with the shorter length of the blouse the midsection is very often open to view (if not the poor unsuspecting woman's bottom when she bends over!) "So, what do I do? That's the way they make the shirts and I can't stand to pull my skirt up around my waist." You must choose. If you truly want to dress in modesty, and please the Lord and not yourself, you can change the way you dress. Many, many women have done so. Get used to wearing your skirt around your waist – or wear a jumper. Search for blouses that are longer, wear a t-shirt under them that is tucked into your skirt, or make them yourself.

The next thought to cover about the blouse is the fabric itself. How thin is it? Can you see through it? I've seen ladies who in every other respect were dressed modestly - the skirt a decent length, the neckline where it should be - but were wearing blouses made of material so sheer that you could read the tag on their undergarments. That is not modest! Hold a garment or fabric that you are considering up to the natural light from a window. If you can see your hand clearly through the fabric, you will be able to see through the blouse while you are wearing it. If you are still unsure, give it the husband test. (Or the mother or sister test for unmarried girls - don't ask your father or brother!) Ask him if he can see through it. This will do two things: it will save you from wearing immodest clothing and it will plant a measure of trust in your husband's heart. He will know that you want to keep yourself for him.

Ladies, it is also not modest to wear a tissue thin blouse over the top of an immodestly cut tank top or shirt. I've seen ladies do this with white shirts over the top of brightly colored tank tops. This has a gaze drawing effect. The person looking is not sure if they are supposed to look at the outer shirt or the inner shirt. Certainly not the inner shirt – it's immodestly cut. But certainly not the outer shirt – it's immodestly thin. You can't take two wrongs and make a right!

Sleeveless blouses are another problem. A woman's bare shoulders are a sexually stimulating sight to a man - they need to be covered up. Not with tiny little "almost a sleeve" sleeves, either. Take it seriously enough to not walk a tightrope with modesty. Sleeveless blouses show skin that should not be seen. Unless that blouse is too tight, which creates other problems, every time you move in it you are at risk of showing off everything under your shirt to the nearest onlooker.

I recently went to a restaurant drive up window with my family. The girl behind the window was wearing a sleeveless top. As she reached out her arm, handing the food out the window, that sleeveless top was like looking down a tunnel all the way to the other side of her shirt! Everyone in the car knew that she had on a black lace bra. I could quote you experience after experience of the same type thing but I'm sure you have seen enough of it to know that I am speaking truth. We expect such things to bombard us in the world but the sad fact is that it is bombarding the church as well.

There are 4 things that we need to discuss about skirts and dresses. Each of these has to do with, again, focal points.

Be careful about the designs and accessories that you wear with your skirts and dresses. Any object – a fancy belt buckle, a bow, a trim on your outfit that slings down on the hips makes your hips a focal point. Patch pockets on the seat of your skirts, especially if those pockets have designs on them, will cause the gaze to direct at your backside. I even recently saw a young woman, in church, in a tight skirt that had an exposed, bright gold zipper that ran straight up the middle of her bottom. The focal point on that garment was pretty obvious. (Have you stopped to consider why clothing manufacturers are selling denim skirts that are purposely faded in the posterior and thighs?) A fly front on a jean skirt is a focal point drawing the gaze to the pelvic area. (One preacher made this graphic point – why does a woman need a fly on the front of her garment?) Obviously the fly is an attempt to do one of two things – resemble male clothing, which is plainly outlined as wrong in the Word, or to draw attention to your sexual organs which is lewd. Another point that will probably make me very unpopular with a lot of Christians is that when you have a skirt that has a slit in it – SEW it SHUT. Don't put an insert in it! Particularly one of a contrasting color! This looks like an arrow pointing straight to your bottom. If the skirt is too tight to sew the slit shut – trash it. Once again, give it a full length mirror test, if you can be honest with yourself. Stand in front of a full length mirror with your eyes closed. Open your eyes and take note of what first attracts your gaze. That is the area of your body that you are drawing attention to. The length of the skirt is another factor. It is the fashion among Baptist women to wear a skirt just barely long enough to cover the knees. When she moves at all, or sits down, that skirt will be moving on up, providing a peep show. (Which by the way I am told is even worse than blatant nakedness, because the shock of lewd clothing will cause most godly men to turn away. A garment that gives occasional flashes of skin that should not be seen stir a man's imagination in a subtle way and cause him to lust before he realizes the danger.)

193

Take the millstones, and grind meal: uncover thy locks, make bare the leg, uncover the thigh, pass over the river. Thy nakedness shall be uncovered, yea, thy shame shall be seen: I will take vengeance, and I will not meet thee as a man. (Isaiah 47:2-3)

God compares uncovering the leg and thigh with nakedness. If you are uncovered in this manner, in the eyes of God you are naked. (No, don't give me a "yeah but" look at the Scripture.) I'm going to make a statement here that is not only not popular in the world, it's not popular in churches, and I doubt seriously that it will be popular with 99% of the people that hear it through these lessons. When – How – Why did the standard of length for a woman's skirt become the knee? This Scripture, that all of our fundamental preachers agree gives the standard of nakedness, does not differentiate between uncovering the thigh and uncovering the LEG - both are considered nakedness in God's eyes.

When I look up the word "leg" in the dictionary it says: The limb of an animal, used in supporting the body and in walking and running; properly, that part of the limb from the knee to the foot, but in a more general sense, the whole limb, including the thigh, the leg and the foot.

The online medical dictionary says: Leg: In popular usage, the leg extends from the top of the thigh down to the foot. However, in medical terminology, the leg refers to the portion of the lower extremity from the knee to the ankle.

The Bible states that uncovering the thigh AND the leg is nakedness. In fact with the way this Scripture is worded if it were not for 1 Corinthians 11:15, I would wear a head covering. A woman's legs are just as much of a point of sexual reference for the eyes of a man as her neckline. Under no circumstances should a woman who professes godliness wear shorts, short culottes, short skirts or slits in their skirts. And like it or not, this Scripture means that we should not uncover the leg – at all.

Whoso causeth the righteous to go astray in an evil way, he shall fall himself into his own pit: but the upright shall have good things in possession. Proverbs 28:10

I have a theory about the length of women's skirts - I believe that the standard for the length of the skirt has been a tradition handed down from

194

some of our "mega churches" and from thence has become considered as a Scriptural standard because the "big name preachers" have not disagreed with it. We don't need to be drawing our standards from any man's tradition - but from the Word of God. Jesus rebuked the Pharisees for making the Word of God of none effect by their tradition.

A little history: Shorter length skirts were introduced into this society as an "opening statement" of the sexual revolution. It was designed to display their invitation for immorality. They were intended to scandalize the "establishment" (those who stood for decency, morals and the American way.) Since that time they have become normal dress in the world and the fashions of the world have long since gone from "creeping" into the churches to taking the churches by storm! Until the 1920's women wore floor length dresses – and never pants – that were not of thin material and not form fitting to the body. During the "Roaring 20's" the dress patterns changed. Even those in the secular society were scandalized by what they saw from fashion designers. A writer for the New York Times in the 1920's stated: "The American woman has lifted skirts far beyond any modest limitation." Another writer, about the same time said, "If dress hems are nine inches off the ground today, there could come a day when our nation becomes so immoral that hems will rise to the kneecaps."

Now some may scoff at the "old fashioned" writers, and think it funny. I call it a shame. If we will take note at how far downhill our society has gone in less than 100 years – are there any bounds to the depravity to which it will stoop in the years to come? But notice that the "immoral" practices of the 1920's are now considered MODEST dress in Independent Baptist circles! I have seen more women than I can count, sitting in church, spending the entire service tugging and pulling at their skirts in an effort to make them look as long while they are sitting down as they were when they were standing up. Why not just wear a longer skirt?

Another commonly accepted, but large immodesty problem, among our women is slit skirts. Again the problem is focal point and teasing glances. The designers use the word provocative to describe a slit skirt – does that tell you anything? Peek-a-boo is a game for babies. See through clothes, the slit skirts, and the lace inserts in a low neckline are peek-a-boo fashions. A preacher brought this to my attention by giving it the man's

195

point of view that we women so often don't see. He said, "When you wear a slit skirt or when you wear see-through lace it makes a man want to look a little harder to see what else he can see." (No, he shouldn't do that - so don't tease him.)

As was mentioned in the survey, over and over again, the modern trend toward women wearing skin tight clothing is a serious problem. It seems that the styles at this time would dictate that young men wear clothing that is falling off of them. Young women wear clothes that look like they've been painted on, or stretched over them with the help of lubricating oil and a shoe horn. The focal point of tight clothing that outlines your figure is pretty obvious. Not only is this immodest, it is not attractive. Let's face it, when you wear clothing that clings to every part of your body, it reveals every imperfection in your figure. If you are a little on the plump side, every tiny bulge will be displayed. If you are really skinny, it is magnified by tight clothing until "if you turned sideways and stuck out your tongue, you'd look like a zipper." Tight clothing leaves nothing to the imagination. If your clothes are too tight, you may as well be parading around in a bathing suit. I heard a preacher who operates a boys' home one time say in a message, "Young ladies, please!! You think you are dressed all right because you are in a skirt - I've got 3 pews full of young men here that I'm trying to teach to live for God and your skirts are so tight I can see your panty lines through them." (He got a lot of criticism for his boldness, but I say, "Amen! It needed to be said.")

It's sad when a man who desires to serve God cannot be free from the flash of flesh in his face even in the house of God! There is something really wrong with the mentality of womankind who will wear clothing that screams, "Look at me!" and then blame the man for looking!! When you wear clothing that can be seen through, or that is so tight that every curve is clearly detailed, you are immodest and not in obedience to 1 Timothy 2.

Analyze the reason for the way you dress. Are you dressing for the Lord? Or to please self?

And whatsoever ye do in word or deed, do all in the name of the Lord Jesus, giving thanks to God and the Father by him.
Colossians 3:17

And whatsoever ye do, do it heartily, as to the Lord, and not unto men;
Colossians 3:23

Another point concerning parenting: Ladies, please - don't dress your young girls in tight, provocative clothing! I recently saw a pretty child of about 8 years old walking through a yard sale. She was wearing a pair of those clingy culottes things that are in fashion right now and a skin tight t-shirt. As usually happens the t-shirt had moved up around her backside and the clingy culottes were outlining her little posterior. At first I paid no attention, until I saw a grown man in the crowd watching her intently. I followed his gaze. Yes! That's perverted and disgusting but Mama had a great deal of the blame. Watch how you dress your children! Don't invite the perverts to ogle your little ones. Consider the example you are to your children in the way that you dress. Train your young men, for their own heart's sake, to turn their eyes away from women who are dressed immodestly. I taught my sons that if they were at a meeting, and a woman got up to sing or testify who was not properly dressed, that they were to find a great deal of interest in their own shoes. That lesson was so ingrained in them that I recently noticed one of my sons, now a grown man, staring at his shoes during a conference we had been invited to attend. I looked around and realized that a young woman had walked by in a very tight, revealing blouse - and I praised the Lord for my son's desire to keep his heart pure.

Does your makeup make a difference? I'm not telling you to never wear makeup. That is entirely between you and your husband and your God. The Word of God does not openly condemn the use of makeup. It, in fact, has very little to say about it at all. It only mentions one woman who wore makeup - Jezebel. Looking at the context of the chapter it is not condemning her for wearing it, it simply mentions that she wore it, but it mentions it for the purpose of revealing the attitude she had. She was trying to be alluring. That's enough for me to decide not to wear it.

Another thought to consider is that makeup is simply not good for your face. Mascara and eyeliner are an eye doctor's nightmare. Foundation cosmetics tend to age your face more rapidly with prolonged use. A woman who never wears cosmetics keeps the fresh, youthful look of her face much longer than one who wears heavy makeup on a regular basis. We are commanded in the Word of God to present our bodies as a living sacrifice and to keep them holy. We are told not to sow to the flesh, because FROM THE FLESH we will reap corruption.

And when thou art spoiled, what wilt thou do? Though thou clothest thyself with crimson, though thou deckest thee with ornaments of gold, though thou rentest thy face with painting, in vain shalt thou make thyself fair; thy lovers will despise thee, they will seek thy life. Jeremiah 4:30

Notice that is says that the face is "rent" (torn) with painting.
Also in researching the origin of makeup you will find that makeup came out of Egypt. Egypt, in the Word of God, is a type of the world and the things that come from Egypt are to be treated with caution by a child of God. I've included this article from the Wikipedia:

Main article: History of cosmetics
The first archaeological evidence of cosmetics usage is found in Ancient Egypt around 4000 BC. The Ancient Greeks and Romans also used cosmetics. The ancient kingdom of Israel was influenced by cosmetics as recorded in the Old Testament—2 Kings 9:30 where Jezebel painted her eyes—approximately 840 BC. The Biblical book of Esther describes various beauty treatments as well. (These were spices and ointments)
In the western world, the advent of cosmetics was in the middle ages, although typically restricted to use within the upper classes. Cosmetic use was frowned upon at some points in history. For example, in the 1800s, make-up was used primarily by prostitutes, and Queen Victoria publicly declared makeup improper, vulgar, and acceptable only for use by actors. Adolf Hitler told women that face painting was for clowns and not for the women of the Master Race. By the middle of the 20th century, cosmetics were in widespread use in nearly all societies around the world.

Another consideration is the chemical composition of makeup. It is a sad fact that has been covered up, then proven, shrugged at and ignored by society at large, that many cosmetic companies use chemicals that are derived from tissue of aborted babies. If, in spite of this, you choose the makeup route, let's take a look at how it should be approached to avoid immodesty.
Your eyes and your lips are the two parts of your face that are the most interesting and alluring to a man's gaze. That is why makeup

manufacturers spend most of their advertising on the eyes and lips. Look again at God's command to us in 1 Timothy.

In like manner also, that women adorn themselves in modest apparel, with shamefacedness and sobriety; not with broided hair, or gold, or pearls, or costly array; But (which becometh women professing godliness) with good works. 1 Timothy 2:9

If your makeup is overdone you will not be sending a message of godliness. Particularly avoid makeup that makes your eyes stand out as the overshadowing feature of your face or that make your lips look wet. You cannot be shamefaced if your face is screaming "look at me, look at my pretty eyes, my luscious mouth." The Bible gives a warning to young men:

For the lips of a strange woman drop as an honeycomb, and her mouth is smoother than oil. Proverbs 5: 3

Lust not after her beauty in thine heart; neither let her take thee with her eyelids. Proverbs 6:25

If that is the warning that God is giving to the young men, then we as women should avoid being placed in the category of the strange woman. We should avoid attempting to make our eyes and lips a point of allurement.

John Bunyan made this statement about the immodesty that he saw in some of the "fashionable ladies" of his day. It is very blunt, but quite an eye opener. "Why are they for going with their … naked shoulder, and paps hanging out like a cow's bag? Why are they for painting their faces, for stretching out their necks, and for putting themselves unto all the formalities which proud fancy leads them to?"

If you need further proof, go take a seat in the middle of the nearest mall and watch the clothing choices of the crowd. Pick out the focal points of the clothing they wear, then compare it with your own wardrobe. You might be surprised to find out that some of the same focal points exist in your own closet. I have seen many of these same type outfits on women who, I truly believe, desire to have God's blessing on their lives yet have not submitted to Him their clothing choices. If only they could understand what they are doing to the men around them!

Submission to your husband should play a major role in your clothing choices. A godly man will be extremely pleased to be consulted about the way his wife dresses. (You don't have to wear his favorite color every day, unless he tells you to. Just get him involved.) Explain that you wish to dress modestly for him and for the Lord. Have him read through the lessons if you choose. Most men would be glad to help their wives because most of them understand what women seem to have a hard time with - that men have a totally different view of the way that women dress than the women themselves do. Be prepared, however, you will draw some opposition from "the sisters" for dressing to please your husband and the Lord.

My husband prefers that I do not cut my hair at all, dye it or perm it. He has sound Biblical basis for this from 1 Corinthians 11:3-15 and 1 Timothy 2:9-10 - and he just likes it better that way. In honor to my husband and my Lord my hair is very long and is in its natural state of color confusion. (We've never been able to decide if it is brown, red or blonde - to which picture is now added a good measure of gray!) I can't count the number of times I have had Christian women make "suggestions" as to what I should do with my hair. These comments are usually preceded with, "I couldn't stand all that long hair – it would drive me crazy!" Many times the comments are punctuated with the remark, "NO man is going to tell me how to fix my hair!" Hummmm...that sounds submissive, doesn't it? I have even had women professing Christ look at me with scorn and criticism and make rude, cutting remarks concerning my hair and clothing choices. I used to be hurt by these comments until I realized that it came from a heart that was more than likely fighting the conviction of the Holy Spirit about their own rebellious form of dress. I've learned to pray for them instead of taking it personally and becoming angry. So be forewarned - choosing to dress for the Lord will not come without cost. Are you willing to identify yourself with Christ at the risk of ridicule from worldly Christians? A submissive, dedicated, godly woman stands out like a billboard in our society - and mediocre Christianity bears its fangs.

A word of caution, however. When God changes your heart in this matter, or in any other matter, and you get the victory for yourself in walking closer to Him in holiness, don't let it go to your head and make a Pharisee out of you. When you see another sister in Christ who has not been taught, or has not surrendered in this area, don't criticize her, even inwardly. She is a matter for prayer and a subject of compassion. Remember that we are supposed to be ornamented with a MEEK and quiet spirit. If you become critical of every woman you see, your heart will become puffed up with pride. God does not honor pride, He hates it. If you are critical and full of yourself, you are just as sinful and guilty as the woman who dresses immodestly.

We've covered a lot in our study on clothing and you are to be commended for sitting through it. With most women this is a brick wall. They won't even stand to listen to it, much less to heed anything that was said. The issue is going to be answered here in our own hearts. Do I desire to be the woman that God wants me to be? Or do I want to be the woman I want to be? There's no other way to look at it. If you will submit, from the heart, to dress the way that God wants you to dress, He will bless and bless and bless your efforts. You will also grow and change to please Him as the Holy Spirit teaches you what is acceptable in his sight. If you will not, then you will answer for your lack of submission when we stand before Him. No one can force you to do it - you've got to submit to His will because of your love for Him and your desire to do things His way instead of your own.

Survey of Christian Men on the Subject of Women's Clothing
(Excerpts from "Dressing for the Lord" from Way of Life Literature):

I sent out a notice to the Fundamental Baptist Information Service e-mail list and asked the following question of the men on the list who are members of fundamentalist and independent Baptist churches: "In your opinion, which of the following items of female dress cause a real potential for lust? Short skirts, tight skirts, slit skirts, long skirts with slits to the knees, sleeveless blouses, low cut blouses and dresses, tight blouses, sheer blouses, T-shirts, V-neck dresses, form-fitting jeans, looser-fitting pants, shorts and one-piece bathing suits." [Pedal pushers and capris were included in the original survey but most of the men did not know what they are, so it turned out that the comments on those items were too irrelevant to include.]

My objective in this is to help girls and women in strong Bible-believing churches to understand how men think, not only men in the world or men in churches in general but men in the very churches they attend. I received a flood of response to this survey. In just one day I received well over 100 responses from men ages 24 to 74 and from many parts of the world – and that was on a weekend – and they are still coming in a week and a half later. This tells me that there is a readiness on the part of men to let women understand how they see this issue. As you will see, the responses were very earnest. The men are discouraged that lust is such a powerful temptation in their lives, and they admitted that it is so. Some of the men literally begged me to tell the women that their manner of dress is important and that they need to understand how men look at things.

One man wrote: "Thank you for this request. This area is the greatest challenge in my life – in all honesty to a brother-in-the-blood."

The following was also typical: "I have been saved for about eight years and the lust issue is huge for me and for all men...I need God every day to help me stay away from lust. Short skirts, tight blouses, slit dresses are all over. You can't look at billboards, grocery store waiting line magazine racks, internet advertisements, walking in the park, or any store. You get my point; it's everywhere...I have to pray every day for God to keep lust out of my way. I wish I was born into a good Bible believing church and was brought up to stay away from lustful sin. To answer your question it would have to be anything short or tight on a woman. I look forward to the cold winters up north when women cover everything up.
Another man said: "That our society drenches every inch of media in sexually explicit advertising is a source of much temptation, sadness and concern for this man. Facing that sort of issue with Christian sisters in a church setting is most grievous.

Most of the men observed that their response to a woman's immodest dress depends on their spiritual condition and acknowledged that they have a responsibility before God not to lust after women regardless of how they are dressed.

For example, one man said: "Men are sight oriented creatures. The Lord has so equipped men to be sexually stimulated visually...Men must govern their own hearts."

Another man said: "My response to immodest is often dependent on the environment, situation and my spiritual defense mechanism at the particular moment. If I have had a wonderful prayer time and clothed myself with all the spiritual armor, I am usually just about OK for anything. But more often than I would like it, I am not prepared or I am in a vulnerable situation; then I better run for my dear life (Gen 39:12.)

Another man said: "While I feel that the Lord has helped me overcome in this area [of not lusting after women] the enemy knows my weakness and still attacks me. In my opinion, the keys to overcoming lust are: 1) Obey God's Word, especially in the command to abstain from the very appearance of evil; and 2) don't put yourself in situations where you will encounter women scantily dressed (i.e. the beach, certain television programs, etc.) Since we are in the world, I know that there is no way to completely avoid the things that tempt us, but if we will stay true to the Word of God and allow Him to help us, we can be 'more than conquerors through Him who loved us' (Romans 8:37.)

Many of the men also observed that this is a heart issue. The following statement by a pastor is typical of those made by many others: "I believe the most important issue in female modesty is the issue of a chaste heart. If the woman desires to please her Saviour and honor her brother in Christ, there is seldom an issue with the clothing she wears. Mandating modest clothing without focusing on creating a chaste heart does little good. If the woman wears 'modest' clothing but is sensual in the way she walks or conducts herself, it will invariably cause a man to lust. I don't need to see skin to cause me to lust. We men have pretty good imaginations."

As to the individual items of dress, the men made the following points. First of all, many of the men replied that all of the aforementioned female dress styles hold a real potential for lust. The following two statements are typical:

"I believe that ALL you had listed cause a 'potential' for lust."

"I think that ALL of the listed items can cause lust. The bottom line for me is that anything that is form fitting, exposing, sheer, or clinging to a woman is immodest and can cause men to lust."

Sheer blouses or dresses are a problem for the vast majority of men. One man said, "I see a lot of Christian women wearing sun dresses in the summer because they are cool. They are also revealing and alluring. Most summer clothes are thin so as to be more comfortable. But you let that woman wearing these clothes stand with a light source behind her (such as the sun) and there is nothing left to the imagination. You can see her form in every detail and it will get men frothing at the mouth, lusting after that woman. Is it the man's fault for not controlling his flesh and desires even though it is there for him to see? Absolutely! But it is equally the woman's fault for not having enough godliness about her to dress modestly in the first place."

Even looser-fitting female pants, while not as much of a problem as form-fitting jeans, hold a potential problem for many men. One man said, "While it is true that some things on your list will draw your attention quicker and cause you to look longer, even 'looser-fitting pants' direct a man's gaze to the area of the hips."

Another wrote: "A few years ago, I preached a message about standards (including music, dress, and others.) I asked for a show of hands as to how many men would admit that their eyes were drawn to a woman's crotch when she wore pants instead of a skirt or dress. More than two dozen hands went up (and who knows how many more were hesitant to make the public confession with their wives right next to them?) The group included many of the finest Christians I know, some of whom are ordained ministers and missionaries."

Many men mentioned the unisex aspect of looser pants on women.

As for V-neck dresses, most men said they are not a problem as long as the v is shallow. A few said the V-neck itself, even if not too low, can be a problem because it acts like an arrow pointing to a place where their eyes should not roam.

As for sleeveless blouses, many of the men mentioned that they can be a problem because they can allow a man to see something he should not see and "the potential for peeking is there." A pastor commented, "There is too much of an opportunity for parts of a woman's anatomy to be inadvertently show through to the public that are only to be revealed to her husband in private."

One man said: "One word about sleeveless dresses or tops. When the woman has her arm raised or in a certain position, the sleeve hole will open in just a way that you can see inside her shirt and see the woman's underwear or even more. No woman, much less a Christian woman, should ever wear clothing that reveals her body."

When it comes to t-shirts on females, the men said they are not a problem unless they are tight or expose the midriff, you can see through them, or they have writings/logos/pictures at the breast level. One pastor said: "It depends on the fit, cut, thickness of the material and color. A modest t-shirt would be loose fitting, not see through, of a thick enough material to truly be modest. Very few t-shirts fit these qualifications."

One man said: "My wife sews attractive vests that she and our daughter wear over t-shirts. It's a way of using clever camouflage to be modest."

One woman mentioned another problem with t-shirts: "I have a problem with smart-alecky t-shirts. I have a hard time finding t-shirts for my daughter sometimes not so much from a tightness standpoint but they have inappropriate sayings on them that encourage a worldly attitude, rebellion against parents, etc."

A man wrote along similar lines in regard to "Christian t-shirts," warning about "Jesus t-shirts like 'This Blood's for you' etc." that really degrade the message of the Scripture."

Comments on the specific items of apparel fell along the following lines: Short skirts, short dresses, and/or shorts – These hold a very serious potential for lust for men.

One man said, "The higher up on a woman's leg, the more lustful/tempting it becomes."

Tight clothing is at least as much of a potential problem for men as skimpy clothing. Most of the men indicated that tight skirts, tight blouses, and form-fitting jeans and one-piece bathing suits hold a "VERY great potential" for lust. One man said tight skirts are "very inviting and a potential for lust."

Another said of tight clothing, "You don't even need to see skin; they provide all the curves." Another said: "I would say the number one problem is any garment that is form fitting, be it jeans, pants, skirt, dress, shirt, whatever. Anything that is tight, no matter how long it is, leaves nothing to the imagination, and that defeats the whole purpose of covering the skin in the first place."
Another said: "One thing I see in my church is tight clothing. Oh, it may very well be covering but it is revealing the shape in a woman. This can be even more tantalizing to a man." Another wrote: "The point is that it is not the type of clothing that can trip a man up, rather it is the amount and the level of cling to the body." One man said that since one-piece bathing suits are "skin tight" he does "not think any red blooded normal man could look purely on a woman attired like this."

Some of the men also mentioned low-riding jeans as a cause for serious concern, because not only do they totally emphasize the woman's figure but they are also suggestive of a bare midriff even if covered with a t-shirt. The t-shirt in such a case is invariably tight, of course. Slit skirts and slit dresses are a problem for man men.
One man answered the question of whether slit skirts are a real potential for lust with the reply, "Oh! Yes!" One man said that slit skirts "tempt your imagination." Another called the slit skirt the "peek-a-boo" skirt, while another said the slit is "designed to catch the eye." A pastor said, "They are a teasing game, catching the attention of a guy's eyes with a promise of more, it is an enticement to sin."

One man said: "My belief is that any slit (whether it be a long, medium or short skirt) provides a flash of skin that is enticing to the eye and the flesh of men. It is the 'forbidden fruit' so to speak, that is covered and when the woman sits or moves just right, that part of the leg is exposed and it is all a man needs - to think about what he just saw or what else he could see." Another man said: "I know that many women cannot begin to understand how that a skirt or a dress that is 2 inches off the floor in length, but has a long slit anywhere on it – front, back or side – can cause a man to lust. They think that we are pathetic, and unfortunately I have to agree."

Another man said: "For me personally, slits draw my eyes where they shouldn't be drawn. If anyone knows anything about advertising, he would know that advertisers use lines to draw people's eyes where they want (company logo, name, whatever.) Slits in skirts do exactly the same thing."

Another observed, "If the slit is there because the dress or skirt is too tight, why not wear a looser skirt?"

Consider some excerpts from the comments made by these men:
"I do believe most women just do not know how men think. Period. I believe that there is a whole segment, group, and class of women, who, if they really understood men, would change their dress code, because they want to please God. Not all women, by far, but some would. They just need to understand it's not just a list of do's and don'ts set forth to force them into 'frumpiness' but a desire of godly men to gain their cooperation in helping them NOT lust, and to not be stumbling blocks, because they just want to please God."

"Many women, usually younger, dress to attract men and do not know how dangerous it truly can be for them. I am a retired criminal investigator and worked criminal work for 17&1/2 years of my career. I think many homicides and serious physical assaults in addition to the obvious sex crimes are brought about by immodest dress and any born again Christian woman should never dress as such. A sexual predator can be turned on, and be as dangerous as a hand grenade with the pin pulled, by a woman that has the one turn on factor for his mind (which is variable with such criminals.) It could be any of the listed ways of dressing."

"I am glad you are addressing this issue. This issue along with worldly music has come into fundamental churches like a tidal wave. Thank you for being a watchman."

"I have to admit some of the dresses that are worn, although the dress hits the floor, and some of the blouses, even though it goes all the way to the neck, are very form fitting. I don't think that women are out to stumble the men of the church, nor am I saying that women need to walk around in sacks. There are sometimes when a lady is doing a special music or something that I have to look away that I may not stumble. In summation I think that all of the clothing you have listed that is form fitting and shows the curves of a woman is a real potential for lust."

"I am a 24 year old, unmarried man. I am very glad that you are asking us men about this issue, because it has been my experience that women truly do not understand the things that can run though a man's head when he sees an immodestly dressed woman. For a God-fearing man this is a true concern. Fashionable clothing is not, as far as I can tell, designed by God-fearing Christians with any interest in modesty. Sex sells and sexy clothing sells. I have talked to women I know about the dress issue and told them that when they wear certain things, no matter how 'covered up' they may be, the fit of the clothing still makes a huge difference. Some women have told me that it is the man's fault for having such a dirty mind or for letting it get to a point where lust becomes a problem. The fact is that men seem specifically prone to these types of thoughts. In North American culture we are inundated with sex. Everywhere we look there is a provocatively dresses (or practically undressed) woman selling something. I think that women (and men) need to seriously consider the way they dress and how it affects members of the opposite sex. The last place I want to have to worry about lust is in my church."

"As Christians, it is not our place to say, "Well, I just don't understand why men can't look at me dressed like this and not battle with lusting thoughts." Instead, we need to take it for a truth when a person of the opposite sex informs us that our dress is causing problems for them and do what we need to do to protect our brothers and sisters from stumbling."

"I am 64 years old now and walking with the Lord Jesus through life. Earlier in my life I was a womanizer as a single man for a long time. My feelings of women dressing immodestly are strong, as I know the sadness that infidelity, lustful sin and adultery bring about to many. Immodest dress is a precursor to the aforementioned activities."

"All men are aroused in one way or the other over revealed flesh. That is exactly why these clothes are made this way. I know some men are more easily aroused than others, but normally any man is naturally inclined (by our sinful nature) to take notice of a woman wearing any garment that is revealing flesh."

"I think it is a shame to come to church after a week in this evil world and want to enjoy a service of worship and praise to the Lord and fellowship among separated people and see women dressing like the world. When you confront them about this you always get the same old line: 'Well if you don't like it, you've got the problem.'"

"Well, I always wonder why a woman who loves the Lord and wants to please the Lord would want to dress like the world and have men looking at her in a carnal way. When I see a woman in a store in town and she is dressed in a certain conservative way, I always think, 'I bet she's a Christian!!'"

"It says a lot about the character of a woman when she shuns the styles of this world and walks in such a way that she wants to let people know that she is different."

"One of the sad things I observe in church is the control that the fashion world has over women and the lack of communication between man and wife. I have been saved for 45 years come August and have been in independent Baptist Church for 40 years. So I see women and teenagers in our church and have to look away or up so as not to be seen looking at how they are dressed. Modesty seems to be an archaic word to many and it grieves me."

"I am 55 years old and I am BROKENHEARTED over the dress of a great number of females in the churches I visit. Oh, if I could only talk to moms and dads. I have never been married but lived in the world many years. I beg you, preacher, tell them that wearing ANYTHING that draws attention to a particular area, accentuating ANY form or flesh, is a great distraction for me. Please, stop wearing TIGHT clothing, exposing flesh, and wearing articles of clothing with writing on them. How many times have I had to turn my eyes away, or worry, did I look too long, did somebody notice me looking? I wish I could talk to a group of women and just tell them, because I know they don't really realize what a distraction it is. [Surely] they don't want the brethren to sin. I can't believe how some of these young girls dress. Don't they know the things that we cherish, we must protect? I don't care about peer pressure! Clothing is an opportunity to share your faith when people see a difference. Remember that man (and woman) looks on the outward appearance. We have to be separated and yes, a 'PECULIAR' people. Men are tempted and aroused by the things they SEE. David was tempted when he SAW Bathsheba; Herod was tempted when he SAW Salome dance; when Samson 'saw a woman in Timnath,' he wanted her because her looks 'pleased' him."

"I want to mention the present trend of embossing brand names across the seat of women's trousers, pants, shorts, or skirts. No imagination needed to explain that."

"I travel a bit, and as I'm walking through a crowded airport looking around, I tend more to notice things like short skirts, skirts or dresses with slits, low-cut blouses or dresses, sheer blouses or tight fitting anything. Clothing that accentuates or draws attention to one part of the body seems more noticeable to me. I believe that clothing absolutely can draw attention to the woman's body and that once attention is there, the potential, perhaps even the likelihood, for lust isn't far behind."

"From what I see in the way many women and teens dress, Christians included, many act like they are 'for sale' or are very ignorant of what they are doing to their image. That's the way I see things on this issue."

"The more skin I see, the more I have to force myself to look away from that individual. It brings back the past [before I was saved.] It seems like some women flaunt their bodies. What they are saying by their clothes is: 'Don't look at my face, look at my body!' I'm all for modesty and I wish all churches had a dress code. Not just in church but also out of church. Skin is a distraction! More skin, more sin!"

"I agree with you about the lack of understanding from most women about the male weakness in the area of lust. The average Christian woman today seems to think, 'If you've got it, flaunt it." I actually had one woman who used to be in my church saying that. God's final act of creation was His most beautiful. A normal man would agree with this. This sets us apart from the animal kingdom. In animals the male is the most attractive. The female is often rather dowdy. Humans are reversed. A godly woman can dress attractively and properly by following a few simple thoughts. Do the clothes she is wearing draw a man's eyes to her face or to her other body parts? Is the clothing she is wearing obviously feminine and modest and not made for men?"

"Thanks so much for addressing this issue. I am a Christian who has been doing street ministry for many years and full time now for 20 years. I am also a single dad (wife died of cancer almost 9 years ago) of four sons, three under 18. I have concentrated on work in the public housing areas. To say I have seen it all would be an understatement. One of the saddest things and hardest to fight against has been the fact that the 'street' and the church now seem to be equal in their approach to female sexuality and its expression. There seems to be no bottom to the level that members of the church are willing to allow in the way of what can be worn to church and church functions. As a man who is deeply concerned that my sons do not get exposed to this type of thing I find myself upset a lot about what goes on. It is obvious that many of these girls are not only not TAUGHT to be modest, but their parents have BOUGHT them the clothes that they wear to flaunt their sexuality in! Sadly enough, I would have to say that there is no part of the female body that I have not seen in church. Short skirts, low cut blouses, halter tops, tiny two-piece bathing suits, and bathing suits with high cut in the back seem to prevail in church activities. To go to the heart of the issue I would have to say that there appears to be many church men who revel in their daughters' budding sexuality."

"To answer your request on women's dress and modesty, I have to paraphrase a statement made many years ago by a Christian minister of national acclaim. His subject was Christian women and the way they dress that would tempt Christian men as well as worldly men to lust after them. It's been so many years ago that he preached the message that I can't quote directly, but in essence what he said was that any Christian man that said he wasn't affected by seeing a

Christian sister in the short skirts, tight skirts, etc. (in other words, most of the items on your list, in fact I would include one or two more) the preacher would pay for that man's physical exam. Blunt, but to the point. We as Christians are not to do anything to cause our Christian brother or sister to stumble, but this subject of modesty (both women and men) is not often preached on. I remember reading an article in a book about how culture has changed in the USA. In the early 1940's a man could be reprimanded on the beach at Atlantic City for not wearing a top to his bathing suit. What we have now is close to nudity, especially in the women. My wife and I will not vacation at the beach so that we don't subject ourselves to the near nudity of the people there. One of the biggest mediums for temptation is the nudity that is seen on television (which we got rid of close to 30 years ago because of commercials and programming.) Next to that are 99% of the magazines articles and advertising. But yet little, if anything, is mentioned from pulpits about the influence of these two mediums."

"All of those items of female dress cause a real potential for lust."

"Why should a man have to battle with lust during a church service when it is hard enough just to walk in a world full of sensuality? If women only knew the snare of temptation that is set before our eyes?"

"Even if it is a fraction of a second and a man turns his head away, the battle can still rage in the mind just from a mere glimpse. I honestly believe that many of them know exactly what they are doing. Why else would they dress like the rebellious world?"

"It seems the last few years as the churches have grown more liberal and the women show more skin, I have to fight harder to keep my mind straight. I am happily married. I do not and will not stray. I wish women could just take the Bible for what it says. Yes, the Lord made us men this way. I think the most beautiful thing God created on this earth is a woman, and Satan knows it, too. That is just the way I feel."

"As a Christian come back from 20 years in the world, I can see this situation very well. I still tend to 'rate' (if you will) women physically by shape and presentation in my mind. This is a battle that must constantly be fought by one who gave in to lust in the past. A woman in a nice dress with little exposed is pleasing to the eye and stops at that."

"I attend a very conservative independent fundamental Baptist church, where the pastor and his wife lead by example. Unfortunately, I see that oftentimes, some of the women in our church, though they always wear dresses or skirts to church and though they are always below the knee, they are still a bit too concerned with 'fashion' and sometimes compromise true modesty for 'looking good' or being fashionable."

"It is often an issue for me. Many of these ladies are dear, sweet Christian women, devoted wives, dedicated servants. I don't believe they INTEND to be a distraction. I just don't think they realize."

"My wife and I are the nursery directors at our church. We are constantly having to interact with workers and mothers. Sometimes I find myself having to do a 'check' on where my eyes are being drawn and where my thoughts are headed. I have to PURPOSE to not think that way, or to just not look at them while I'm talking to them, or distract myself with something else (hummm, that wall needs a new coat of paint, or that floor needs vacuuming, or we are out of paper towels.) I'm sure they would be mortified if they realized they were even remotely emitting a 'sexy' quality. That's not to say some women don't intend to look sexy. One woman in particular who is very attractive (even my wife says so,) USED to dress very stylish, in expensive, designer clothes that were hip, cool, young, modern but seemed clueless as to the biblical boundaries she was overstepping. After our pastor preached on the subject of modesty my wife and I noticed –IMMEDIETLY – that this lady's wardrobe changed completely. It was like the light went on and she responded with humility and gratitude for the message. Now, she still looks stylish, but is much more conservative, appropriate and modest in her attire. It's truly a relief. Now, when we see her coming, we're actually glad to see her because we know she's not going to make us feel uncomfortable because of her sexy-ish clothes."

"I would agree that while some women are out and out Jezebels, there are others who do not understand how a man is affected by a woman's modesty (or lack thereof.) One of my major concerns is that we have strayed from the question of how to standardize modesty. Almost anywhere I go anymore I hear the argument on the length of skirts, 'It's below the knee.' When did the definition of modesty begin with how far below the knee it goes? Why is it just length? Formfitting, slit-skirted, bare legs, and everything else you mentioned in your list are a magnet for a man's eyes. While this has not been a problem at our church, it is becoming an issue with churches I would never have expected to see it in. I get irritated when I have to look in another direction rather than see an immodest woman in church. The point of the irritation is not that I am looking away but the fact that I have to do so in Independent fundamental circles. I guess I get more and more frustrated with dress standards. We preach of the immorality of the world, television that is filled with homosexuality, nudity and the internet filled with almost any type of perversion you want. Our society has degenerated to animal-like sexuality where there are no rules and little discussion of consequences. Our answer should to be to show how different we are from them (which is becoming less and less.) I do not care how different our ladies are from the world; this is not the standard of comparison. The standard of comparison is how much they are like Christ...and He is nothing like this world. 'Ye therefore, beloved, seeing ye know [these things] before, beware lest ye also, being led away with the error of the wicked, fall from your own steadfastness.' (2 Peter 3:17)

"Almost all of the styles you listed serve to in some way accentuate, reveal, or tantalize the senses of men. Men are very liable to visual temptation. Even Job realized that (Job 31:1) The Psalmist did, too (Psalm 101:3.) The ladies need to know that there is a need to have a heart of modesty that will give them the desire to strengthen and honor their brothers in Christ. If that happens, modesty will be a matter of heart and dress and not simply a legalistic issue."

"I suspect I have to deal with this most every day of my life. Consider the magazines in the grocery store checkout area. Most Christian women are oblivious to modesty, but the folks that design most of the clothes in most clothing stores where Christian women make purchases are not ignorant of what they are doing. The modestly dressed individual is a rare breed in this part of the country. I do know a few families, very few, who have decided to be different but they cause me to look in amazement."

"I am a red blooded, fully functional, American man who desires to have his thoughts and words be acceptable to God. I have been happily married for 28 years. The Biblical issue of modesty is best understood by an understanding of defrauding. No one should take any action whereby he causes desires to be raised in another that cannot be righteously satisfied. That our society drenches every inch of media in sexually explicit advertising is a source of much temptation, sadness and concern for this man. Facing that sort of issue with Christian sisters in a church setting is most grievous. I believe the phrase 'long, loose and lots of it' should be the motto of Christian women's apparel. Before knowing her husband, my bride had no idea of how men think or how easily stimulated they are. I hope my candor may be of some value to the Christian sisters who are trying to live holy lives. I try to tell young ladies that I can influence for good that the kind of fish you catch depends on what you bait your hook with and where you cast your line. If you can't catch a man in church with a modest dress on, you don't want him anyway!"

"You are absolutely right about women not seeing these dangers. They can demand Bible verses to back up the assertion that certain clothes cause lust all day long, but the truth is that if these clothes cause men to lust they are participating in the problem whether or not there are specific Scriptures to exclude every piece of clothing that designers can conceive."

"In my personal opinion, I think the styles that expose the bosom or the tight form of the bosom present the majority of the problem because it is more accepted to show that area in our society as opposed to the upper thigh or the lower buttocks."

"Personally, I see women (including independent Baptist church-goers and staff) causing potential for lust in all the clothing you listed. The point is that it is not the type of clothing that can trip a man up; rather it is the amount and the level of cling to the body. When I see women dressing as I described above, I can't avoid wondering why they are 'advertising' their flesh. Is it because they are lacking in Christian character?"

"My wife was taught as a little girl that all attention should be drawn to her face and that rule has been a great guideline."

"It's not always what the attire is but how it is worn and the woman herself. Excessive use of perfume and make up—both designed to draw men; they should be used with wisdom. Also, flirtatious natures and wanting to be noticed by the opposite sex should be reigned in." "It is the duty of every husband to make sure his wife is properly dressed, not only for church but all the time. I have been blessed with a modest wife. Men are weak in the area of sex and need 'the handbrake' of a modest woman to keep him on track and his thoughts in line."

"I am certainly not proud to have to say that all of the above items of clothing on women cause a real potential for lust, but for me it is the case. Of all of my close brothers in the Lord whom I have talked with on this subject over time, all are in agreement that they struggle with lust. It is so few women, at least where I am, that dress modestly or even have a single clue that there is a Biblical instruction for them to do so. I am so thankful for my pastor's wife and her decision to dress modestly."

"It is amazing to me that husbands, fathers, etc. would allow their women out in public wearing some of the things women wear. Have they no idea of the thoughts of other men? Shame on them!"

"There is a term 'not leaving anything to the imagination.' Our Father knows, as does any man, that men do not need any encouragement at all, let alone a less than reverent dress style. The fleshly man is full of imagination. I cannot think of even one of the styles listed that are appropriate for Christian women. Unfortunately, I see them in churches and 'Christian Schools' every day."

"Blessings to you for writing on this subject. There is nothing I detest more than women dressed immodestly anywhere, but most especially in church. This is one more way for Satan to take men's minds off of the worship of their Heavenly Father! Women should not wear anything which exposes or draws a man's attention to 'those' areas that are conducive to male lust. Oh how I wish modest dressing would come back into style! That both men and women would have more self-respect in general and particularly more respect of the Lord's house."

"Whatever standard the parent lives before and requires of his/her children, the easier it will before the child to maintain that standard. Usually the child never has higher standards of the parent. If we expect lawyers, ambassadors, etc. to look respectful and above the normal standard, shouldn't Christians do the same?"

"Another apparel item that may be worth mentioning is knee-high leather boots. These seem to be more and more prevalent among Christian women. In my opinion, these boots scream sensuality and are a real potential for generating lust. I may be completely off base on this as my view is certainly tainted from years of pornography, womanizing, immorality, spending a lot of time at bars and etc. (from my teen years until my mid-twenties when I was saved.) During those days, however, when a woman wore knee high boots, it would certainly attract attention for all of the wrong reasons. Perhaps Christian women are not aware of this? Overall, on the issue of modesty, I completely agree that many women do not understand how men look at things in this realm. I suspect for many men, including me, that lust is a daily battle. I desire for my church family and Christian friends to be a safe haven from temptation."

"If such things draw the attention of normal, godly Christian men, by definition they are immodest, no matter what women think."

"When my wife and I were first married, she wore pants. I didn't tell her to stop, although she would have if I had told her to. She would have quit wearing pants but she would have resented me for telling her to do so. She had to quit wearing them because she was convicted by the Holy Spirit and God's Word. She was convicted and she quit wearing pants. In fact, she dresses so modestly that people stare at her because she dresses differently and not because she is showing something off. I am proud of her stance as a Christian because she dresses this way in obedience to the Word of God and not only in obedience to me."

217

"I don't know how women can 'not' know the impact their dress has on men. In fact, I believe they do (more than they say or let on.) One thing I see in my church is tight clothing. Oh, it may very well be covering but it is revealing the woman's outline. This can be even worse. I once was at a conference and the preacher asked a very strong Christian couple (wife modestly dressed) 'Who do you dress for?' Her answer was her husband. The preacher and the congregation gave their 'Amens.' I thought about that answer and it was an answer I would have wanted my wife to give until just a few years before. Now she knows I would want her to dress for the Lord Jesus Christ Himself. I have the potential to be carnal and in the flesh and to want to see her in less modest apparel. That would never be the case with our Lord. Thus I told her to dress for Jesus Christ."

"Our church teaches and preaches separation. Our pastor has even compiled a small booklet on modest dress. Having said all that, we have had and still do have problems. In order to be a choir member or teach Sunday School, etc., we must sign a form saying we agree to the dress standards as well as many other standards of conduct. What I have seen is, yes, they are wearing dresses but many are far from modest. I have had my wife ask me, 'Did you see what so and so was wearing?' I am honest with her and I tell her, 'of course I did!' I am a man and when a woman exposes 50% of her breasts I can't help but notice. I told her I don't ogle but it is a part of a woman that men find attractive, so here I am in God's house trying to worship God and hear from His Word and I see these things. But she is wearing a dress!! Form fitting clothing is another area that is a problem. A lady can actually be wearing a reasonably nice dress that meets the standard – at least in her mind it does – but the problem is that it is at least a size too small for her! These folks are rarely confronted because they are wearing a dress, you know! I believe we easily forget modesty and become lost in the 'I'm wearing a dress' attitude. To be honest I have seen more modest pants on many lost ladies than the dresses on our standard-signing church ladies. I'm not for pants, I'm just referring to our hypocrisy! It shows either a lack of discernment on their part or a worldly desire to show off their body – maybe both. Sorry to vent but this has hit close to home as I have tried to protect teenagers from what they see in church. I believe there is a tremendous lack of understanding on the part of most women about what they wear and why. As I said, our church teaches and preaches on these things and they do a good job teaching. It is a spiritual issue. They know the facts. It is accepting them and living by them that is the problem. I have heard, 'they just want us to look like old women.' If that means to dress modestly then yes, please try to look at the older women who are trying to teach the younger, as Titus says, through example."

"As I was not saved until I was an adult, I was like most men; I enjoyed the sight of the female form. Without Christ, I had no reason not to indulge my lusts when I looked at immodestly dressed women. There is no shortage of flesh in our culture; the movies, TV, music videos, internet, etc., all promote it. After I was saved, God began to show me through His Word to flee youthful lusts and to be like Job who made a covenant with his eyes not to look upon a maid. You listed several types of clothing and asked which ones were areas of temptation. My answer would be 'all of them!' As my wife and I began to grow in the Lord, I made the comment to her that, 'if the average woman knew how the average man thinks it would cause her to dress a lot differently.' I don't think women realize just how much they expose themselves by the style of clothes they wear (or don't wear as the case may be.)"

"The stark difference between Biblical modesty and femininity was illustrated one night as another preacher and I, along with our wives and families, were on the street in a large city near our home preaching and passing out gospel tracts during a music festival. Two young women, who were dressed very provocatively, walked by and received the cat-calls and lewd remarks of a couple of young guys. The boys then turned and saw my wife standing there (she is 32) dressed in a modest skirt and top and said, "Oh, sorry ma'am!" Ladies need to understand that how they are dressed says a lot about who they are and determines to some extent how they will be treated. Scripture backs this up (Proverbs 7, Genesis 38:15-16.)"

"Pastors need to deal with this issue as more than just as a 'when you come to church' thing. I believe we have created a double standard in our independent Baptist churches in that the only time dress is dealt with is when people are taught that they ought to come to church 'dressed right.' Not many deal with the fact that believers

219

are to glorify God in all things, every day, including how we dress. Christian women have a responsibility before the Lord to be obedient to the Bible's admonitions concerning dress. They also have a responsibility to their brothers in the Lord, not to cast a stumbling block before them in the way that they dress."

"I am 60 years old and even as a younger, unsaved man, it always seemed strange to see churchgoing women dressed in that manner (and I understand many felt they needed to do so to attract a man.) Now, in the more liberal churches and some so-called fundamental ones, the manner of dress seems to be according to one's own preference and not based on the Bible's teaching of decent dress. I'm also still amazed that some church-going men like their wives to dress in that way."

"I became a born again believer in Jesus Christ when I was 34. Our family left the Methodist church and switched to a large popular Southern Baptist church. We eventually left the Southern Baptist church and one of the biggest reasons is because the women dressed so immodestly. I felt I was in a lingerie show. I would have to walk the halls of the church with my head hung to avoid the display of flesh. We became quickly disappointed that the church undermined our own family's standards. Two years ago, our family finally switched to a fundamental independent Bible believing Baptist church and we really love serving the Lord and being with believers of like precious faith and with standards. I believe if godly women understood the effect they can have on a godly man they would dress differently. I have daughters and I constantly have to instruct them on what men think of immodestly dressed women and correct their dress."

"Thank you for addressing this serious problem. I agree that most Christian women do not seem to understand how that the way they dress affects men. Unfortunately, some do understand and they enjoy dressing in a way that attracts the attention of men. We are living in the last part of the last days. Demon influence and demon possession is rampant. Evil triumphs when the church does nothing. One sign of demon activity is nudity and lewd dress. Men respond by sight. Sight arouses their sexual drive. Anything that exposes, highlights, or outlines the torso and thigh is lustful dress. The Word of God is clear that a man who lusts after a woman is guilty of adultery along with her. I told my people last Sunday that if the woman dresses inappropriately and goes to town, causing men to look and lust, that they will be held accountable for participating in committing adultery."

As a man, a Christian and a pastor, I believe modesty is perhaps the most important issue in dress, whether among the church or otherwise. I'm telling you, MEN NOTICE, MEN LOOK AND MEN LUST, EVEN THE GOOD ONES. I know many women say, 'Well that's their problem, not mine!' but while we men will answer for our lust, the ladies will answer for doing something that causes another to fall into sin. Ladies, understand, your dress DOES affect us. And as such, you should carefully consider what you wear. Men are created in such a way as to be stimulated by sight – so when you see a lady, pretty, or sometimes not, we are stimulated by the sight of their flesh. It's just the way we are."

Ladies, please dress with modesty. Dress as you would if Jesus were sitting next to you. And He is, by the way, both because the Christian is indwelt by the Holy Spirit and because He has promised to be there when two or three are gathered together in His name. Jesus is sitting next to you!"

"I am a member of a fundamental church and am sad to say that many of these worldly ways are finding their way into our church. May God send His Holy Spirit to move in our midst so that a revival would break forth."

Lesson Fourteen Review

1) Write the memory portion for this week

_____
_____
_____

2) We have a _____ before God to never set a
_____ in the path of our brother in Christ. We have a
responsibility before God to _____

3) What is a "focal point"?

_____
_____

4) Designers focus on those areas of a woman's body that is the most
_____ to a man, because they know that is what sells.

5) God equates uncovering the leg and thigh with _____

6) Give the standard dictionary definition for the word 'leg.'

_____
_____
_____

7) Give the medical definition for the word 'leg.'

_____
_____
_____

8) List 5 things that are 'focal point' problems in the blouse or shirt:

_____
_____
_____
_____
_____

9) List 4 'focal point' problems with the skirt or dress:

_____

_____

_____

_____

10) There is something really wrong with the mentality of womankind who will wear clothing that screams, "look at me!" and

_____

_____

11) When you wear clothing that can be seen through, or that is so tight that every curve is clearly detailed you are _____ and not in _____ to _____.

12) The only woman the Bible mentions that wore makeup was

_____

13) The origin of makeup was the country of _____

14) _____ to your _____ should play a major role in your clothing choices.

15) Be prepared, to draw some _____ from _____ for dressing to please your husband and the Lord.

16) Who can force you into submission in the area of your clothing?

_____

A Woman Among all Those
Lessons in Christian Womanhood

Lesson 15

Her husband is known in the gates, when he sitteth among the elders of the land. Proverbs 31:23

I therefore, the prisoner of the Lord, beseech you that ye walk worthy of the vocation wherewith ye are called, Ephesians 4:1

At first glance, this verse seems odd, even out of place. Why, in the middle of all the attributes of the virtuous woman does it mention the prestige of her husband? For a man to be known in the gate, in Bible times, was a position of leadership in the community. The men who sat in the gate were the ones who gave their opinion in cases of judgment. They were county commissioners or governors if you will. We remember from our study of Ruth that when Boaz sought to purchase Elimilech's property and the gain of Ruth as his wife he went to the gate and called for the elders to witness the deal. Small matters of judgment and decision were given to the elders in the gate because only really large matters were worth the tedious journey to take them to the king or prophet. I mentioned in a previous lesson that the virtuous woman's husband was "known in the gate" on her merit, not on his own. The fact that he sat among the elders of the land showed that his family was in order and his wife was what she ought to be. Only those who had good moral character, proven honesty and solid families were allowed to be among the elders in the gate. A man with a shameful family life would not be considered for the position. Therefore the position of the Virtuous Woman's husband as one that sat in the gate is a direct reflection on her character, as well as his own.

A gracious woman retaineth honour: and strong men retain riches. Proverbs 11:16

The word gracious means: Favorable; kind; benevolent; merciful; disposed to forgive offenses and impart unmerited blessings.

What a mouthful!! So in order to retain honor a woman must have these attributes. She must be kind - benevolent - merciful - disposed to forgive offenses and impart unmerited blessings. (No wonder we don't fully realize the awesomeness of what we are saying when we say that God is gracious. We just touch the tip of the iceberg by saying it is "unmerited favor.") It is one thing to have a claim to being honorable – but to retain it is another thing entirely. A person may make a good first impression but reputation comes with time and proof. The virtuous woman obviously had proved herself as a gracious, honorable woman.

A virtuous woman is a crown to her husband: but she that maketh ashamed is as rotteness in his bones. Proverbs 12:4

Notice that it does not say in this verse that the crown involved belongs to the woman, but to her husband! Your virtue will be an ornament on the head of your husband. It will honor him.

The woman I have chosen for our example this week is Zipporah. In studying this I found something I consider unusual. Why was Miriam the leader of the women of the children of Israel? Why Moses' sister, and not his wife? There must have been a reason. Perhaps we can find that reason in Zipporah's character.

Exodus 2:21, 6:20, 24-26, 18:1-6.

When Moses reached the backside of the desert in Midian he found that the priest of Midian had 7 daughters. Zipporah was chosen as his bride. Everything went well until God called Moses to go back to Egypt. In the inn along the way we see that Zipporah saved Moses' life by circumcising her son with a sharp stone. Her reaction to the event showed that she vehemently objected to the procedure. Why should her son be made to suffer discomfort because of the commands of Moses' God that his people be peculiar? She couldn't turn her fury on God, so instead she turned it on Moses. "A bloody husband" doesn't sound like a term of endearment.

The next time she is mentioned is all the way out in the desert, just before Mt. Sinai, after the children of Israel are well on their way to the promised-land. The Bible says that he had "sent her back" to Midian. Why? Perhaps it was for her protection – but probably not. By this time

225

Moses had found that he could trust God. Perhaps he knew she could not handle the pressure. But whatever the reason - she was not there with her husband during the time in Egypt, yet we see that it was his original intent to take her.

After this time she is not mentioned again at all. It is mentioned in Numbers 12:1 that Moses had taken another wife. Again, why? Did she die? Or did he send her away again? Or was this woman taken as a second wife?

Could Zipporah have been considered as the leader of the women in the children of Israel instead of Miriam? I think she could have been. It could very well be that God removed her from the picture for the majority of Moses' life and ministry because He did not want her to be a hindrance to his plans for Moses' life. What did Zipporah do that made her a weight to her husband instead of a blessing? What kept her from being his crown?

First - She chose her child over her husband.

An awful mistake for any woman to make is to place her child above her husband in the home relationship. The responsibility for rearing, disciplining, feeding, clothing and educating your children can be overwhelming – taxing physically, taxing emotionally and if we are not very careful it can be taxing spiritually. It can also ruin a marriage. Am I saying that children are not good for a marriage? No! Children are one of the biggest blessings to a home. The Bible says they are God's reward. It says we are blessed to have a "quiver full of them." So what am I saying? Do not place your children before the Lord or before your husband in your affections. Your relationship with God is paramount and your husband is your priority. Make sure that you keep your relationship with your husband warm and loving, companionable and friendly. Treat him with respect and honor. Do not shove him aside, spending all of your devotion on your children. If your children's wants and needs come first while your husband's needs are neglected your home is not in the order that God planned for it to be. I know, personally, of a woman who threw herself, body and soul, into her children's lives at the expense of her marriage. Her husband was ignored and the children were everything. Then as happens to us all in course of time, her children grew up, found mates and careers and left home. Now she had neither husband nor children – for he couldn't take the neglect. She was at such a loss for what

226

to do with herself after they were gone that she had a complete mental breakdown. She had ruined her marriage and her mind. (Yes, she professed Christ. So very sad.)

Zipporah despised the command of God because her child was made uncomfortable by it. Many a woman has torn down the godly standards of a home because she did not want her children made uncomfortable by them. I have known of pastors and their wives who held to godly standards of dress and conduct until their own children became teenagers – then when the standards became a "personal pinch" they dropped those standards, not only in the home but in the church as well. This is hypocrisy. Many a missionary is not on the field serving God as He should because either he or his wife refused to "put their children through that hardship." An attitude like that raises the child to the position of an idol in your life. (Anything or any person that you place above God in your devotion is an idol.)

We can, with God's help, and we must if we are to be right with God, uphold the standards of Christianity in our home and teach our children that God's Word is supreme. We must teach that the husband is the head of the home and his word is the law to be followed, cheerfully and submissively, by every member of the family. It is not hard (nor is it wrong- indeed it is very right!) to teach a child that God has first place in our lives, that Daddy is Mommy's sweetheart and as such deserves as much love and devotion as can be lavished on him. In fact, they like the idea when they are very young and want to get in on the "welcome home wagon" for Daddy when he comes in. It gives a child a sense of security to know that their parents love each other and live for each other. When this is the established order of the home, the children expect for Daddy's needs and wants to be of utmost importance in the home. They expect for his rules to be followed and his wishes honored. When they are older it becomes a pattern for their own lives. They will develop more stable households themselves if they have seen a godly pattern in the lives of their parents.

And these words, which I command thee this day, shall be in thine heart: And thou shalt teach them diligently unto thy children, and shalt talk of them when thou sittest in thine house, and when thou walkest by the way, and when thou liest down, and when thou risest up and thou shalt bind them for a sign upon thine hand, and they shall be as frontlets between thine eyes. And thou shalt write them upon the posts of thy house, and on thy gates.   Deuteronomy 6:6-9

Secondly - she criticized him for the command of God. Moses was seeking to do right. Zipporah did not like what was shaking her world so she lashed out at Moses. In the process she made a difficult task even more unpleasant. This does not in any way resemble the help that a woman should be for her husband. The Bible warns us against being a nag, against being critical and contentious.

A foolish son is the calamity of his father: and the contentions of a wife are a continual dropping. Proverbs 19:13

A continual dropping in a very rainy day and a contentious woman are alike. Proverbs 27:15

Another woman in the Bible who was guilty of something similar was Michal. 1 Samuel 19:11-17; 2 Samuel 6:16. Michal was willing enough to save David's life when her father was seeking to destroy him. But when she was faced with her husband, in the prestigious position of being the recently crowned king of Israel, publicly abandoning himself to whole hearted worship of his God, her pride couldn't handle it. She was embarrassed by his lack of dignity and with haughty disdain she openly criticized him for it.

One of the worst mistakes a woman can make in her relationship with her husband (or a husband with his wife) is to publicly criticize him. This is damaging to the marriage relationship, it does not follow the command of God to wives to show reverence for their husband and it is not even common courtesy. If done in the presence of his friends and church family it will cause them to lose confidence in him and will cause them to lose confidence in her as well. If done in the presence of their children it will break down the entire family structure. If you have criticism for an action or attitude that your husband has displayed: first, take it to the Lord and make sure that the problem is not your own attitude. Secondly, if you must carry it further, take it to your husband in private. Do so in a spirit of meekness and reverence – not in brawling criticism.

Proverbs 21:9 and 25:24 both say the same thing: It is better to dwell in the corner of the housetop, than with a brawling woman and in a wide house. The next thing to do is to zip your lip. Criticizing your husband to others is a major error in your marriage. Yet, how many women have I heard who not only criticize their husband to others but openly belittle him and embarrass him in a crowd! Whether in seriousness or as a jest, this is wrong! wrong!! wrong!!! The Bible places the husband as the head of the home, the head of the woman and in the position of lord in the family. We are to reverence him.

I am not saying that you cannot be playful and tease. Let's not have a solemn, sober-sides, always serious, boring marriage. Yuk! But there is a distinct difference between playful banter and criticism; between playfulness and embarrassing someone to amuse yourself. Use the rule of thumb that has been used so many times to teach our children the difference between teasing and picking on another – It is only fun if BOTH people are enjoying it – otherwise you are being a bully. No, I'm not saying that you cannot be playful but I am saying that you should be extremely careful about what you say that smacks of criticism - especially if your husband is in the ministry. If you are a preacher's wife and you criticize your husband to members of your congregation or make him the object of crude jokes you will tear down his influence before the people he is serving.

Another reason to watch what we say when it resembles criticism, is that we are commanded in the Word of God to love our husbands as brethren.

Finally, be ye all of one mind, having compassion one of another, love as brethren, be pitiful, be courteous. 1 Peter 3:8

Notice that it says be courteous. The context of the chapter is the husband and wife relationship. Love as brethren. Sometimes we forget that our husbands are our brothers in Christ and that all of the Scriptures that relate to how we should treat our brothers in Christ also apply to our husband. We are also commanded to treat others as we would be treated ourselves.

And as ye would that men should do to you, do ye also to them likewise. Luke 6:31

We dislike to be criticized, to be the brunt of jokes or to have our personal matters spread around for public scrutiny. We need to treat our husbands with the same consideration for their feelings.

Years ago I found myself faced with a difficult situation. A lady in our church was continually complaining about her husband. He could do nothing right in her eyes and she vocalized it at every turn. She did not seem to really realize what she was doing, it had just become a habit. I prayed about the situation and the Lord gave me an answer. Every time she began to complain, I turned the subject by praising my husband for something. After a while she couldn't bear it and realized that she had some things she could praise her husband about too. Let's face it ladies – along with the obvious fact that it is damaging to your marriage and your husband's testimony to criticize him – no one really wants to hear it, either! It will give you a reputation that you do not want as well. The woman that I mentioned had ruined her own testimony among many people because she was always belittling her husband.

The third thing we see about Zipporah is that she was not there for his comfort during the time in Egypt.

How can you be a help, meet for the needs of your man, if you are not there when he needs you? A woman's first responsibility and priority should be to meet the needs of her husband. Yes, other things do press on your time and attention. A mature man will understand the demands on your attention, especially if you have small children at home. Sometimes the children's needs are more pressing and immediate – that does not mean they are more important. I would never suggest that you neglect the needs of your children in any way. A father who loves his children would not want you to, either. However, if your interests and activities are taking priority something is wrong. If everyone else's wants and needs come first and your husband gets the leftovers when you are too distracted or too tired to really care, then your priorities are out of line.

A godly woman will do her best to adjust her schedule so that her husband has her best. She will see that he has her undivided attention when he needs it. Save some time just for him. Listen to him. Be a companion. Be a friend. Be a comfort when he needs it. You're not interested in what he's interested in? Grow up and get involved in it anyway so that you are making yourself a companion to your husband. You really can do some things that you are not particularly interested in for the sake of friendship. And you can do it with a good attitude. Let's face it ladies – we do that with our lady friends. We do it for our children. We go places with them or involve ourselves in activities that are not our favorite things in order to be a companion. But when it comes to our husbands for some reason we feel that he should be governed by our likes and dislikes instead of the other way around.

I know of a lady whose husband is an avid hunter. She started hunting with her husband to keep him company – now she loves it as much as he does. I know of other wives whose husbands are sports fans. They will go to the games with them to be a companion. You don't have to fish – you can go and sit in the boat and enjoy the river's breeze with a book. Many a time I have carried two glasses of iced tea to the yard and sat down at the edge of the driveway and handed tools to my husband as he lay under the car. You don't always have to be doing what you like to do, you can share his interests just out of a desire to be a companion. If you do not become your husband's best friend, someone else will. And that someone else will claim a great portion of his time and attention that you could have. Don't neglect the opportunity to be his companion and then complain that he spends his time elsewhere.

Why are so many couples getting a divorce after 20+ years of marriage? They marry because of physical attraction or infatuation. As soon as they are married they have careers to pursue and then children to raise. After all the kids are gone and they retire, they sit back and take a good long look at this person they have lived with for many years but never really gotten to know. Then they suddenly realize, "You know what? I really don't like you!"

Next - Zipporah was not a leader of the women because she was simply not available for the job. Ladies, it is our responsibility to follow our husbands wherever and however the will of God leads him. It is our responsibility to see to it that we, ourselves, walk closely to the Lord so that we are a help and not a hindrance to his work. (Remember: Worthy of the vocation wherewith ye are called.) How many testimonies are there of women who have turned their backs on their husband as he announced a call to preach or a call to the mission field? I have heard more than one man sorrowfully say, "She left me because she wouldn't be married to a preacher." How could a woman who claims that she loves God and loves her husband make that husband choose between her and the will of God for his life? Selfishness!! Without a doubt, no question about it, when God calls your husband somewhere - your job is to follow. Not to question, not to barter and bargain, not to whine, complain and make it harder. Your job is to follow. Your job is to serve the Lord with all of your heart, soul and mind. In serving and caring for your husband's needs you are fulfilling your primary service to God. Serve Him in the church as well - as your husband permits and as the Lord directs. The problem with Zipporah is not that Moses was not willing to see her serve God wholeheartedly but, apparently, that she chose not to do so.

I have mentioned before that you should make your talents and skills available for the Lord's use. As a very young Christian the Lord placed in my heart a desire to sing His praise. I had been very much steeped in ungodly music before my salvation - it was my god. As the Lord made His miraculous change in my life I wanted to know more of the hymns and spiritual songs than I did of the ungodly ones and I wanted to sing for His glory. There was only one problem. I couldn't carry a tune in a bucket! Then a preacher preached about turning your talents over to the Lord for His use and he made a statement to the effect that if you did turn it over to God, the Lord would grow that talent to His design and desire and make of it what He wanted. At the altar that day I told the Lord that if he would give me a talent to sing, I would always use it for Him. I told him that if I began to use it for self or Satan, I desired that He would take it away. The Lord blessed that request. I have been able to use my voice for His glory. I am not an isolated case. Many a Christian has found that if they will commit themselves to Christ, He will take the little that they have and prosper it for His use. The problem is not that God is not able to use us – the problem is that we choose not to be used.

A preacher recently opened my eyes to something I had never noticed. When Moses was standing before the burning bush and God commissioned him to go to Egypt, he had the perfect opportunity to ask God to remove the speech impediment and make him more plainly understood. Instead, Moses chose to use the impediment as an excuse to try to get out of following the will of God. Do we ask God to make us more usable? To give us the skills we lack that we might be of more service to Him? Or do we instead whine, "I can't do that. Wish I could but I can't, so God will have to get someone else." Most of the great things that have been accomplished for the glory of God throughout history have been done by people who did not have the ability to do what they did. Moses did not have the ability to be a spokesman for God before Pharaoh. Peter and John were ignorant and unlearned. The Apostle Paul said that when he was weak then he was strong because he knew that the power in him was of God and not his own.

And he said unto me, My grace is sufficient for thee: for my strength is made perfect in weakness. Most gladly therefore will I rather glory in my infirmities, that the power of Christ may rest upon me. 2 Corinthians 12:9

Many a Christian, myself included, have been put in the position of teaching or leadership and the cry of their hearts have been "Lord, help me! I can't do this!" And His answer to a willing servant is:

I can do all things through Christ which strengtheneth me. Philippians 4:13.

For if there be first a willing mind, it is accepted according to that a man hath, and not according to that he hath not. 2 Corinthians 8:12

Unfortunately, a great deal of the time we are not used of God simply because we do not want to be used of Him. Our mind is set on self – not service.

Take a look at Miriam. What made her the choice as leader among the women of Israel?

Availability – She was simply there when she was needed and willing to do what needed to be done. It wasn't a matter of great ability, education, skill or wisdom. Remember that, before Moses showed up out of the desert, she was simply an Israelite slave, the daughter of an Israelite slave.

Love for the Lord – We see that she loved God in her willingness to wholeheartedly worship and we see that she knew the Word of the Lord, because she was called a prophetess.

And Miriam the prophetess, the sister of Aaron, took a timbrel in her hand; and all the women went out after her with timbrels and with dances. And Miriam answered them, Sing ye to the LORD, for he hath triumphed

233

gloriously; the horse and his rider hath he thrown into the sea. Exodus 15:20-21

You do not need special skills or talents. You do not need higher education and massive Bible knowledge. All you need is to love the Lord and to make yourself available to Him for His service. All you need is to keep your priorities straight and to support your husband in his service for the Lord. Our memory passage says that we should walk worthy of the vocation to which we are called. Our first vocation – our primary job, if you will – is to be an help (right there, available, for whatever the need may be) meet (suitable, right for, designed for) our husbands. We need to walk worthy of that vocation, remembering what it takes to retain honor: to be favorable, kind, benevolent, merciful, disposed to forgive offenses and impart unmerited blessings. Do we apply those good graces to our husbands? Or are these things special privileges only for those outside our families?

There are many examples we could use from the Word of God that illustrate the point that the virtuous woman's husband will be known in the gates on her merits……Eve: for what was Adam known? Bringing sin upon all mankind because of the influence of his wife. What was her downfall? She was deceived. She disobeyed the command of God. She listened to someone's "new idea" instead of believing what she had been taught from the Lord and the man who walked with the Lord in the garden each evening. Eve found a 'better idea' and talked her husband into it.

Pharaoh's daughter….Solomon's wife: for what was Solomon known in the gates? He was the wisest man who ever lived, yet was brought to the lowest point by his wife. She brought her idols into her marriage and ruined the wisest man on earth. She let Solomon "have his religion" but chose to cling to her old ways instead of embracing God. Little by little, she roped him into her idolatry and brought the whole nation into idolatry. (A classic example of what happens to those who are unequally yoked to unbelievers.)

Did not Solomon king of Israel sin by these things? yet among many nations was there no king like him, who was beloved of his God, and God made him king over all Israel: nevertheless even him did outlandish women cause to sin. Nehemiah 13:26

I see an example here of three reactions to God's command on a man's life....Zipporah and Michal criticized their husbands openly for God's call on their lives. Eve gave her husband the choice "God or me," and Pharaoh's daughter subverted her husband little by little by the idea of "You have your beliefs and I have mine." The result was different for each of the men because of the choice they made. Adam sinned and passed his sin to all mankind. Solomon sinned and the kingdom was divided. David put Michal away as his wife and served God anyway. Moses served God in spite of Zipporah and for many years of his life without her. But in each case he was known in the gates due to the actions of his wife.

If our husband was sitting in the gate – what would be the talk of the town?

Lesson Fifteen Review

1. Write the memory portion for this week.

_____
_____
_____

2. The virtuous woman's husband was "known in the gate" on _____ merit.

3. List 3 reasons why Zipporah was not a leader among the women of the children of Israel

_____
_____
_____

4. List 2 reasons why Miriam was chosen as the women's leader.

_____
_____

5. Was Miriam chosen because of her special talents, education or abilities? _____

6. Before Moses showed up Miriam was simply an

_____

7. Many women tear down the godly standards of a home and church because they do not want their children to be made _____ by them.

8. One of the worst mistakes a woman can make is to publicly _____ her husband.

9. A woman's first responsibility and priority is to _____

10. You should be a _____ to your husband, his best _____.

11. You should make your _____ and _____ available for the Lord's use.

11. You should make your _____ and _____ available for the Lord's use.

12. You do not need _____ and massive _____ to serve God. All you need is to _____ and to make yourself _____ to Him for His service. All you need is to keep your _____ straight and to _____ your _____ in his service for the Lord.

13. What does it take to retain honor? _____
_____
_____

14. We should apply these good graces to our _____ and not just to those _____ our homes.

15. Most of the great things that have been accomplished for God throughout history have been done by people who

_____.

16. What was Adam "known in the gate" for?

_____

What did Eve have to do with that?

_____

17. What was Solomon "known in the gate" for? _____

_____

_____

What did his wife have to do with that?

_____

18. What was the result of Zipporah's wrong response concerning the ministry God had given Moses?

_____

_____

19. What was the result of Michal's open criticism of her husband because of his love for and worship of God?

_____

_____

A Woman Among all Those
Lessons in Christian Womanhood

Lesson 16

Scripture Memory: She maketh fine linen and selleth it, and delivereth girdles unto the merchant. Proverbs 31:24

I will therefore that the younger women marry, bear children, guide the house, give none occasion to the adversary to speak reproachfully. 1 Timothy 5:14

Proverbs 31 says a lot about the labors of a virtuous woman. She is very obviously a hard working woman in every respect. Let's take a look at those labors in order as they appear in the passage.

Vs. 13 - She seeketh wool, and flax, and worketh willingly with her hands. We have learned from this that she is not lazy, she's a willing worker.

Vs. 14 - She is like the merchants' ships; she bringeth her food from afar. So her labor extends to feeding her family with the very best that she can provide them.

Vs. 15 - She riseth also while it is yet night, and giveth meat to her household, and a portion to her maidens. So we see that she will not lay in bed when there is work to be done and she does not leave her work for others to do.

Vs. 16 - She considereth a field, and buyeth it: with the fruit of her hands she planteth a vineyard. She uses her skill for the betterment of her family, not for selfish gain.

Vs. 18 - She perceiveth that her merchandise is good: her candle goeth not out by night. She's diligent and careful with her shopping and with all money matters.

Vs. 19 - She layeth her hands to the spindle, her hands hold the distaff. She uses her special skills for the Lord and her family.

Vs. 21 - She is not afraid of the snow for her household, for all her household are clothed with scarlet. She cares for her family's clothing, making sure that her children are provided for to the best of her ability.

Now we have this week's verse. She maketh fine linen and selleth it, and delivereth girdles unto the merchant. Notice that every one of her labors is not only **for** her home but also done **in** or **from** her home.

This is a touchy subject and a difficult one to approach in today's modern society. Today's lesson deals with women in the workforce. We have dealt with it a little in an earlier lesson. But as the Lord has brought it up again in this verse, He must want us to cover it more thoroughly. First of all - I want to stand on record, without apology, to say that I am against women working outside the home. I also want to say that I believe just as emphatically that she sometimes, in our society, has no choice. I believe with all of my heart that one of the great downfalls of our society is women in the workforce. It has contributed to the destruction of not only the family unit as God planned for it to be but our economy as well. If women were at home, caring for the home and instructing the children there would be enough jobs to go around for the men who needed them. Our cost of living would be lower, supply and demand would be more in order and the children would be raised with the ideals of their parents, not with the ideals of "society."

I am not an old woman, yet I remember as a child that it was not a normal thing for a mother to work outside the home. "Stay at home moms" were so much the norm when I was young that the term wasn't even the cliché that it is now. It was very rare for a child to be going home to an empty house or to a babysitter because Mom was at work. Now it is an almost unheard of thing for a family to have a "stay at home mom." She's the oddball, the exception to the rule and is often looked down on by society as a freak, a "brainwashed fundamentalist" or backward to normal society.

The economical demands that a woman being in the workforce places upon the family sometimes doesn't even repay the woman for working. It requires in many instances things that were never required before such as day care and babysitting fees, extensive wardrobes for work, a second car, etc. Not to mention that it is a universal, and Biblical, fact that we will extend our style of living to match our income.

Hell and destruction are never full; so the eyes of man are never satisfied. Proverbs 27:20

239

Therefore, when the income increases so do the desires of what to do with that income. Then, when those things are purchased, the inevitable result of covetousness comes in: in our mind they become necessities and we begin to be a slave to the things that we want. We feel that we cannot do without those things and so we **have** to work to maintain a certain standard of living. Covetousness is a grievous sin in the eyes of God. It is listed as the 10ᵗʰ commandment.

Thou shalt not covet thy neighbour's house, thou shalt not covet thy neighbour's wife, nor his manservant, nor his maidservant, nor his ox, nor his ass, nor any thing that is thy neighbour's.   Exodus 20:17

Covetousness is defined: A strong or inordinate desire of obtaining and possessing some supposed good; usually in a bad sense, and applied to an inordinate desire of wealth or avarice.

Inordinate means: Irregular; disorderly; excessive; immoderate; not limited to rules prescribed, or to usual bounds.

Avarice means: Greediness or insatiable desire of gain.

So covetousness is, in it's broad since, greatly desiring something. Most of the time that it is used in the Word of God it is used in a negative sense and then it means greediness or wanting something that we should not necessarily have. Many times it is a sin that we overlook or shrug off with an "everybody does it, so what's the big deal?" attitude. However, it is not a sin that God shrugs at and we need to attempt to learn the mind of God that we may please Him and not ourselves.

Mortify therefore your members which are upon the earth; fornication, uncleanness, inordinate affection, evil concupiscence, and covetousness, which is idolatry: Colossians 3:5

But fornication, and all uncleanness, or covetousness, let it not be once named among you, as becometh saints; Ephesians 5:3

Let your conversation be without covetousness; and be content with such things as ye have: for he hath said, I will never leave thee, nor forsake thee. Hebrews 13:5

So God is telling us that covetousness is something a Christian should mortify (kill) in their lives. He says it should not once be named among us – it's not becoming to a saint to be covetous. He says that our manner of life should be without covetousness, and we should be content with what we have.

But godliness with contentment is great gain. 1Timothy 6:6

Consider this as well: covetousness is one of the things that disqualifies a man to pastor a church.

A bishop then must be blameless, the husband of one wife, vigilant, sober, of good behaviour, given to hospitality, apt to teach; Not given to wine, no striker, not greedy of filthy lucre; but patient, not a brawler, not covetous: 1 Timothy 3:2-3

We are told to avoid the company of a brother in Christ who is covetous.

But now I have written unto you not to keep company, if any man that is called a brother be a fornicator, or covetous, or an idolater, or a railer, or a drunkard, or an extortioner; with such an one no not to eat. 1Corinthians 5:11

So it is clear that God considers covetousness as being quite a bit more serious than we do. Look at the category that He places it in; right alongside fornicators and idolaters! Why don't we consider it in the same mindset that God does? It is listed as one of the sins of the last days.

This know also, that in the last days perilous times shall come. For men shall be lovers of their own selves, covetous, boasters, proud, blasphemers, disobedient to parents, unthankful, unholy,   2 Timothy 3:1-2

It is natural for those who love their own selves to be covetous and to be all the rest of the things listed in that verse. It is natural for them to think that it is normal behavior – no big thing. It's a big thing to God. Why such a big thing? Let's take another look at this passage:

Mortify therefore your members which are upon the earth; fornication, uncleanness, inordinate affection, evil concupiscence, and covetousness, which is idolatry: Colossians 3:5

The Word of God says that covetousness is idolatry. How so? We desire the things we are coveting so much that we set the commandments of God aside. The will of God takes a back burner and the things that we are after are of such primary concern that God's commands are overlooked in order to gain them. Therefore those things become idols in our lives.

I'm not by any means saying that every woman who works does so because of covetousness. I am saying that many times when women choose to work, covetousness is the reason. And I am saying that a lot of times we don't need a lot of the things that we think we need. If our priorities were as God would have them to be, we could really do without a lot of the things that we think are so important in order to be right with God.

Another thing that sometimes drives a woman into the workforce, when she does not have to be there, is a sense that being a housewife is second rate. The woman feels that the man has the better life because he's not "stuck at home." This is another area where godliness with contentment should reign. We **can** be happy in the sphere that God has planned for us if we will realize that the will of God is always best for our lives. The unisex movement is wicked and destructive to the basics of Christianity and the home. And like it or not, women in the secular workforce is a foundation stone of the unisex movement.

The demands that women in the workforce places upon the emotions of the women themselves, in a lot of instances, is contrary to what God had designed for them. She becomes torn between her loyalty to her husband, home and children and her loyalty to her job. Many times she is frustrated and feels a failure because she feels that she cannot do everything that is required of her.

The sacrifice of the children in the home on the altar of women working is an even greater evil. Children are left alone or with a babysitter or day care. Then they, almost always, begin to develop attitudes and actions that are contrary to the way that the parents would have them behave. A lot of children are in public school, placed there for the convenience of a working mom, when the mother could home school or when they could be placed in a Christian school. Some preachers have likened this to offering them as a sacrifice to Moloch. It is a pretty accurate comparison. They are taught in public school to ridicule and scorn Christianity. They are taught to embrace New Age philosophy. They are taught that homosexuality is an acceptable alternate life-style. They are taught that Godly morals and purity are obsolete and unnecessary. They are taught a slanted version of history and science that omits Biblical accuracy. They are taught to scorn basic skills of mathematics, spelling and vocabulary, in preference to "social skills." I cannot understand the mindset of American Christians, who truly love their children and love the Lord yet place those children in public school. There is really no excuse today for a person to be ignorant of what the public education system is doing to our children. But a lot of folks seem to have their heads in the sand and simply don't want to know. Probably because sending them to public school is more convenient.

When a woman works, the husband also suffers from the wife's lack of attention. His needs are neglected. Many times the wife becomes resentful of the double duty of job and household chores and feels that her husband should take up the slack. A lot of times there will be jealousy involved, if the wife works with men. Or sometimes just jealousy of her time that should belong to him. Many a marriage has broken up because of a woman's job.

Another difficulty that a woman faces, who must work outside the home, is that it has a tendency, in some, to make submission to the husband/head of the home that much harder. A woman who works outside the home can develop a certain sense of independence that is not in keeping with God's design for her. So here she is faced with another battle with her attitude! The devil will be sure to stir up trouble (he loves to wreck Christian homes.) When he does, it will be so easy to flare up with the attitude, "I am my own independent person, I earn my own living, you could not make it without my income," etc. We have covered thoroughly that a woman is to be in subjection to and to reverence her husband. So we know that when independence causes an un-submissive attitude we are in the wrong. Still another problem that faces women in the workforce is that they sometimes find themselves having to be submissive to another man other than their husbands.

Wives, submit yourselves unto your **own husbands,** as unto the Lord. Ephesians 5:22

When the boss crosses the authority of the home, it will create an uncomfortable choice in the minds of a woman. Do I follow God's order in my home? Or do I jeopardize my job? Not only is the outside job damaging to the home structure, it is clear in Scripture what God sees as a woman's responsibility.

I will therefore that the younger women marry, bear children, guide the house, give none occasion to the adversary to speak reproachfully. 1 Timothy 5:14

Remember – we are learning in this course God's ideal for women and seeking to be in submission to His will for us as virtuous women. If God said that our ideal was to marry, bear children and guide the house, what right do we have to pick up the world's philosophy that it is demeaning to be a housewife?

In a perfect society the ideal would be for no woman to work outside her home. The plan of God, plainly outlined in Scripture, is for the husband to be the authority and the provider for the home. It is for the woman to be in submission to her husband and enforce his authority with her children as she guides and teaches them. It is for her to give her labor to her husband, children and home. The children are to be in obedience to parents, to reverence and respect them all of their lives and to care for them, if needed, in their old age.

That said and covered, let me now say this: I am fully aware that we do not live in a perfect society. There are a lot of things that drive a woman into the workforce today. I know that a lot of our fundamental preachers will say that under no circumstances should a woman work, that a man who does not completely support his family and have his wife at home does not properly have his house in order, etc. etc. blah, blah. However, I'm trying to deal with real life in these lessons, not with "ideals." Yes! Given what **should** be – a woman should be home. However, I cannot be so impractical as to criticize a woman for working. There really are things in today's society that come up that require a woman to work – just as there were instances in the Bible of women who worked.

Whether or not you work is going to be a matter between you and your husband and the Lord. The Word of God says that you are to be a help (a support person, a completer, a mate) meet (right for, suitable for, designed for) **your** husband. It says that you are to be in submission to your own husband. If your husband desires for you to work – no one has a right to say otherwise to you. I will say this - if you don't have to work outside your home - don't. Even if you don't have children at home you will have trouble in many ways if you work outside your home.

I will also say that if you have small children (preschool age) unless you have absolutely no choice (such as being a single mom) please! please!! please!!! don't work! Try to do things in the home to boost your income if you can but don't leave your children for someone else to raise. (That includes grandparents!) If there is any way at all that you can cut corners and do without whatever you don't absolutely need, in order to stay home, you will never regret the sacrifice you may make in order to be a real mother to your children. If you have school age children and you **must** work, seek to do things **in** the home or **from** the home that will bring in income, or at the very least strive for a job that will have you working during their school hours and home when they are home.

I look back at my life as a young girl and realize now that the sin that I got into dated from the time as a teenager when my mother got a job and I was left on my own for many hours at a time. If you leave your children alone, you are leaving them for the devil to attack.

The rod and reproof give wisdom: but a child left to himself bringeth his mother to shame. Proverbs 29:15

If you leave them with a babysitter or day care, you are giving them to someone else to raise. Touch base with reality and realize that someone else will raise them with their own methods and beliefs - not yours. Are there examples in the Word of women who worked? Yes, but very, very few. Most women who are mentioned in the Bible are "keepers at home." It mentions that Priscilla worked with her husband in a business from their homes as tent makers.

And found a certain Jew named Aquila, born in Pontus, lately come from Italy, with his wife Priscilla; (because that Claudius had commanded all Jews to depart from Rome:) and came unto them. And because he was of the same craft, he abode with them, and wrought: for by their occupation they were tent makers. Acts 18:2-3

It mentions Lydia as a seller of purple.

And a certain woman named Lydia, a seller of purple, of the city of Thyatira, which worshipped God, heard us: whose heart the Lord opened, that she attended unto the things which were spoken of Paul. Acts 16:14

It mentions that the daughters of the priest of Midian were the ones who kept the sheep.

Now the priest of Midian had seven daughters: and they came and drew water, and filled the troughs to water their father's flock.
Exodus 2:16

It also says that Rachel kept the sheep as well.

And he said unto them, Is he well? And they said, He is well: and, behold, Rachel his daughter cometh with the sheep. Genesis 29:6

(By the way, when Moses showed up and when Jacob showed up, they took over keeping those sheep!)

Ruth had the necessity of gathering food to maintain herself and Naomi.

And Ruth the Moabitess said unto Naomi, Let me now go to the field, and glean ears of corn after him in whose sight I shall find grace. And she said unto her, Go, my daughter. Ruth 2:2

Notice, however, each of these ladies are earning an income either **in** their homes or **from** their homes. Part of the reason for this is that they had a very different type of society in Bible days than we do now. Even the men labored mostly from their homes. Farming, ranching, or home-based business was the almost exclusive way of earning income. It is not surprising that the women and even the children were totally involved in the process. Anyone who knows what it is to farm knows that it is the entire family that works the farm! We know that women carried goods to market, they worked in the fields with the sheep and goats, spun, weaved, sewed, etc. So they were to some extent involved in the income of their families – but we also see plainly from Scripture that her home is her primary responsibility.

That they may teach the young women to be sober, to love their husbands, to love their children, To be discreet, chaste, keepers at home, good, obedient to their own husbands, that the word of God be not blasphemed. Titus 2:4-5

The Virtuous Woman was earning money - not as her own "independent" income - but as supplementary income for the benefit of her family. She was doing it in such a way that she did not lose her womanhood or challenge her husband as the head of the home and earner of the bread for the family.

Don't step out of your sphere as a woman in order to add income to your family. Some women feel that they have to prove that they are as capable as a man to handle a job in a "man's world." That philosophy is worldly and part of the feminist movement, which has no place in the attitude of a virtuous woman. Be a lady. Don't be afraid to be a lady. There are very few ladies left in our society. I was so saddened by the comment of one of my students in recent years. She was a beautiful young girl and when addressed by the term "young lady" snapped her head around and said with scorn, "I'm not a lady, I don't want to be a **lady!"** What has happened to our society when young girls think it is an insult to be called a lady??

My dad once took a flight from Florida to Kansas. He was severely handicapped and needed help aboard the plane. The woman sitting in the seat next to him was very helpful. She literally picked my dad up and moved him! Her comment was, "I'm very strong. I pull concrete for a living." Although thankful for her help – such things certainly do not leave a womanly impression! My dad was laughing and shaking his head and holding out his arms to give the impression of the muscle bound woman who could pick up a man and move him around.

The unisex movement has stolen something very precious from womankind. They have hyped up the emotions of women by making them feel that they are inferior to men if they did not try to hold down a man's job and dress like, talk like, and act like men. It does not challenge a woman's intelligence, nor her abilities, to retain her femininity. I have the joy and privilege of being the "queen" of my home. My husband and sons treat me with the utmost care and consideration - and I like it that way! I would not trade my favored position with any one of the "career women" who are out to prove that they can "hold their own in a man's world." (My husband can hold it for me - that's okay by me!) I have not lost my identity - they have. I know exactly who I am and I don't have to fight with anyone to prove it. Those who must work from the home should seek in every respect to continue to be a lady.

Now let's deal with some practicalities: There are a lot of ways in which a woman can add income to her home without losing her womanhood. First of all, we see clearly from our Proverbs 31 passage that the ideal is that she work **in** the home. Remember that Priscilla (Acts 18:3) worked with her husband as a team in their tent making business. Our Virtuous Woman did spinning, weaving, and garment making as well as using the produce of her vineyard.

Some ideas for what you can do in your home to make extra money are: babysitting, sewing, crafts, cooking (watch the laws - sometimes the health department will not allow someone to sell home cooked items and sometimes the law will not allow you to babysit more than a certain number of children in your home,) typing or computer work, tutoring, raising garden produce to sell.

For many years my mother sewed dolls and made crocheted crafts all winter and in the spring and summer took them to craft shows and set up a booth to sell them. She would save the money from her craft sales until the end of the season and then use it to purchase the materials for the next winter's sewing. Then she used her profit for her desired project. One year it paid for a vacation for the family. One year it refurnished her living room.

One dear Christian lady that I know home schools her children and takes children into her home to babysit to earn some extra for the household. Another had sewing skills and took out an ad in the local shopper paper to advertise that she would do simple alterations. She was soon so busy that she had to have help to do it all, so she had a widow lady in the church take some of her excess work. I remember an elderly widow during my childhood who took in ironing to boost her income. Another pastor's wife does computer work and typing. If you play an instrument or sew well you can give lessons in your home. Where there is a will, there is a way.

The next favored choice would to be to work from the home. This is where you are still primarily at home but you work away from home for some hours of the day, usually for yourself, not an employer. Lydia worked from her home as a seller of purple. Acts 16:14. Purple in the Bible is not a color but a type of cloth of high quality. We do not know if Lydia made the purple herself. She may have been collecting it from other ladies who made it and taking it to market as an agent for them. Some ideas for what you can do from your home to make extra money are: cleaning, yard work, babysitting, sitting for or running errands for the elderly or handicapped, There are other things you can do, both in and from the home, if you are determined that God would have you stay there. If you pray and seek His face, He will provide the means and the opportunity to do His will.

Now that I have told you the ideal, we will deal with those who work outside the home as part of the secular work force. As I said, we do not live in a perfect society. If our society were what it ought to be; income would be from primarily agricultural sources, families would stay intact, people would be true to God, country and family values. Fathers would work and support their families, mothers would stay at home and teach and train their children, and children would be obedient and respectful.

However - that's not the way things are. People are sinners and sin has taken its toll on our society. So what do you tell a single mother with small children? She has to work – she has no choice. What do you tell a widow who has no family that will care for her needs? She has to work, too. What do you tell a woman whose husband cannot work for health reasons (or who will not work because he's not what he should be?) And what do you tell a struggling family in the economy of our time (which is getting worse by the day) who cannot meet the basic needs of rent, food and utilities on one income or who have been used to an income, and have bills requiring an income, that they no longer have due to job loss, layoffs or inflation? Sometimes the mother has to work in that situation as well. NOT, however, as often as they CHOOSE to work in order to have nicer things, independence and freedom from the home scene. It should be a last resort - only on her husband's request and/or approval, never at the expense of the welfare of her children. If you are working in order to afford some of the "finer" things of life, then you are choosing covetousness over the will of God.

If you HAVE to work outside the home, it would be preferable to choose a ministering type of work - working with children, teaching, nursing home, etc. Other than that, choose a job that preserves your femininity. Go ahead! Be a stereotype! Get a job as a secretary, a bank teller, a receptionist. Avoid anything that steals your identity as a woman; such as driving a dump truck, standing on the side of the road holding a sign for a construction crew, doing concrete or drywall work, etc. (I know of women who do all of those things and more!) Ladies, doing work like that not only falls short of the goal of making you "equal with a man," it also subjects you to their ridicule behind your back. A man has no respect for, jeers at and sometimes has an almost stand-offish fear of a woman who flexes her muscle and elbows her way into a stereotypical man's job. Be a woman. Be a lady.

I would also recommend that you avoid working a job, if at all possible, where you are primarily working around men. (Many times a woman working in a factory finds this as a problem.) This is for several reasons. You cannot work around lost men without hearing a great deal of crude jokes, profanity, and such like. Lost men also have no sense of propriety about who they flirt with and very seldom care if you are married or not. If you are the only, or one of few, women working where there are a lot of men you will become a target. At best you will hear a lot of junk you would rather not hear. At worst you will be subjected to suggestive comments and propositions. This is in spite of the sexual harassment laws. If you maintain your Christian standards and openly disapprove of such behavior, you will possibly be ridiculed and perhaps even persecuted on the job because of it. Christian men are targeted on the job because of their standards – and a woman in such an environment is an invitation to trouble.

If you must work in the secular work force, be careful. Choose your job with Christ and your testimony in mind. Make sure that your husband approves of not only you working, but the job environment that you choose. Consider the requirements of the job. Will you still be able to be faithful to church? Will you be able to maintain godly standards of dress and action? Too many women take a job where they are required to sell alcohol, tobacco products, lottery tickets, etc. The Bible specifically prohibits us from being involved in the distribution of liquor.

Woe unto him that giveth his neighbor drink, that puttest thy bottle to him and makest him drunken also, that thou mayest look on their nakedness! Habakkuk 2:15

Lay hands suddenly on no man, neither be partaker of other men's sins: keep thyself pure. 1 Timothy 5:22

Most of the time if you take a job where you are required to sell the items mentioned above you will also be in violation of your church covenant.

Above all else, pray. Ask the Lord to make your job an outlet for witnessing and a testimony of His grace in your life. Ask him for strength for the double duty that will fall on your shoulders. Ask Him for a sweetness of temper when you return home tired and your time is still in demand. Ask Him to help you not to shirk your first responsibility to your husband and children. And if your heart is in the right place....ask Him to work a miracle in your finances so that you will not always have to work.

Our Virtuous woman was not afraid to dirty her hands. She was a keeper at home, an help meet for her husband, a mother to her children and still managed to add income to her household. And she did it all while maintaining her femininity. She was a lady – a gracious woman in every sense of the word. And the Bible promises that a gracious woman will be honored.

A gracious woman retaineth honour: and strong men retain riches. Proverbs 11:16

251

Lesson Sixteen Review

1. Write the memory portion for this week.

_____

_____

_____

2. List the 8 things we have learned about the virtuous woman's labor.

_____

_____

_____

_____

_____

_____

_____

_____

3. Every one of the virtuous woman's labors is not only _____ her home but also done_____ her home.

4. The 10th commandment is:

_____

_____

5. Define Covetousness

_____

_____

_____

6. Define Inordinate

_____

_____

_____

7. Define Avarice

_____

_____

_____

8. Covetousness is the same in God's sight as _____.

9. The Bible tells us to _____ ourselves from a covetous brother in Christ and tells us that it _____ a man to pastor a church. Covetousness is one of the sins of the _____ days.

10. List 3 reasons why it is an undesirable thing for a woman to work outside the home.

_____

_____

_____

11. List 3 things that a woman can do **in** her home to earn money for her family. _____

_____

_____

12. List 3 things that a woman can do **from** her home to earn money for her family.

_____

_____

_____

13. Those who work outside the home should make every effort to continue to be a _____

14. If you are working in order to afford some of the _____ of life, then you are choosing _____ over the _____.

15. Working outside the home should be a _____ only on her husband's _____ and never at the expense of her _____.

16. List 4 jobs that would be best chosen for those who must work outside the home.

_____

_____

_____

_____

17. Choosing to hold down a job that is considered a "man's job" will open a woman to several undesirable things. List them:

_____

_____

18. If you must work in the secular work force choose your job with _____ and your _____ in mind.

19. List 5 things that you should ask God for if you have to work:

_____

_____

_____

_____

_____

20. The Bible promises that a _____ woman will retain _____.

A Woman Among all Those
Lessons in Christian Womanhood

Lesson 17

Scripture Memory for the lesson: Strength and honour are her clothing; and she shall rejoice in time to come. Proverbs 31:25

Only let your conversation be as it becometh the gospel of Christ: that whether I come and see you, or else be absent, I may hear of your affairs, that ye stand fast in one spirit, with one mind striving together for the faith of the gospel; Philippians 1:27

Why does it say that her clothing is strength and honour? It's something she is putting on purposely. Something she has sought out and chosen. Something she has labored for. Your clothing is what people see. It's how you present yourself. It says a lot about your personality, your self-respect, your beliefs and your attitudes. Here's how the virtuous woman presents herself to others. This lesson has to do with our testimony before the world and our fellow believers.

First, she is clothed with strength. This is not referring to outward strength, but inward. It is a quiet sense of confidence. Not brassy or showy - just strength. No one has to guess that the virtuous woman is strong. It's her clothing, it's easy to see. She does not have to tell someone she's strong, it shows as plainly as the clothing she wears. She has confidence that she's saved, confidence that she's in the will of God, confidence in her role as a woman. She has the ability to help others because she has experienced the help that God can give.

Many times a person will get the impression that a Christian woman is an underdog. Because she is in submission to her husband and she is not in the forefront of everything, vying for attention, they feel she is insecure, ignorant, and unable to hold her head up in society. Unfortunately, that sort of underdog type behavior is sometimes purposely portrayed by women in an effort to seek godliness and is mistaken for meekness in women. We have mentioned before that God tells her to be strong and that meekness in the Word of God is not synonymous with weakness. Nothing

255

could be further from the truth. That is not Christian womanhood. There is no shame in taking the place and fulfilling the role that God has planned for you. In fact it is a high, not easily attained, goal. (Who can find?) There is a balance to everything in the Word of God. I am not by any means telling you to jump up and assert your rights. (We've already covered that.) But God does not intend for you to walk around hanging your head down in insecurity. However, many a woman seeking godliness finds herself battling insecurity. They feel that they don't measure up. Why? We reach for a goal much beyond ourselves.

The problem comes in when we begin to think that we can reach that goal by our own power. When we fail to attain that goal, or we fall in the attempt to reach it, we feel like a failure. How can a woman have confidence that way? The first step toward confidence is to realize that you do not have to climb this ladder yourself and you do not have to pull yourself up by your own bootstraps. The Lord desires to make you into a virtuous woman and if you submit yourself to Him, He will guide you every step of the way as you reach for the goal.

Being confident of this very thing, that he which hath begun a good work in you will perform it until the day of Jesus Christ: Philippians 1:6

For it is God which worketh in you both to will and to do of his good pleasure. Philippians 2:13

The next step toward confidence is to realize that this is a never ending process. Many people become frustrated because they are not reaching maturity fast enough to suit them. Completed Christian growth is not something that we will ever reach, this side of Heaven. You will always have some more to learn, another step to take toward maturity. You will always have to go back and learn the same lessons again that you thought you already knew. And you will from time to time fall short of the goal. Am I telling you not to strive? To give up because the goal is unattainable? No, in no way!!! Every victory that we win, every step toward the mind of Christ in our lives is a jewel of pleasure in the eyes of our Lord.

So where does that strength, that confidence, come from that the virtuous woman is supposed to attain? We get it from God, of course. The Bible says that the **Lord** is clothed with strength - Psalm 93:1. We understand that our righteousness is a robe that God gives to us that we cannot get any other way. This strength is also a gift from God that we will only get from Him. What a burden it lifts to realize that we do not have to struggle and claw our way to the top of the ladder! **God** is ready and willing to do the work in us if we will just submit to the hand of the potter.

The LORD God is my strength, and he will make my feet like hinds' feet, and he will make me to walk upon mine high places. To the chief singer on my stringed instruments. Habakukk 3:1

He giveth power to the faint; and to them that have no might he increaseth strength. Isaiah 40:29

Trust ye in the LORD forever: for in the LORD JEHOVAH is everlasting strength. Isaiah 26:4

God is my strength and power: and he maketh my way perfect. 2 Samuel 22:33

The way of the Lord is strength to the upright: but destruction shall be to the workers of iniquity Proverbs 10:29

First: Confidence in your salvation will provide a measure of strength. There is no weaker Christian than one who doubts their salvation. That's why the devil loves to try to make us doubt. If the devil cannot keep a person from getting saved, he will spend the rest of their lives trying to defeat them as a Christian. The best tool he has is to make them doubt their salvation. If he can keep your mind in turmoil, wondering if you are saved, then he has you right where he wants you. You will be ineffective for Christ because you won't feel that you can minister to anyone else when your own spirit is insecure.

Part of the armor of God in Ephesians 6 is the Helmet of Salvation. Why a helmet? Because assurance of your salvation keeps your mind. It is defense against the devil's attacks. Draw close to God, spend time in prayer, cling to the church, love the Word of God. The easiest Christian for the devil to attack with doubts is the one who is not reading their Bible nor spending time alone with God as they should, or the one who is slipping away from church. The Word refers to us as a body, fitly joined together, where the weak parts are supported in strength by the stronger ones. You will be a much more confident, secure Christian as you draw closer and closer to God and His church. If you battle doubts, ask God to help you. Be open and honest with Him in prayer and ask Him to show you your salvation and give you something from the Word of God that you can refer back to when the devil comes at you. You must be secure in your salvation in order to take the next step toward clothing yourself with strength.

Secondly: Recognize that the power for your Christian walk rests in Him and not yourself.

It is God that girdeth me with strength, and maketh my way perfect. Psalm 18:32

My flesh and my heart faileth: but God is the strength of my heart, and my portion forever. Psalm 73: 26

We cannot walk this pathway on our own. We do not have the ability to be Christians. To live a Christ-like life and battle the devil, the world and our own flesh takes power far beyond what we will ever have. But the joy of it all is that we don't have to. The only job we have is to submit ourselves to Christ and trust Him to handle it. In ourselves we are nothing. In Christ we can do anything.

Thirdly: We will get it with experience. Walking with God day by day, through the good and the bad, will prove to you that God is faithful and can see you through each situation. As you experience the grace of God in your life you will gain a confidence in His love and care. No one likes to go through hard times. No one likes tribulation. But the fact of the matter is that you cannot mature as a Christian without it. Have you ever purchased "hot house" flowers and tried to plant them in your garden? What happens to them? As soon as the sun or wind get a little rough with them, or they experience a good, heavy rainfall, they die. Why? Because they have never been exposed to adverse conditions. God could raise us as "hothouse" Christians - never allowing us to experience any hardship - but we would be weaklings, unable to stand up to anything. Hardships strengthen the faith - if we will acknowledge that God is in control and plans for our best in every situation. Tribulation and trouble are the necessary sandpaper that smooths the rough edges and forms us into a masterpiece of beauty for our Savior.

That the trial of your faith, being much more precious than of gold that perisheth, though it be tried with fire, might be found unto praise and honour and glory at the appearing of Jesus Christ: 1 Peter 1:7

Blessed be God, even the Father of our Lord Jesus Christ, the Father of mercies, and the God of all comfort; Who comforteth us in all our tribulation, that we may be able to comfort them which are in any trouble, by the comfort wherewith we ourselves are comforted of God. 2 Corinthians 1:3-5

Here again is a wonderful joy. We do not have to 'go it alone' through our trials and temptations. Christ has promised never to leave us nor forsake us. People have said to me, as they have looked at some of the things that God has brought us through, "I don't know how you held up, how you kept going." I always tell them that there is a place in the lowest of valleys where the hand of God is more real and the touch of God is more sweet than in any other place. But there is a price for that sweet touch - you must travel the valley to get there. Don't be afraid of what God may put you through as a Christian. He is completely trustworthy and He will see you through, every step of the way, to the end of the journey and into glory.

So what steps do we take toward strength? Remember that the fear of the Lord is the beginning of wisdom and the Bible says there is strength in wisdom.

Counsel is mine and sound wisdom: I am understanding; I have strength Proverbs 8:14 (In the context of the chapter this is wisdom talking.)

1) Wisdom will cause you to increase strength.

A wise man is strong; yea a man of knowledge increaseth strength. Proverbs 24:5

So in order to gain strength we must seek after wisdom. This comes from studying the word of God, listening to the preaching of the Word of God and then applying it to our lives. A foolish Christian is one who listens to the Word preached, sees that it is right according to the Word of God and then will not apply it to their lives.

But be ye doers of the word, and not hearers only, decieving your own selves. James 1:22

A Christian who will not allow God to change and mold his life to the pattern of the Word will stagnate, begin to find fault with the church, the preacher and every Christian around him who is trying to live right. This person will eventually either cause problems in the church or get out of church completely - or both. They will not ever attain the strength we are talking about. You must not just read and hear the Word. You must live it.

2) It also tells us to ask Him for it.

In the day when I cried thou answeredst me, and strengthenedst me with strength in my soul. Psalm 138:3

That's pretty simple. But the Bible says that we have not because we ask not. We are to wait upon God if we would have strength.

But they that wait upon the LORD shall renew their strength; they shall mount up with wings as eagles; they shall run and not be weary; and they shall walk and not faint. Isaiah 40:31.

You don't become a mature Christian in a day - or even a year. God grows you step by step and He provides you with the teaching you can handle. The Lord likens Christian growth to a child's development. At first they can only tolerate milk and then you introduce foods a little at a time as their system can handle it. Eventually they are feeding themselves. But you do not give a newborn baby a steak to suck on. Wait for the Lord to give the growth you need. I've seen so many young Christians experience what I call "growing pains." They want to grow up in the Lord faster than they can handle it and wonder why they do not have the instant maturity of a Christian who has been saved 30 years. Wait on God. Learn and grow eagerly, but don't chafe if some things only come with time.

3) He tells us to have quietness and confidence in the Lord

For thus saith the Lord GOD, the Holy One of Israel; In returning and rest shall ye be saved, in quietness and in confidence shall be your strength: and ye would not. Isaiah 30:15

We need to spend time alone with God. To develop our relationship with Him. We cannot gain the strength that we need as a Christian if the only time that we give Him is our time at church. It is important to gather together, to feed on the Word and to fellowship with one another. We cannot thrive without it. But just as important is our private time with God.

The woman I have chosen for our example for this lesson is Mary, the sister of Martha and Lazarus. Luke 10:38-42, John 11:1-3, 19-32, John 12:1-8 Mary's testimony of strength was firmly established - but where did she get it? She spent every moment that she could at the feet of Jesus. She did not push herself to the forefront, but she was obviously confident of her relationship with the Savior. When we see her mentioned for the first time she is at the feet of Jesus. She was so intent upon soaking in every word that He said, she was neglectful of her sister and her guests. (Jesus refused to rebuke her for it.) Next we see her falling at His feet in agony for His comfort at the death of her brother. Then lastly we see her at His feet again in adoration as she anoints His feet with a precious, costly ointment and wipes His feet with her hair. Notice the progression. She learns of Him, believes in Him, then finds He can be trusted even when things don't look right and her whole world is in chaos. Then she turns her confidence in Him to service and adoration. That is the Christian walk in a nutshell. She clung to Him and we should also. We are told to seek His face continually.

Seek the LORD and His strength, seek his face continually.
1 Chronicles 16:11.

4) We are told to rejoice in the presence of God.

Glory and honour are in his presence; strength and gladness are in his place. Give unto the LORD, ye kindreds of the people, give unto the LORD glory and strength. 1 Chronicles 16:27-28

All of these things are steps of faith - steps of growth. Little by little as we seek wisdom, pray for strength, wait upon God, spend time alone with Him, learn from Him and seek His face, we will grow in Him. With that growth the confidence will come. Truly we will have the strength that

God wants us to have when we realize that our sufficiency is in Christ alone and not in ourselves.

Not that we are sufficient of ourselves to think any thing as of ourselves; but our sufficiency is of God; 2 Corinthians 3:5

Once we have attained a measure of strength as a Christian what should we do with the strength we receive? How should it be used? Certainly not for self! Give it back to the Lord. In way too many people that measure of confidence that the Lord gives is snatched up for selfish use and then it becomes abominable pride. God cannot and will not bless a life filled with pride!

Christians are dropping out like flies all around us in this Laodicean church age. Part of the reason is that they attain a certain level of confidence as a Christian, then forget that their strength and sufficiency is not in themselves but in the Lord. They lift their heads in pride and the Lord has to knock them down to size to keep them from stealing His glory. Through His power, experience and the Scriptures, God gives you the confidence to walk with Him in a measure of maturity. Be careful to use the knowledge He has given you, the wisdom you have attained and the strength that you have for His honor and glory. Realize that you are nothing on your own, nothing without His power, nothing that **any** other Christian could be and will be by the same God given method. Notice that Psalm 96:7 repeats what we learned in 1 Chronicles 16:28.

Give unto the LORD, O ye kindreds of the people, give unto the LORD glory and strength. Psalm 96:7

So give it back to God from your heart, in full acknowledgement of where you got it.

5) Next you must love God with it.

And thou shalt love the Lord thy God with all thy heart, and with all thy soul, and with all thy mind, and with all thy strength: this is the first commandment. Mark 12:30,

Use the strength that God has given you and love Him with all your might. Put some effort into your love for God. Be a servant, willing, obedient and faithful to His service. Using our strength for His honor and glory means dying to self and serving Him by serving others. He said that the greatest among His children is the servant of all!

I will go in the strength of the Lord God: I will make mention of thy righteousness, even of thine only. Psalm 71:16

So we are to use that confidence, that strength, in our witness to others - making mention of God's righteousness and not our own.
Then there is one of the most important and most overlooked responsibilities of the church - edification of the saints. The Lord desires that we clothe ourselves with strength because a strong Christian is a support to others who are weaker.

For the perfecting of the saints, for the work of the ministry, for the edifying of the body of Christ: Ephesians 4:12

Let no corrupt communication proceed out of your mouth, but that which is good to the use of edifying, that it may minister grace unto the hearers. Ephesians 4:29

What's the result of that strength? What will be the gain of becoming a strong Christian? Obviously, we should seek strength because God commanded it. He said that if we would be a virtuous woman, it should be our clothing. But what are the immediate results?

#1 Blessing.

Blessed is the man whose strength is in thee; in whose heart are the ways of them. Psalm 84:5

#2 It will cause you not to faint in adversity.

If thou faint in the day of adversity thy strength is small.   Proverbs 24:10

#3 It will cause you to not deny His name.

I know thy works: behold, I have set before thee an open door, and no man can shut it: for thou hast a little strength, and hast kept my word, and hast not denied my name. Revelation 3:8.

#4 It will give help in time of trouble.

But the salvation of the righteous is of the LORD: he is their strength in the time of trouble. Psalm 37:39,

God is our refuge and strength, a very present help in trouble. Psalm 46:1

#5 - God will get the glory because we openly acknowledge that strength comes from Him and not ourselves.

And he said unto me, My grace is sufficient for thee: for my strength is made perfect in weakness. Most gladly therefore will I rather glory in my infirmities, that the power of Christ may rest upon me. 2 Corinthians 12:9

So first, she is clothed with strength. Secondly, she is clothed with honour.

Honour means: reputation, or good name.

Testimony means: a solemn declaration or affirmation made for the purpose of establishing or proving some fact. Or it means witness; evidence, proof of some fact.

So not only does the virtuous woman have confidence in herself, others have confidence in her as well. She can be trusted. She has a good testimony. Her whole life is clothed with the idea that she trusts God and she can be trusted in return. You will never notice in the Word of God that anyone had any doubt that Mary of Bethany was a disciple of Jesus Christ. Honor has to do with our personal integrity. How do we uphold the name of Christ? Do we carry the name "Christian" in all honesty? Or does the name 'hypocrite' rest on the tip of the tongue of those who know us behind the scenes? A woman's testimony is a fragile as an eggshell. A good testimony is delicate and must be preserved. A poor testimony is like a rock. A poor testimony is a reflection on you, your family, your church, your pastor and your Lord. That is why the Lord said:

Abstain from all appearance of evil.1 Thessalonians 5:22

I am not referring to slander. Any Christian who tries to live for God will eventually become the target of slander. The devil may target you, as you seek to be obedient to the Word and will of God, because he does not want you to be an influence to others for their good. One of his favored tricks is to undermine a minister of the Gospel by attacking his family with slander; particularly if he can stir up some self-righteous, hypocritical, saved person to do the job for him. Or he may target you in an effort to stunt your growth before you can gain that strength that you need in order to be effective for Christ. There is a distinct difference between the unrighteous tale bearing and tattling that is so unfortunate amongst the body of Christ and the true testimony of a believer who is striving with all their might to serve God. The Bible does tell us that slander will happen. We will cover the subject more thoroughly in a future lesson. The Bible makes it plain that not only are we not to slander one another, but that we should also not be surprised when it happens to us. Look at how Job's best friends took the occasion of his trouble to accuse him falsely.

So when I refer to upholding a testimony, understand that I am not saying that you should be able to keep other people from being able to speak evil things about you - there's no way you can stop that from happening. You can, however, keep your heart right before God. You can walk uprightly and honestly before God and others. Then you can trust God with your testimony and let Him handle the rest. That's why strength and honour are her clothing. You may find yourself needing all the strength that God has to offer in order to trust Him with your honour. That is also why she shall rejoice *in time to come*. A good testimony is not built overnight. It happens through time and trial.

So many times people excuse their poor testimony by saying, "I know that I am saved, it doesn't really matter how I look on the outside, because God sees the heart." Oh, yes! It is true that God sees the heart. Which means that we should be more righteous - not less! Take a look at what Jesus told the Pharisees:

Woe unto you, scribes and Pharisees, hypocrites! for ye make clean the outside of the cup and of the platter, but within they are full of extortion and excess. Thou blind Pharisee, clean first that which is within the cup and platter, that the outside of them may be clean also. Matthew 23:25

Notice that he did not tell them that it did not matter what they looked like on the outside. He told them that the matter of the heart should come first <u>that the outside may be clean also</u>.

Then there are those who excuse themselves by saying, "We cannot possibly shape ourselves to please everyone. We would whittle ourselves away." No, you cannot please everyone. But you can seek to please the Lord. His desires for you to live a holy life are plainly stated in the Word of God.

But as he which hath called you is holy, so be ye holy in all manner of conversation; Because it is written, Be ye holy; for I am holy.
1 Peter 1:15 – 16

Seeing then that all these things shall be dissolved, what manner of persons ought ye to be in all holy conversation and godliness,   2 Peter 3:11

If so be that ye have heard him, and have been taught by him, as the truth is in Jesus: That ye put off concerning the former conversation the old man, which is corrupt according to the deceitful lusts; And be renewed in the spirit of your mind; And that ye put on the new man, which after God is created in righteousness and true holiness. Wherefore putting away lying, speak every man truth with his neighbour: for we are members one of another. Be ye angry, and sin not: let not the sun go down upon your wrath: Neither give place to the devil. Let him that stole steal no more: but rather let him labour, working with his hands the thing which is good, that he may have to give to him that needeth. Let no corrupt communication proceed out of your mouth, but that which is good to the use of edifying, that it may minister grace unto the hearers. And grieve not the holy Spirit of God, whereby ye are sealed unto the day of redemption. Let all bitterness, and wrath, and anger, and clamour, and evil speaking, be put away from you, with all malice: And be ye kind one to another, tenderhearted, forgiving one another, even as God for Christ's sake hath forgiven you. Ephesians 4:21-32

The passage above summarizes what it means to have a good testimony. Be a Christian. Be different. Don't lie to each other. Don't sin in anger, forgive quickly. Don't give place to the devil. Don't steal - work and give instead. Watch your mouth - use it for the benefit of others and not their destruction. Don't grieve the Spirit of God. Put away the things that would make you a grouchy, hateful, angry, vengeful person. Instead be kind, tenderhearted and forgiving.

She's not necessarily rejoicing right now - she will in time to come. Why is she not rejoicing now? Because it comes with time. Because it's not always easy to cover yourself with strength and honour. It's not always easy to focus on the reward when you are in the midst of the labor. Building virtue is a time consuming process. It does not happen in a few days and it does not happen without a few failures. Don't be impatient for reward.

And beside this, giving all diligence, add to your faith virtue; and to virtue knowledge; and to knowledge temperance; and to temperance patience; and to patience godliness; And to godliness brotherly kindness; and to brotherly kindness charity. For if these things be in you, and abound, they make you that ye shall neither be barren nor unfruitful in the knowledge of our Lord Jesus Christ.
2 Peter 1:5-8

One step at a time. Clinging to Christ all the way.

Lesson Seventeen Review

1) Write this lesson's Scripture passage:

_____

_____

_____

_____

2) Why does it say that her clothing is strength and honour?

_____

_____

_____

3) The strength we are talking about here is a quiet sense of

_____

4) A Christian woman is not an _____

5) The first step toward confidence is to

_____

_____

6) The next step is to

_____

_____

7) Where does that confidence come from?

_____

8) The first source of strength is _____

9) If the devil cannot keep a person from getting _____, he
will spend the rest of their lives _____ and the
best tool he has is to _____

10) List 3 things that will help you battle doubts:

_____

_____

_____

11) The second source of strength is to recognize _____

_____

12) The third source of strength is:

_____

13) List 5 steps toward
strength:_____

_____

_____

_____

_____

14) List 3 things we should do with the strength we receive:

_____

_____

_____

15) What are 5 results of strength in our lives?

_____

_____

_____

_____

_____

16) Honour means:_____

_____

_____

17) Testimony means: _____

_____

_____

18) Honor has to do with our _____

19) A good testimony is _____

20) A bad testimony is _____

21) Why does the Bible say that she shall rejoice in time to come?

_____

_____

A Woman Among all Those
Lessons in Christian Womanhood

Lesson 18

Scripture memory for this lesson: She openeth her mouth with wisdom: and in her tongue is the law of kindness. Proverbs 31:26

Let your speech be always with grace, seasoned with salt, that ye may know how ye ought to answer every man. Colossians 4:6

Oh! The dreaded tongue! This is a lesson that will probably take a jab at all of us in one manner or another! In fact the Bible says:

For in many things we offend all. If any man offend not in word, the same is a perfect man, and able also to bridle the whole body. James 3:2

James chapter 3 is an entire chapter devoted to the tongue.
(Read James 3)

The Word of God has so many things to say about the tongue! It is easier to sin with our tongue than in just about any other way. But look at our virtuous woman. When she opens her mouth you can expect wisdom. In her tongue is - not just kindness - but the law of kindness! That means that when she opens her mouth you can always expect what comes out of it to be kind. Others can use her as the rule by which a Christian woman's manner of speech should be patterned.

And be ye kind one to another, tenderhearted, forgiving one another, even as God for Christ's sake hath forgiven you. Ephesians 4:32

Her speech is always with grace - She doesn't just give to people, with her tongue, what they deserve. She's sure to be kinder than they deserve (remember that grace means that we have received more than we deserve.) How many times have we heard the phrase "They have earned a piece of my mind so they're going to get it!" That's the attitude that our flesh likes. However, it is not in keeping with the way God says a virtuous woman ought to be. "Seasoned with salt." The Bible refers to salt in various ways, but used as a metaphor - a type - it is only used twice. Once is in Matthew where Jesus calls us the salt of the earth and the other is here in Colossians 4:6. Salt has several properties that we should look into if we are to understand fully how to season our speech with salt.

1. Salt is a seasoning:

Can that which is unsavory be eaten without salt? or is there any taste in the white of an egg? Job 6:6

What does a seasoning do? It is a compliment to the food. It brings out the full flavor of the food it is sprinkled on. It is not the salt itself we are interested in tasting but the good flavor of the food enhanced by the salt. If the salt is overdone, the food is ruined and no one wants it. Our speech should be a complement to our godliness, it should bring out the full flavor of our Christianity. It should not overpower. We should be extremely careful as Christian ladies not to talk too much - a poor character trait, unfortunately, that women are particularly known for.

But let it be the hidden man of the heart, in that which is not corruptible, even the ornament of a meek and **quiet** spirit, which is in the sight of God of great price. 1 Peter 3:4

And that ye study to be **quiet**, and to do your own business, and to work with your own hands, as we commanded you. 1 Thessalonians 4:11

Both of these verses refer to more than just being quiet with your voice - although that is a great part of it - but also quiet with your manner of life; not being of a rowdy, antagonistic behavior with your nose always in someone else's business.

Look at the woman that God chose to be the mother of His Christ. When faced with things that she did not understand, what was her reaction? Luke 1:26-38; Luke 2:19. My! That poor girl's world was suddenly turned upside down. Not only did she see an angel - but who was going to believe this story?? Notice that her reaction was not hysterical, argumentative, or in any manner selfish. She submitted to the will of God calmly, with very little to say. Then when the child was born - the very same night he was born - her birthing room, such as it was, was invaded by a bunch of smelly shepherds who came on the run from the fields, babbling about seeing angels. Strangers, crowding into the already crowded stable, wanting to look at her new born baby. She kept these things, and pondered them in her heart. She may not have understood - but she quietly submitted to the Lord.

Look at her again in John 2:3-5. Her quiet confidence in Jesus' ability again shows that she was a woman of few words. In fact we never read that she had much to say at all - except one place. In Luke 1:46-55 is the longest speech of any kind we see come out of Mary. It is praise to God.

In the multitude of words there wanteth not sin: but he that refraineth his lips is wise. Proverbs 10:19 (Or in today's vernacular, a fool's keyboard is known by a multitude of keystrokes.)

For a dream cometh through the multitude of business; and a fool's voice is known by multitude of words. Ecclesiastes 5:3

As a general rule, we talk too much. Seldom do you find any woman – any person for that matter - who would not be better off if they were quieter than they are. That's why the Bible says we should study it. (And for some of us it's a harder study than for others!) Practice. Teach yourself to be quiet. Don't feel like you always have to express your opinion. Minding your own business is the first step. Unless expressly asked for, don't give your advice or your opinion on someone else's matters. (Of course, your opinion is worth its weight in gold but the other person may not have the depth to understand that yet!)

This is advice that should be particularly heeded by those of us who have married children. Don't be free in handing out unwanted advice. I try (try, mind you!) to only give the advice that I am asked for. Remember how you felt about advice that you received as a young adult - how much unwanted advice did you heed? And how did you inwardly respond to those who were offering it? One of the hardest things that a parent of adults has to do is to step back and let those adult children make mistakes. (Another quick hint - "I told you so" is not in keeping with kind speech seasoned with salt either!) Along with simply talking too much, which puts us at, not just the risk of, but according to the Scriptures we just read, the surety of sin, the Bible gives us a warning against prating.

The wise in heart will receive commandments: but a prating fool shall fall. Proverbs 10:8

He that winketh with the eye causeth sorrow: but a prating fool shall fall. Proverbs 10:10

Prate means: To talk much and without weight, or to little purpose; to be loquacious; as the vulgar express it: to run on. To utter foolishly. Continued talk to little purpose; trifling talk: unmeaning loquacity.

Loquacious means: Talkative; given to continual talking. Apt to blab and disclose secrets.

We should avoid prating as the very opposite of Christian Womanhood. Empty headed, babbling conversation is sure sin. When you talk without thinking, you are just about certain to say something stupid, hurt someone's feelings or make a fool of yourself in some way. We should learn to curb the tongue in the manner of empty talk.

2. Excessive amounts of salt are destructive:

And Abimelech fought against the city all that day; and he took the city, and slew the people that was therein, and beat down the city, and sowed it with salt. Judges 9:45

(He sowed it with salt because with that excessive amount of salt in the ground nothing would grow.)

Too much salt ruins food. Large amounts of salt ruins the ground. The reason the Dead Sea is called the Dead Sea is because it has such a high salt content that nothing can live there. Too much talk ruins your testimony! Too much talk spoils your influence with others. Too much talk makes your personality overbearing and hard to put up with. Too much talk will retard your spiritual growth. How many times have we as teachers told our students that they cannot learn with their mouth in constant motion? How many times have we told them that the reason that God gave them one mouth and two ears is that He wants them to hear twice as much as they speak? We should be careful to apply those truths to our own lives. We will learn more of God and the things of God if we listen more and talk less.

On the other hand, salt itself is a very necessary part of our lives. It is part of our very makeup, part of the chemistry of our bodies and carries with it essential nutrients that we cannot live without. It was an essential part of the sacrifices to God.

And every oblation of thy meat offering shalt thou season with salt; neither shalt thou suffer the salt of the covenant of thy God to be lacking from thy meat offering: with all thine offerings thou shalt offer salt. Leviticus 2:13

Properly placed speech, in the proper amount, is so necessary in our service to God!! How can we witness without it? How can we edify the saints of God? How can we comfort those who are in any trouble? How can we testify of His grace and goodness in our lives? Our God is perfectly balanced and He seeks for us to be in balance as well. To say that we should not talk at all, or that we should refrain from using our voice in God's service, is as wrong as to say that we should rattle on and on with no control. But we need to realize that we are given the power of speech for the purpose of serving God, not for the pleasing of our flesh.

The tongue of the wise useth knowledge aright: but the mouth of fools poureth out foolishness. Proverbs 15:2

A word fitly spoken is like apples of gold in pictures of silver. Proverbs 25:11

3. Salt is a preservative:

Canned, bottled and dried foods all contain salt in one form or another in order to preserve the fresh taste of the food and keep it from spoiling. If your speech is seasoned with salt you will seek to preserve, not to tear down. To edify, not to weaken, a brother in Christ. One of the most overlooked jobs of a Christian is edification.

To Edify means: To build, in a literal sense. To instruct and improve the mind in knowledge generally, and particularly in moral and religious knowledge, in faith and holiness.

Let us therefore follow after the things which make for peace, and things wherewith one may edify another. Romans 14:19

Wherefore comfort yourselves together, and edify one another, even as also ye do. 1 Thessalonians 5:11

Instead of all the ways that we are prone to use our mouths toward one another: gossip, backbiting, talebearing, malice, anger, just plain talk, talk, talk - The Bible says that we are to use it for edification; for building one another up in the faith.

Too often an older Christian loses the picture of the journey toward maturity upon which God has brought them. They forget that they were once a baby Christian, ignorant of the ways and workings of God. They forget that they did not get birthed into the family of God with a proper measure of holiness already in place. So, they begin to use their mouths for the purpose of tearing at young Christians who have not attained their spiritual level. That's pride - and it's ungodly!! Our job as older Christians is to support the weak, to edify one another, to comfort and heal. And yes, to teach. And even in some instances to rebuke but not for our own gratification - for their benefit. It should always be done in love and kindness, always mindful that pride can bring us to the same point of sin. No matter how far down the road to spirituality we think we are.

The proper way to edify is to, first of all, consider yourself.

Brethren, if a man be overtaken in a fault, ye which are spiritual, restore such a one in the spirit of meekness; considering thyself, lest thou also be tempted. Galatians 6:1

(I once heard a preacher say that you cannot know that you are spiritual – that if you know it, it is pride and then you are no longer spiritual. Well, I guess if he means that you cannot consider yourself on a higher plane than others, he's right. However, if none of us were ever to know that we had reached some spiritual maturity, who would lead? We would never be able to follow the command in the verse above - who would restore if no one knew they could?)

And why beholdest thou the mote that is in thy brother's eye, but considerest not the beam that is in thine own eye? Or how wilt thou say to thy brother, Let me pull out the mote out of thine eye; and, behold, a beam is in thine own eye? Thou hypocrite, first cast out the beam out of thine own eye; and then shalt thou see clearly to cast out the mote out of thy brother's eye. Matthew 7:3-5

First determine if you have reached the spiritual plane to which you are trying to bring your brother up. Don't criticize sin in his life if you don't have victory over it yourself. Don't try to build him up if you aren't built in that area yourself. This does not mean that you cannot edify someone unless you have "spiritually arrived." The Apostle Paul said he had not "arrived" spiritually, so there's not much hope any of the rest of us will. Yet, we are told to edify one another. So what do we do? We stand on the Word of God. It is our final answer in all matters of faith and practice. If the Bible says it - then it's right. It's not unrighteous judgment if it comes from the Word of God. Unrighteous judgment comes from our own opinion or from judging others when we are doing the same things.

Edification means to encourage your fellow Christian to do right, to provoke him to good works, to stir him up to godliness, faith and charity. That is, according to the Word of God, one of the primary reasons for going to church.

And let us consider one another to provoke unto love and to good works: Not forsaking the assembling of ourselves together, as the manner of some is; but exhorting one another: and so much the more, as ye see the day approaching. Hebrews 10:24

4. Salt has healing properties:

Salt is used in so many ways to heal. Having grown up on the Gulf Coast, I know from experience that a dip in salt water will promote the healing of any cut or sore. Saline solution that is in most throat and nasal sprays are primarily salt water. We are told to use warm salt water for a sore throat; cold sores, or any problem in the mouth!

So many times though, our mouths are used to hurt, not to heal. We do not have the time in this lesson to cover all of the things we should avoid in this area, but we'll cover it in the next lesson. Remember that our Virtuous Woman's tongue contains the "law of kindness." James says that it is a shame when out of the same mouth proceedeth blessing and cursing - these things ought not to be!

If our speech is seasoned with salt it will be a healing balm and even when it is used in rebuke or teaching it will be for the purpose of healing not hurting. One of the greatest ways that our speech promotes healing is to witness of the saving faith of Jesus Christ.

But sanctify the Lord God in your hearts: and be ready always to give an answer to every man that asketh you a reason of the hope that is in you with meekness and fear: 1 Peter 3:15

5. Salt is an irritant.

If you don't believe it - go ahead and do what I suggested and take a dip in salt water when you have an open sore! Or swish some warm salt water in your mouth when you have a bad cold sore! Oh, yes! It irritates! In strong enough concentrations it will also cause burns on your skin. It can even remove paint and erode concrete!

When we witness for the Lord Jesus Christ, or when we seek to speak up for godliness and righteousness, it will irritate those who don't want to hear it. Used in the proper proportion it is the greatest healer ever known. It heals a sin sick soul. But conviction of sin comes as part of the process - and conviction is a very uncomfortable feeling. When made uncomfortable by conviction, the one witnessed to, or the one rebuked for sin, often lashes out at the one doing the witnessing. Expect it. It will happen. Look what happened with the apostles and with Stephen.

And to him they agreed: and when they had called the apostles, and beaten them, they commanded that they should not speak in the name of Jesus, and let them go. And they departed from the presence of the council, rejoicing that they were counted worthy to suffer shame for his name. Acts 5:40-41

When they heard these things, they were cut to the heart, and they gnashed on him with their teeth. Acts 7:54

There are many instances throughout the Word of God where the conviction of sin made people react with anger, and even violence, toward the one witnessing. In fact the Lord told us not to be surprised when it happens. We could name countless incidences in our society today where people are criticized, persecuted and even jailed for witnessing for Christ or rebuking sin. However, don't refuse to witness because you make someone uncomfortable by it or because someone gets angry. Don't back away from taking a stand for righteousness and holiness. We should never set out to make someone angry on purpose. If they get angry when you are obeying the Savior by witnessing, do not be surprised or back away. You would not refuse to submit someone you love to medical treatment because they feel irritated or uncomfortable by the way that the medical staff treats them. You subject them to the treatment even when they don't understand why they are being made uncomfortable. Why? Because you know that in the end you are looking for healing. The Gospel is the same. It makes us squirm in discomfort as we recognize our sin and compare it to the holiness of our God. It sometimes irritates as we desire to hold on to that sin like it was something worth having. But the end result, if we accept the truth, is the complete healing, the saving of a soul. Use that salt!!

6. Salt is a cleansing agent.
Because my parents owned a pet store when I was growing up, I was raised with a knowledge of the cleansing properties of salt. Aquariums are properly cleaned with non-iodized salt, because it leaves no harmful residue that is toxic to the fish, like soap will. Not only does the chemical makeup of salt clean and sterilize but it also has a grainy, gritty texture that scours away dirt.

Our speech should be a cleansing agent. We should speak the truth and avoid, not only lying, but all types of corrupt communication. If we recognize that our speech as Christians is a reflection on our own testimony, on our family, our church, our pastor, and our Lord, then we will be very careful that our speech is not corrupt. We are to be an example, a pattern to follow, for younger Christians as well. When our speech is corrupt we are far from a cleansing agent in their lives.

Wherefore putting away lying, speak every man truth with his neighbour: for we are members one of another. Ephesians 4:25

Let no corrupt communication proceed out of your mouth, but that which is good to the use of edifying, that it may minister grace unto the hearers. Ephesians 4:29

Be not deceived: evil communications corrupt good manners.
1 Corinthians 15:33

Nothing ruins a testimony faster than rude, crude speech out of a Christian - particularly a Christian woman. Nothing ruins a testimony more permanently than a lying Christian. Speak the truth, keep your speech clean and gracious. Not only does this mean don't use swear words; it also means don't use rudeness, euphemisms (substitute words used in the place of swear words,) crude or worldly phrases and off color jokes. If you do use this form of speech, your manners will be corrupted, your testimony ruined and you will be mocked as a hypocrite.

I was speaking recently with a young Christian woman. In her speech she repeatedly used a phrase that was very worldly and uncouth. It was not a cuss word, but a phrase that had been derived from an abbreviated cuss word, and is commonly used in worldly speech. When gently rebuked for her phrase, it came to light that she had no idea what it meant. It had been taught to her by a preacher that she looked up to! We really need to watch our mouths for the sake of those that are listening and learning from us as well as to keep ourselves clean and pure before God.

7. Salt melts ice.

If you live in a cold area you are very familiar with salt being spread on sidewalks and roads. It not only melts the ice that is already there but it helps to keep ice from forming where it should not. What happens when the ice forms? Someone is in danger of slipping and falling.

Our speech should be directed at keeping hearts tender and warm toward God. Not just in the hearts of others but in our own hearts as well. How? Testify of the Lord's grace and goodness. Praise His name openly. Not just in church. (It is so sad that openly praising God in church is beginning to be a rare thing.) Openly praise Him wherever you are. Make the goodness of God a part of your everyday conversation. If God has blessed you, tell someone (and don't necessarily wait until that someone is a fellow believer. Those to whom you are witnessing will listen to you tell them how good God is to you. It will be an excellent testimony before them.) If you have learned a special truth about Him, share it. In openly using your voice in the praise of God, you will identify yourself with the Lord without question. It will make you a bolder witness and will cause you to keep a check on your own heart. God will not allow you to openly praise Him if you have sin in your life without revealing it to you. As soon as your mouth opens in praise, God will sprinkle some salt on the ice on your heart and open your sin to view so that you can get right and have closer fellowship with Him.

O magnify the Lord with me, and let us exalt his name together. Psalm 34:3

Remember how Mary praised the Lord in Luke 1:46-55. Praising God seemed to be the only thing that caused her to be very vocal in her speech. She was quiet and thoughtful. Slow to fret and complain. Slow to take offense, willing to give direction to others to follow the Lord's commands, and very vocal in her praise.

1 Thessalonians 5 gives us a good outline to follow for the use of our mouths. We'll close this lesson with it:

Now we exhort you brethren, **warn** them that are unruly, **comfort** the feebleminded, **support** the weak, **be patient** toward all men. See that **none render evil** for evil unto any man; but ever **follow that which is good,** both among yourselves, and to all men. **Rejoice** evermore. **Pray** without ceasing. In everything **give thanks:** for this is the will of God in Christ Jesus concerning you.   1 Thessalonians 5:14-18

Toward others: Warn, comfort, support, don't retaliate, be patient, follow that which is good
.
Toward God: Rejoice, Pray, Give thanks

That ought to keep us busy.

Lesson Eighteen Review

1) Write this lesson's Scripture passage:

_____

_____

_____

_____

2) What does prate mean? _____

_____

_____

_____

3) What does loquacious mean? _____

_____

_____

_____

4) What does edify mean? _____

_____

_____

5) List the 7 properties of salt discussed in this lesson.

_____

_____

_____

_____

_____

_____

_____

6) The Bible says that is we are able to _____ the tongue we would be a _____ man, and able also to _____ the whole body.

7) When the virtuous woman opens her mouth you can expect _____.

8) Others can use the virtuous woman as the rule by which a Christian woman's _____ should be patterned.

9) Grace is: _____

10) Our speech should be a _____ to our godliness, it should bring out the _____ of our Christianity. It should not _____

11) 1 Peter 3:4 and 1 Thessalonians 4:11 refer to more than just being _____ but also quiet with _____.

12) _____ is the first step in studying to be quiet.

13) List 2 things that too much salt will ruin:

_____

_____

14) List 3 things that too much talk will ruin:

_____

_____

15) If your speech is seasoned with salt you will seek to:

_____

_____

16) List several things that are the job of an older Christian:

_____

_____

_____

_____

17) Why will our speech be an irritant?

_____

_____

_____

_____

18) Nothing ruins a Christian's testimony faster than:

_____

19) Our speech should be directed at keeping

_____

20) List 2 benefits of making a habit of openly praising God.

_____

_____

A Woman Among all Those
Lessons in Christian Womanhood

Lesson 19

Scripture Memory: She openeth her mouth with wisdom; and in her tongue is the law of kindness. Proverbs 21:26

He that keepeth his mouth keepeth his life: but he that openeth wide his lips shall have destruction. Proverbs 13:3

When I began to study this subject, I knew there was a lot of material in the Word of God concerning the tongue and warnings about misusing the tongue - but I did not realize how really huge a subject it is! There is, in fact, so much in the Bible about this subject that we cannot possibly cover it all in these lessons. We can only scratch the surface. God gives admonition upon admonition about our tongues but it is a completely overlooked subject a lot of times. Why? Probably because it is a sin that almost all of us are more than prone to in one area or another - and many times preachers don't preach and teachers don't teach on subjects they don't have victory over themselves!! If we took that attitude with this subject, however, it would probably never be taught. The book of James tells us that if we would learn to control the tongue, we would be perfect and able to bridle the whole body. Recognizing our failings in this area does not excuse us from learning it from the Bible, from seeking to apply it to our lives, or from teaching it as part of the whole counsel of God. If that were so, the Lord would not have included it in the Word of God. (And oh, my! Did He ever include it! I took a rough count of the verses I looked through for this lesson. 234 verses that were admonitions concerning speech, the tongue, the mouth and the lips and I know I did not get to them all!) He intends for it to be taught and learned. In our last lesson we studied the proper use of the tongue. This week we'll go more in depth in some ways we should not use it.

Who has not been the victim of an unkind, unruly tongue? The tongue has destroyed more Christians than persecution from outside the church. How many churches have suffered because of unruly tongues? How many pastors have been hindered in their work for God because of malicious tongues? How many people have we met on visitation, over the years, who have told us, "I used to go to church, I used to be faithful to every service, I was a Sunday School teacher, etc. etc. - but then I got hurt by what someone said?" Now, truly, they have no excuse. They should have had more Spiritual maturity. (Although many times the ones attacked in this manner are baby Christians or Christians who have not grown in the Lord.) They should have understood that **God** did not hurt them. They should have understood that they should put it behind them and go on for Christ. But even more, the one who was careless or malicious with their tongues will be to blame at the Judgment Seat of Christ for the destruction of their brother with their tongue. I have known of several cases over the years where these offended ones have come back to the Lord and sought to pick up the shattered pieces of their Christian life. They have all given testimony that they regret the time that they have wasted. Even sadder are the ones who never return.

I have outlined this lesson all in "B's" just for fun. (We need something on the lighter side for this one!) The ways not to use our tongue would be: Boastingly, Blabbering Boisterously, Blasphemously, Badgering and Berate-ingly, or Bellyache-ingly.

Boastingly:

Pride is an abomination to the Lord. Pride spawns a lot of ugly results coming from the mouth. God considers proud speech foolish.

In the mouth of the foolish is a rod of pride: but the lips of the wise shall preserve them. Proverbs 14:3

We are not to be boasting of our abilities. If you are to be praised, let someone else do it.

Let another man praise thee, and not thine own mouth; a stranger and not thine own lips. Proverbs 27:2

Most of the time when pride swells the heart and erupts from the lips it forms an unrighteous attempt to put yourself on a pedestal at someone else's expense. But look how God feels about it:

These six things doth the LORD hate: yea, seven are an abomination unto him: a proud look, a lying tongue, and hands that shed innocent blood, An heart that deviseth wicked imaginations, feet that be swift in running to mischief, A false witness that speaketh lies, and he that soweth discord among brethren. Proverbs 6:16-19

The LORD shall cut off all flattering lips, and the tongue that speaketh proud things. Psalm 12:3

These are murmurers, complainers, walking after their own lusts; and the mouth speaketh great swelling words, having men's persons in admiration because of advantage. Jude 1:16

We need to avoid the "I" disease. If our speech dots too many "I's" we need to slow down, take a deep breath and talk about someone else - preferably the Lord.

Miriam was guilty of boasting of her position with God, and it caused her to think evil of Moses and to criticize him in front of the children of Israel in an effort to promote herself. The result was that she suffered the humiliation and pain of 7 days shut out of the camp as a leper. Numbers 12:1-16

Miriam's digression into pride is all too common. First we are allowed to use what meager talents we have for the glory of God. God takes those things and magnifies and molds them to suit His purpose. Then when we see the results of what God has done with us, we begin to get the big head and think we're really something. That causes us to look down on others and want to promote ourselves above them. So.... then the tongue comes into play, and we cut at that person with it in an attempt to discredit them and make ourselves look better (which usually has the opposite effect.) As a result of this, we cause God to have to step in and abase that pride.

For whosoever exalteth himself shall be abased; and he that humbleth himself shall be exalted. Luke 14:11

We need to be careful not to allow pride into our lives that will cause our mouths to sin. It has been said that anyone who has to step on someone else to make himself look bigger is a mighty small person. A proud heart will also stir up trouble. When we begin to think more of ourselves than we ought, it will, many times, give way to envy of others who have what we consider to be a favored position. Then we begin to use the tongue contentiously. The attitude seems to be that if we belittle someone else, it will make us look more acceptable in the eyes of those we are trying to impress. Not only is it ungodly, it doesn't work! That kind of attitude generally tears us down in the opinion of others. It doesn't build us up.

Only by pride cometh contention: but with the well advised is wisdom. Proverbs 13:10

Cast out the scorner, and contention shall go out; yea, strife and reproach shall cease. Proverbs 22:10

In Genesis 16:1-4 is the story of Hagar and Abram. Notice that Hagar was a maidservant and totally humble in her attitude until she conceived. Then she despised Sarai. We don't know what she said to Sarai – but it was enough to get her in a lot of trouble. Then her attitude was reflected in her son's attitude which got them both sent away from Abraham's house.

And Sarah saw the son of Hagar the Egyptian, which she had born unto Abraham, mocking. Wherefore she said unto Abraham, Cast out this bondwoman and her son: for the son of this bondwoman shall not be heir with my son, even with Isaac. Genesis 21:9-10

Other instances in the Bible are Hannah and Peninnah, and also Rachel and Leah who were provoked by envy to say unkind, hurtful things in an attempt to gain more favor for themselves. In every instance their boasting and belittling did not work. It only caused a great deal of trouble for themselves.

For I say, through the grace given unto me, to every man that is among you, not to think of himself more highly than he ought to think; but to think soberly, according as God hath dealt to every man the measure of faith. Romans 12:3

For if a man think himself to be something, when he is nothing, he deceiveth himself. Galatians 6:3

A lot of times, too, the person boasting of their abilities is lying. Why do they do that? Probably a sense of insecurity. They do not feel that who they are, or the abilities that they have, are interesting enough or dramatic enough so they come up with all sorts of tall tales about themselves. Even small children know that lying is a sin. It is a sin of the old nature to be untruthful. It doesn't belong in a Christian's life.

Lie not one to another, seeing that ye have put off the old man with his deeds; Colossians 1:9

Our next "B" is **Babbling Boisterously:**

We covered prating and talking too much in the last lesson. Remember that prating means "much talk to no purpose." The Bible warns us against foolish speech. A good study that really helps to build character, is to go through the Word of God and look carefully at all of God's warnings against fools and foolishness. Then compare it to His admonition on wisdom.

Fool is defined: a person who is somewhat deficient in intellect, but not an idiot; or a person who acts absurdly; one who does not exercise his reason; one who pursues a course contrary to the dictates of wisdom. In Scripture, fool is often used for a wicked or depraved person; one who acts contrary to sound wisdom in his moral deportment; one who follows his own inclinations, who prefers trifling and temporary pleasures to the service of God and eternal happiness.

God gives serious warnings about foolish speech.

The heart of him that hath understanding seeketh knowledge: but the mouth of fools feedeth on foolishness. Proverbs 15:14

A fool's mouth is his destruction, and his lips are the snare of his soul. Proverbs 18:7

The words of a wise man's mouth are gracious; but the lips of a fool will swallow up himself. Ecclesiastes 10:12

The tongue of the wise useth knowledge aright: but the mouth of fools poureth out foolishness. Proverbs 15:2

So in looking at the verses above we can see that foolish speech is speech that does not seek knowledge. It is speech that doesn't care how to use knowledge but just opens the mouth and lets fly whatever chooses to come out. In our school room is a large sign that says: "Before you say what you think - think!" We would all do well to follow that advice. We all talk about "having our foot in our mouth." It comes from allowing our mouths to run ahead of our minds. We may see it as a joke, but God gives it a much more serious aspect:

The heart of the wise teacheth his mouth, and addeth learning to his lips. Proverbs 16:23

The heart of the righteous studieth to answer: but the mouth of the wicked poureth out evil things. Proverbs 15:28

God says that it is unrighteous not to think before you speak. That's pretty serious.

Job's wife was told that she spoke as one of the foolish women when she told Job to "curse God and die." Her emotions were out of control and she opened her mouth and spoke without thinking.

I once knew a man who would never immediately answer a question that he was asked. It did not matter if you were asking his opinion of the weather. He would stop, look for a minute at his feet as though processing the question through his mind, then offer a carefully considered answer. I thought it was just a quirk in his personality because I am so used to people (myself included) who just give an "off the cuff" answer for most things. I learned, later, that he had been prone to a hasty and violent temper when he was young. God had taught him to be cautious about his speech by being slow to answer and considering carefully what was said before he gave his answer to anything he was asked.

One of the strongest cautions about rash speech in the Word of God is about making rash vows before the Lord:

Keep thy foot when thou goest to the house of God, and be more ready to hear, than to give the sacrifice of fools: for they consider not that they do evil. Be not rash with thy mouth, and let not thine heart be hasty to utter any thing before God: for God is in heaven, and thou upon earth: therefore let thy words be few. For a dream cometh through the multitude of business; and a fool's voice is known by multitude of words. When thou vowest a vow unto God, defer not to pay it; for he hath no pleasure in fools: pay that which thou hast vowed. Better is it that thou shouldest not vow, than that thou shouldest vow and not pay. Suffer not thy mouth to cause thy flesh to sin; neither say thou before the angel, that it was an error: wherefore should God be angry at thy voice, and destroy the work of thine hands? For in the multitude of dreams and many words there are also divers vanities: but fear thou God. Ecclesiastes 5:1-7

Obviously, God does not take empty promises lightly. He takes it very seriously when we come before Him and make a promise to Him. He expects us to follow through with what we say we will do.

A church hosted a camp meeting once, where several men began to promise financial support to the camp for the construction of a needed building. This offering was not "promoted" but was spontaneously started. Once started, everyone seemed to want to get in on the bandwagon. Enough money was promised to pay for the building and then some. However, in actuality, only about 1/5 of the promised money ever came in. Those men openly lied to God. Yet, I was appalled when I found that the host preacher had never expected to see much of the money that was promised because that same scene is repeated many times. People make God all sorts of promises, that they do not intend to keep, so that they will look good in the eyes of other people. I wonder sometimes if those people really believe in God at all! They certainly do not have the proper amount of fear of our living God or of the judgment that the word of God says is sure to follow! Ananias and Sapphira made that same mistake – and it cost them their lives. Acts 5:1-10

A big mistake that a lot of women make is to promise their children things with which they do not intend to follow through. Or they sometimes make a rash promise to them that they later find too difficult to fulfill. Sometimes it is a rash threat of discipline that they later regret and so don't follow through. This breaks a child's trust in you. One character trait of my mother's, that I will always remember, was that if she told you, "I promise," she would keep that promise at all cost. I remember, as well, that she was extremely cautious about giving that promise in the first place. Many times I can remember her saying, "No, I believe that we will do (this or that) but I cannot promise you because I am not totally sure I can hold to it." I trusted my mother implicitly to keep her word because she had proved to me over the years that she always kept her promises.

No matter to whom you are speaking, the Word of God tells you that you should be completely honest in what you say. It says that you should not ever make promises that you do not intend to keep. The Word of God tells us not to swear (at all!) that we will do something - why? Because we should be so honest that saying to someone, "I will do this," should have the same bond over us as if we signed a contract.

But let your communication be, Yea, yea; Nay, nay: for whatsoever is more than these cometh of evil. Matthew 5:37

This brings us to our next "B" – **Blasphemously**

The word Blasphemy means: An indignity offered to God by words or writing; reproachful, contemptuous or irreverent words uttered impiously against Jehovah.

There are more ways to blaspheme God than to curse, swear and talk filth. I'm sure that we are all aware that those things have no place in the life of a child of God. But we also blaspheme God when we say one thing and do another (hypocrisy.) When we tell lies, when we refuse to be in submission to our God given authority. We belong to God and when we, as His purchased, redeemed possessions, speak in ways that discredit Christianity, we have - as he told King David – given the enemies of God occasion to blaspheme. By doing so, it is the same as uttering those blasphemous words ourselves.

Sound speech, that cannot be condemned; that he that is of the contrary part may be ashamed, having no evil thing to say of you. Titus 2:8

Let no corrupt communication proceed out of your mouth, but that which is good to the use of edifying, that it may minister grace unto the hearers. Ephesians 4:29

But now ye also put off all these; anger, wrath, malice, blasphemy, filthy communication out of your mouth. Colossians 3:8

Surely no Christian would be guilty of "filthy communication," right?

Why, then, did God feel that the admonition was necessary? I've known many, many a Christian to use euphemistic words and phrases, to tell off color jokes, to make references to personal matters that should be kept to themselves. (I've even heard all of those things come from the pulpit!) Christians pick up phrases from the world and sling them around as though they were acceptable speech. A lot of times they don't even know what the words mean. They just use them because they hear other people use them. A good rule to use here is: if you don't know what something means, or what the origin of it is, it is best to not use it at all. Sometimes those of us who were not raised in Christian homes have grown up hearing and using phrases that are worldly and a poor testimony without realizing it. I can remember more than one time as I have grown up in the Lord that I have had to confess in shame that I found terminology in my vocabulary that was not pleasing to the Lord. Once you realize that something is not holy about your speech, you should be willing to purge it from your speech for God's sake.

The word Euphemism means: a figure in which a harsh or indelicate word or expression is softened, or rather by which a delicate word or expression is substituted for one which is offensive to good manners or to delicate ears. (In simple terms, a euphemism is a substitute for a cuss word.)

Blasphemy can be as much our manner of life as our words - The Bible says that open sin in our lives blasphemes God. When we claim the name of Christ with our mouth and deny Him with our works we have blasphemed His name. Why? Because what we say and do is a direct reflection on our Lord. A lot of times the only thing that people know about God is what they see in the lives of Christians - I have told my students, "Please, if you are going to go out of here and live for the devil, if you are going to wallow in sin – please! tell everyone that you are a Buddhist -- don't claim the name of Christ!"

Wherefore the Lord said, Forasmuch as this people draw near me with their mouth, and with their lips do honour me, but have removed their heart far from me, and their fear toward me is taught by the precept of men: Therefore, behold, I will proceed to do a marvellous work among this people, even a marvellous work and a wonder: for the wisdom of their wise men shall perish, and the understanding of their prudent men shall be hid. Isaiah 29:13-14

What do we mean by **Badger-ingly and Berate-ingly?**

As we mentioned before, our speech should be alway with grace, seasoned with salt. The virtuous woman's tongue contains the law of kindness. The tongue should never be used as a weapon. However, it is the best known weapon of the Baptist Church. If you badger your family or friends with your tongue, you will cause them to be weary of your presence. No one likes to be subjected to the presence of a person with is always picking and nagging at others. No one likes to be in the presence of a person who is always antagonistic and looking for a fight. And no one likes to spend time with someone who is always belittling them.

Put away from thee a froward mouth, and perverse lips put far from thee. Proverbs 4:24

Perverse

Perverse means: Literally, turned aside; hence, distorted from the right. Obstinate in the wrong; disposed to be contrary; stubborn; untractable. Cross; petulant; peevish; disposed to cross and vex.

Froward means: Perverse, that is, turning from, with aversion or reluctance; not willing to yield or comply with what is required; unyielding; ungovernable; refractory; disobedient; peevish; as a froward child.

So a froward mouth is one that is not, and refuses to be, under control. And perverse lips are those that tend to be stubborn, bad tempered and ill natured. We are commanded to put those things – not just away – but FAR away. One of the worst things that a woman can do is to use her tongue as a vent for her emotions. Particularly if she has unstable hormone levels. A woman with PMS or going through menopause is a hormonal time bomb with a very short fuse. If you have this problem you must seek to get it under control before you will be able to adequately control your tongue. It is not, absolutely not, acceptable in a virtuous woman to use her unstable hormone levels as an excuse to let her tongue lash out at others as a weapon. (Many times 'PMS' is just an excuse for a spoiled brat to turn loose of her tongue at the expense of everyone around her.) It was mentioned in a previous lesson that if you are having emotional or hormonal problems it would be better to go off by yourself and be as quiet as possible. Try to, quietly, explain to your husband or children that you are not the master of your attitude at the moment and need some time alone. Better to be abnormally quiet than abominably mouthy.

There are things that you can do to bring your spirit under control. The first is to realize that your emotions are out of whack - it's not them, it's you. Then pray for the Lord's help. Seek nutritional help. Eat right, get enough sleep, drink enough water, take some vitamin supplements, take a remedy for PMS or menopause. Then when you sometimes fail in all of your efforts to keep that wicked little wiggler in your mouth from doing its damage - go to the one you have mistreated and be woman enough to apologize.

A word fitly spoken is like apples of gold in pictures of silver. Proverbs 25:11

Set a watch, O LORD, before my mouth; keep the door of my lips. Psalm 141:3

Another ungodly manner in which the tongue is used is when it is unleashed in anger. The Lord admonishes us to control our tempers. Remember that the book of James says that a fountain cannot turn out both sweet water and bitter. Yet, a lot of Christian women do just that with their tongues. They are **so** sweet that, as the expression is, "honey wouldn't melt in their mouths,"- until you make them angry -- then look out! You don't want to be in the same room! That's not a good testimony. That is not having a godly control over your spirit.

Be ye angry, and sin not: let not the sun go down upon your wrath: Ephesians 4:26

Be not hasty in thy spirit to be angry: for anger resteth in the bosom of fools. Ecclesiastes 7:9

An angry man stirreth up strife, and a furious man aboundeth in transgression. Proverbs 29:22

It is better to dwell in the wilderness, than with a contentious and an angry woman. Proverbs 21:19

Another weapon-like use of the tongue is slander. Backbiting, whispering, gossip and talebearing are all in the same category. This is where so many Christians' lives are ruined. My pastor/husband likes to quote a preacher from many years ago who reportedly preached a message on gossip, which was beginning to be a problem in his church. One of the women, who had been the most guilty, came forward during the invitation, crying, "Pastor, I want to lay my tongue on the altar." He said, "Well, we've only got 20 feet, but if you double it up, it should fit!" (Who knows if the story is true? Pastors back then were extremely blunt, and not very politically correct – and people got right with God, instead of getting mad.)

Slander means: A false tale or report maliciously uttered and tending to injure the reputation of another by lessening him in the esteem of his fellow citizens, by exposing him to impeachment and punishment, or by impairing his means of living; defamation. Those who slander are filled with pride, and are seeking the destruction of their fellow Christian. They do not necessarily care whether or not what they are saying is true - it is done in malice and hatred.

Jezebel paid for the slander of Naboth. Her malicious plan was to have him killed so that her wimpy husband could have Naboth's vineyard. 1 Kings 21:1-15 The plan worked just fine. Her husband got the vineyard, and she had proved that no one could cross the king and get away with it - except that God saw - and God's judgment was very sure.

And of Jezebel also spake the LORD, saying, The dogs shall eat Jezebel by the wall of Jezreel. Him that dieth of Ahab in the city the dogs shall eat; and him that dieth in the field shall the fowls of the air eat. But there was none like unto Ahab, which did sell himself to work wickedness in the sight of the LORD, whom Jezebel his wife stirred up. 1Kings 21:23-25
When we are prone to slander others our intent may not be to see that person die physically - but are we so puffed up in our own importance that we do not care if they die spiritually? Do we care about their feelings? If we are virtuous women, we will avoid even stepping to the threshold of slander of others - because in her tongue is the law of kindness.

He that hideth hatred with lying lips, and he that uttereth a slander, is a fool. Proverbs 10:18

The next cousin of Slander is a Backbiter, or Whisperer.

Whispering is: The act of speaking with a low voice; the telling of tales, and exciting of suspicions; a backbiting.

So to tell tales on people for the purpose of making someone doubt their character is slander, backbiting and whispering. Slander, backbiting and whispering are generally the results of malice.
Remember that we have defined malice as: Extreme enmity of heart, or malevolence; a disposition to injure others without cause, from mere personal gratification or from a spirit of revenge; unprovoked malignity or spite.

Malice is a sin of the old nature. It is to be put aside as babyish and unfit for the life of a Christian. If you harbor hatred in your heart toward a brother or sister in Christ, and you desire their destruction, then you are holding a root of bitterness. The Bible says you are just as guilty before God as a murderer.

Whosoever hateth his brother is a murderer: and ye know that no murderer hath eternal life abiding in him. 1 John 3:15

Notice that malice and evil speaking go hand in hand.

Wherefore laying aside all malice, and all guile, and hypocrisies, and envies, and all evil speakings, As newborn babes, desire the sincere milk of the word, that ye may grow thereby: If so be ye have tasted that the Lord is gracious. 1Peter 2:1-3
Gossip and slander are not necessarily the same thing, although both are evil. Slander has a purpose of hatred behind it, while gossip generally comes from an uncontrolled mouth in the head of a person who is idle. Although it is not Bible, it is certainly true that an idle mind is the devil's playground, and idle hands are the devil's workshop.

The definition of gossip is: One who runs from house to house, tattling and telling news; an idle tattler.

As parents, we know that if our children are kept busy they get into less trouble. We know that their time must be structured. If they have too much time on their hands they will quarrel with each other and they will come up with all kinds of mischief. It is never surprising to us when we find out that a child is in trouble when we know that child is left alone and allowed to choose for himself how he will spend his time. Why do we not realize that the same is true of ourselves? If we would be busy about the things of God we would have less time to quarrel with each other, less time to criticize and complain and less time to come up with mischievous things to do. We would not have so much time to gossip and tell tales and we would sin less. I had a pastor once who said, "If you are sitting down rowing, you can't rock the boat." His meaning was pretty clear. Those who cause the most trouble in churches are the ones who work the least and talk the most. Look at this admonition given specifically to women:

And withal they learn to be idle, wandering about from house to house; and not only idle, but tattlers also and busybodies, speaking things which they ought not. I will therefore that the younger women marry, bear children, guide the house, give none occasion to the adversary to speak reproachfully. 1 Timothy 5:13-14

God obviously intends for us to keep busy enough to not have time for idle, unrighteous speech. My husband and I have a close, dear friend who is also a pastor. He has weathered the storm of more church troubles than most pastors would ever want to see. He made the comment to me one time, "I have never had a family leave my church when it was the man's idea to leave." It has always, every time, been the ungodly, ungovernable mouth of the woman that has caused the problem. Bickering, complaining, whining, gossiping women are not virtuous women.

Another sin of the mouth that comes from idleness is talebearing. Talebearing and gossip differ very little, and are used synonymously a lot of times. The only difference I see is that talebearing, generally, is telling the truth on someone when it should not be told, where gossip doesn't really care whether what is told is true or not.

Talebearer: A person who officiously tells tales; one who impertinently communicates intelligence or anecdotes, and makes mischief in society by his officiousness.

Basically a talebearer is one who can't keep secrets. He's heard something and has to spread it. Whether or not it will hurt the person involved, a talebearer has an uncontrollable urge to tell what they know just because they can tell it. Particularly so, if what they are telling will create a sensation. There is a common, not very flattering joke that says, "The three fastest forms of communication are telephone, telegraph and tell-a-woman." A person who cannot keep secrets is not to be trusted. If you hear something about someone, true or not, it needs to be kept to yourself if there is no godly reason for it to be told.

A talebearer revealeth secrets: but he that is of a faithful spirit concealeth the matter. Proverbs 11:13

The words of a talebearer are as wounds, and they go down into the innermost parts of the belly. Proverbs 26:22

Where no wood is, there the fire goeth out: so where there is no talebearer, the strife ceaseth. Proverbs 26:20

Talebearing creates strife, and it is a wound inflicted by someone who is of an unfaithful spirit. Sometimes that is a wound from which the other person never recovers.

So where do you draw the line? Sometimes it's hard to tell when something should be communicated and when it should not. First of all, use the same rule again that you use with your children. Is it tattling? Tattling is telling something about someone just for the purpose of telling it. It is telling just to be mean. Do you have a reason to be saying what you are saying? If you do not, it is idle speech and probably will hurt someone. But we also tell our children that it is not only okay, but necessary, to tell if someone is going to get hurt, if property is going to be damaged or loss suffered in some other way.

I found out about a situation once that was going to be devastating to the church if it was allowed to continue. It was not told to me but something that I walked in on unexpectedly. The person involved confessed to me what was going on. I dearly loved this person and tried to reason with them concerning what was happening. They would not listen and brushed me aside. What did I do? I went straight to my husband and then to my pastor and told what I knew. Did it cause a blow up? Yes, and I lost a friend. I still regret the loss of that friend. I do not, however, regret what I did because the church did not suffer the harm that was coming. (By the way, my husband and pastor were the ONLY ones that I told.)

Is it okay to communicate prayer requests for others? Hummmm....... A lot of times prayer requests are thinly veiled talebearing. Do they want it communicated? Now we certainly ask for prayer for those who are lost or backslidden. And they, almost all of the time, did not ask for that prayer request. We understand that this is necessary and not talebearing. But what of other issues? It never hurts to ask. "Do you want me to keep this to myself, or do you care if others know?" Then it should be all right to communicate a prayer request for that person. Did they tell you in confidence? Or did they tell other people as well? If they are not concerned with keeping it a secret you MAY BE safe in telling it. But it is still safer to ask.

This brings us to our last "B" (Whew! Finally!) **Belly-ache-ingly.**

Constant, continuous complaining. Never satisfied, always whining about something.

I had a friend once who never saw a bright side to anything. She complained so much that I finally had to distance myself from her company because her attitude was rubbing off on me. Nothing ever pleased and nothing ever suited. Even the best of things had a dark cloud over it if you looked long enough! She actually seemed to seek for things to complain about. This is not the attitude that the Lord wants us to have at all! People who are always complaining not only make themselves miserable, they make those around them miserable. A complaining attitude is many times simply a bad habit (an ungodly habit, I might add.) It is also contagious. If you don't believe it, go into a classroom full of children who are busy and peaceful and get one of them complaining about something. Before very long every child in the room will be unhappy in some form or other. They are either catching the attitude and complaining themselves, or they are unhappy because everyone else around them is unhappy.

The same holds true in our homes. If we have a cheerful, merry heart it will bubble out of the mouth with joy and praise. This attitude and pattern of speech will fill our homes with joy and happiness. Let someone come into the home with a sour attitude and a complaining spirit! Then see how fast all that happiness is quenched and everyone is at odds with one another!

A merry heart maketh a cheerful countenance: but by sorrow of the heart the spirit is broken. Proverbs 15:13

All the days of the afflicted are evil: but he that is of a merry heart hath a continual feast. Proverbs 15:15

A merry heart doeth good like a medicine: but a broken spirit drieth the bones. Proverbs 17:22

We are to be a rejoicing people. Our hearts are supposed to be full of joy and love and we are to be eagerly looking for the Lord's return. The peace of God is supposed to rule in our hearts.

And let the peace of God rule in your hearts, to the which also ye are called in one body; and be ye thankful. Colossians 3:15

Rejoice in the lord always: and again I say, Rejoice. Philippians 4:4

Rejoice evermore. 1 Thessalonians 5:16

What creates a whining, complaining attitude? Selfishness. We have our mind so self-absorbed that we cannot be pleased. What gives us the right to be so focused on ourselves that we think everything has to be done to our satisfaction? The Lord firmly judged the Children of Israel for complaining.

And when the people complained it displeased the LORD: and the LORD heard it; and his anger was kindled; and the fire of the LORD burnt among them, and consumed them that were in the uttermost parts of the camp. Numbers 11:1

He takes it pretty seriously, doesn't He? Our lives are supposed to be ruled by peace and our mouths are supposed to be always open to the praise of God. A down in the mouth, bitter, complaining attitude is a poor testimony. It is a bad reflection on the Savior. Why should people want what we have if we are always bellyaching about something?

Neither murmur ye, as some of them also murmured, and were destroyed of the destroyer. 1 Corinthians 10:10

What do we have to complain about? We are rescued from Hell and promised eternal life in the glories of Heaven. We have a tender loving Shepherd to guide us through each step we take here, who has promised He will never leave us nor forsake us! We are blessed far more than what we deserve!

Do all things without murmurings and disputings. Philippians 2:14

All things: That doesn't give us much room for complaint, does it? There is so much more that I could have given on the tongue! But this will suffice. We probably have enough here to keep us busy for the rest of our lives. Remember that the virtuous woman's mouth opened in wisdom and in her tongue is the law of kindness. Perhaps therefore, in a nutshell, it would do us well to simply follow this advice: If we don't know what we are talking about we should be silent – and if it's not kind it should not be coming from our tongues.

Let the words of my mouth, and the meditation of my heart, be acceptable in thy sight, O LORD, my strength, and my redeemer. Psalm 19:14

Set a watch, O LORD, before my mouth; keep the door of my lips. Psalm 141:3

Lesson Nineteen Review

1) Write the Scripture memory verses for this lesson:

_____

_____

_____

_____

2) What does 'prating' mean?

_____

3) What does 'fool' mean?

_____

_____

_____

4) What does 'blasphemy' mean?

_____

_____

_____

5) What is a Euphemism?

_____

_____

_____

6) What does 'froward' mean?

_____

_____

_____

7) What does 'perverse' mean?

_____

_____

_____

8) Define 'slander'

_____

9) Define 'whispering'

_____
_____
_____

10) Define 'malice'

_____
_____
_____

11) Define 'gossip'

_____
_____
_____

12) Define 'talebearing'

_____
_____
_____

13) Name the five 'B's that we should avoid in our speech and tell briefly what they mean

_____
_____
_____
_____
_____

14) Most of the time when a person is boasting it is an unrighteous attempt to put themselves on a _____ at someone else's _____.

15) God says that it is _____ not to think before you speak.

16) We should be so honest that saying _____ should have the same bond over us as if we had _____

17) Name 2 ways in which we might be guilty of blaspheming:

_____

_____

18) The best known weapon of the Baptist Church is the _____

19) Name the weapon-like uses of the tongue listed in this lesson:

_____

_____

_____

_____

_____

20) What is the difference between talebearing and gossip?

_____

_____

21) People who are always complaining not only make themselves _____ they also make _____

22) What creates a whining, complaining attitude?

_____

23) How many things in our lives should be done without murmurings and complainings? _____

24) What is the the simple advice to follow from our virtuous woman on how to control our tongues?

_____

_____

_____

A Woman Among all Those
Lessons in Christian Womanhood

Lesson 20

Scripture Memory: She looketh well to the ways of her household, and eateth not the bread of idleness. Proverbs 31:27

By much slothfulness the building decayeth; and through idleness of the hands the house droppeth through. Ecclesiastes 10:18

Do you look at your service to your family as your service to God? Look around your home and imagine that you are keeping it clean, decorated, organized, and running smoothly for the Lord - how does it measure up? The Virtuous Woman is a busy woman. She's not just looking to the ways of her household. She's looking well to them. Ask God to give you a fervent love for your home, and a desire to make it all you can make it for your family. Keep yourself busy. It is very rare that there is not enough in a household to do to keep a woman busy. If we examined ourselves honestly we would probably see that when we find ourselves "bored" it is not because we have nothing to do. It is usually because we have nothing that we WANT to do.

If you are one of those extremely rare individuals who is so organized that you have your whole home under control and you have so much time on your hands that you don't know what to do with it, then you may need to seek for an outlet of service in order to keep your mind in order. However, most of us are not blessed with that problem. No, when we spend our time on frivolous things, it is because we have let something more important go in order to amuse ourselves idly.

She eateth not the bread of idleness. What does the bread of idleness do? We eat because we are bored, not because we are hungry. Here's a no-brainer - - we get fat. I'm not saying that this is the only way in which we can gain unwanted weight, - there are lots of ways that it happens but this is definitely one way. Having time on your hands that is not filled with activity causes you to seek for something amusing or flesh satisfying to do and most of the time we eat when we are not really hungry. The things that we eat at those times are usually munchies and goodies, not healthy food. Then when we have filled ourselves with those things, we lose our desire for the healthy, necessary food.

Not only can the bread of idleness be physical junk food, but spiritual junk food as well. The Word of God is likened to our necessary bread. When we feed our senses on things that overshadow the Word of God in our lives, it is spiritual junk food. When you are idle, you are giving place to the devil and you are more likely to fill your mind and heart with the things that are empty space fillers. Then when your mind becomes absorbed with those "mind munchies" you will lose your desire for the spiritually healthy and more necessary food. This is a weight that drags us down in our service for God and our family.

Wherefore seeing we also are compassed about with so great a cloud of witnesses, let us lay aside every weight, and the sin which doth so easily beset us, and let us run with patience the race that is set before us, Hebrews 12:1

There are some things that we collect in our lives that are just excess baggage. These are things that may not be, in themselves, sinful. They are, instead, unnecessary things that slow down our service to God and cause us to be less effective. The end result of this IS sin, because of our attitudes. We could have done better for our Master, had we been willing to lay those things aside, and concentrate upon the things that really matter. Choosing to give the Lord less than your best is sin. These weights are not necessarily the same for all of us - but they have the same results. They are empty time wasters or they are things that focus our attention on things that do not really matter, thereby taking our minds off Christ. (Spiritual junk food.)

Picture in your mind a scene that is true behind more doors than many would believe. A home in chaos. Housework undone, laundry piling up, children ignorant, uncared for and left to amuse themselves as they choose and in the midst of it all find a very unhappy, overweight, spiritually immature woman. Not because she has done her best and cannot keep up but because she is the author of her own unhappiness. She spends her times in frivolous things, while the things that really matter lie waste. We might not necessarily fall into that category of extreme - but do we idly waste the time that God has given us? Can we do better for our Master?

307

Television, romance novels, daydreaming, video games, excessive sleep, etc. are huge wasters of the time that the Bible tells us is so precious.

The Lord is coming back - soon! We don't have much time left to serve Him. Our world is getting crazier by the moment and we, as the Children of God, are going to have to either take a stand for Christ or fall by the wayside. There will very soon be no middle ground. We MUST take our Christianity more seriously and with a much more dedicated, sober minded attitude than is generally displayed in this Laodocean age. When we stand before Him at the Judgment Seat of Christ, He is going to require an account from us of how we spent our time here - are we idle? The days are evil, people need to be saved. We need to be a pure and holy people before the Lord. The Lord has given us a physical and a spiritual responsibility to our husband and our children and to the church. The Bible tells us that if we are really looking for the Lord's return we would seek to purify our lives.

Redeeming the time, because the days are evil. Ephesians 5:16

And every man that hath this hope in him purifieth himself, even as he is pure. 1 John 3:3

Walk in wisdom toward them that are without, redeeming the time. Colossians 4:5

To redeem something means: To rescue; to recover; to deliver from. To redeem time, is to use more diligence in the improvement of it; to be diligent and active in duty and preparation. Do you spend your time in things that are pure? Purifying yourself as you are expecting the Lord's return? There are so many ways in which idleness is a breeding ground for sin. The Bible gives us several warnings against being idle and slothful because of the sin that it spawns. We need to take a close look at some of the bi-products of slothfulness and idleness.

Slothful means: Inactive; sluggish; lazy; indolent; idle.

Idle means: Not employed; unoccupied with business; inactive; doing nothing.

Slothfulness casteth into a deep sleep; and an idle soul shall suffer hunger. Proverbs 19:15

As the door turneth upon his hinges, so doth the slothful upon his bed. Proverbs 26:14

A slothful person is a person who would rather laze around and sleep than to do anything productive. And idle person is one who spends their time doing nothing that has any purpose. A spiritually slothful person is one who is too lazy to seek diligently after maturity in Christ, too interested in pleasing and appeasing the flesh to labor and spend themselves for the cause of Christ. And a spiritually idle person is one who fills their time with frivolous things that are unnecessary for the cause of Christ.

The slothful man roasteth not that which he took in hunting: but the substance of a diligent man is precious. Proverbs 12:27

He also that is slothful in his work is brother to him that is a great waster. Proverbs 18:9

Slothfulness causes a person to waste the resources that he has. He's too lazy to get up and do what is required. A slothful woman will allow food to rot in her refrigerator because she is too lazy to prepare it, then wish someone would take her out to eat. A slothful woman will let her laundry pile up until she has nothing to wear and then complain she has no clothes. She will let the dust and clutter collect and then day-dream of a housemaid. Spiritual slothfulness causes us to waste the talents and abilities that God has given us. It causes us to allow the home and the house of God to fall apart before us and we have an attitude of apathy.

Apathy means: Want of feeling; an utter privation of passion, or insensibility to pain; applied either to the body or the mind.

Apathy is an "I don't care" attitude. We have no right, as Christians to that attitude. Our lives should be governed by Romans 12:1-2 and 1 Corinthians 6:19. We are purchased possessions of the Saviour and every moment of our lives belongs to Him.

The way of the slothful man is as a hedge of thorns: but the way of the righteous is made plain. Proverbs 15:19

One bi-product of slothfulness is confusion. Sloth becomes a habit and like most bad habits, it turns around and bites. A slothful person becomes dull witted and can't concentrate on things requiring any energy. He's sleepy-headed. A spiritually slothful person cannot think with any energy on spiritual things. She is too lazy to put those spiritual things to practice in her life. As a result she is easily swayed into any false doctrine. The slothful person also easily drops out of church with very little provocation, sometimes over the most foolish things.

The slothful man saith, There is a lion without, I shall be slain in the streets. Proverbs 22:13

A slothful person is an excuse maker. He's always got a reason - usually one that makes no sense - for being lazy. And just as ridiculous as someone refusing to get up and go out of doors because they're afraid of lions in the city, a slothful person's excuses are too obvious for any really thinking person to swallow. Spiritually slothful people are the ones who "would have, could have, should have" done this or that for the Lord, but - well - they were hindered, or they didn't have opportunity, etc. etc.

A slothful man hideth his hand in his bosom, and will not so much as bring it to his mouth again. Proverbs 19:24

The desire of the slothful killeth him; for his hands refuse to labor. Proverbs 21:25

I went by the field of the slothful, and by the vineyard of the man void of understanding; And, lo, it was all grown over with thorns, and nettles had covered the face thereof, and the stone wall thereof was broken down. Then I saw, and considered it well: I looked upon it, and received instruction. Yet a little sleep, a little slumber, a little folding of the hands to sleep: So shall thy poverty come as one that traveleth; and thy want as an armed man.
Proverbs 24:30

This is definitely the biggest bi-product of sloth: loss. Loss of what could have been. He's lazy, so he goes without - at least the Bible says that a lazy person should go without and not be petted and pampered by the government. Be assured, God's judgments are more righteous. A spiritually slothful person will not have the spiritual food necessary for their growth because they're too lazy to feed themselves, too lazy to labor spiritually and will not take care of their spiritual business. The end results of this are saved people who never grow to maturity and a church full of people who have to be chased and babied to keep them in church. What right does the owner of the vineyard mentioned in this passage have to complain that he has no crop? What right does a spiritually slothful person have to complain when God does not bless? What right does a woman who fritters away her time have to complain that her household is in chaos? Whether it is physical labor or Spiritual labor, God tells us that we should be careful to labor with our might.

Not slothful in business; fervent in spirit; serving the Lord;   Romans 12:11

And whatsoever ye do, do it heartily, as to the Lord, and not unto men; Colossians 3:23

Slothful people tend to be great day-dreamers. Daydreaming is a huge waste of time - and a breeding ground for sin. Covetousness at best, immortality at worst - the mind needs to be kept under lock and key for the Lord. We are commanded to control it, and to bring it into subjection for Christ's sake.

Casting down imaginations, and every high thing that exalteth itself against the knowledge of God, and bringing into captivity every thought to the obedience of Christ; 2 Corinthians 10:5

The final bi-product of slothfulness that we will discuss is that we will be under tribute. That's because there's been no training, no labor and no watchfulness. Therefore when the enemy comes through, it's an easy takeover. When the devil attacks a spiritually slothful person, it's an easy takeover, because there's been no grounding in the Word of God, no loved and nurtured labor for the Lord, no watching for the Lord's return. Notice in the next verse that the stone wall of the slothful man's vineyard is broken down. It's an easy mark for any thief or spoiler. This vineyard could represent your home or it could represent your life as it bears fruit for the Lord. We need to be diligent, not slothful.

The hand of the diligent shall bear rule: but the slothful shall be under tribute. Proverbs 12:24

Now let's take a look at idleness. Idleness and slothfulness are almost the same thing, and both have serious repercussions. Whereas a slothful person may just laze around, an idle person may fill his life with activity - but it's empty activity that has no productive or eternal purpose. We have talked about this warning in 1 Timothy given specifically to women.

And withal they learn to be idle, wandering about from house to house; and not only idle, but tattlers also and busybodies, speaking things which they ought not. 1Timothy 5:13

Idleness causes us to lose control of our mouths and speak things we ought not. It is the breeding ground for gossip, tattling and a busybody attitude. A sure fire way to get yourself in trouble with your mouth is to be idle. If you are having trouble controlling your tongue, a good cure is to get busy about some things that really matter. All that we should need to know about whether or not it is a sin to be idle is found in Ezekiel:

Behold, this was the iniquity of thy sister Sodom, pride, fullness of bread, and abundance of idleness was in her and in her daughters, neither did she strengthen the hand of the poor and needy. Ezekiel 16:49

If abundance of idleness was one of the causes of the sinful lifestyle of Sodom - we certainly should do our best to be as productively busy as we can possibly be. The saying, "we should avoid it like the plague," certainly fits here. Immorality is definitely one bi-product of idleness. Either immorality in the actual commission of the flesh or immorality in the mind. When the mind is unoccupied with business, it becomes depraved in the things that it falls into. And the devil will make sure that it does. Lot's daughters are a good example of this. Genesis 19:29-36

Now these girls are an extreme, of course. They had been raised in one of the wickedest of all the cities ever known. Their mother had loved the things she was leaving behind in that wicked city so much that she turned to look back, which was her destruction. Their father had loved money and prestige so much that he had sacrificed his family for it. We could say that they had been raised in such a way that what they did was a natural

312

by-product. Their minds had been allowed to feed on filth, and that certainly planted the seed for their immorality. However, the fact that they were living in a cave with little or nothing to do, day in and day out, certainly contributed to their depravity of mind.

We do not need to look very far for the seed of immorality to be planted in our minds. It is plastered everywhere we look. Television portrays it, magazine stands scream it out and billboards wave it to passers-by. It is much easier in our world to live an immoral life than a moral one. So it is no wonder that we have a real battle keeping our minds in any form of purity at all. The sin comes in when we willingly take that display of immorality into our senses. When we purposely view those programs, read those books and magazines full of immoral stories, listen to country or pop music that exalts extra-marital relationships. We fill our minds full of junk and then wonder why we can't keep our thoughts pure. And - like it or not - the thoughts of the heart are the same in God's eyes as the commission of the flesh.

Ye have heard that it was said by them of old time, Thou shalt not commit adultery: But I say unto you, That whosoever looketh on a woman to lust after her hath committed adultery with her already in his heart. Matthew 5:27-28

What about "Christian" romance novels? Examine your books. Do they portray things that are not in keeping with godly principle? Do they present physical scenes before the imagination that do not need to be shared? Even if those things in the book are between man and wife - why are we being made privy to things that are private? And where does it cause our imaginations to go? Is this a book you would want your unmarried teenager reading? Also, many times those romance novels give an unrealistic view of life. I spoke with a young woman once who had been totally absorbed in reading every Christian romance novel she could get her hands on. Finally one day she, in tears, destroyed every one of them. Her testimony was that the male characters in the book had caused her to look at her husband with a critical eye. He did not measure up to the "perfect" men in those books and she found herself comparing him to them in her imagination. (Once she had purged them from her home, she also realized that she had let very necessary work go and time that she could have spent fellowshipping with her family, in order to have more time to read them.) Another young unmarried lady had given testimony of

313

reading those Christian romance novels and allowing her imagination to carry her further when the book stopped short with only a suggestion of the scenes. She found her mind in places that it did not belong.

We need to minutely careful about our "pastimes." Do the things that we use for our relaxation or for our amusement fill our minds with spiritual junk food that plants the seed of sin in our minds? We must be careful about what we pump into our minds. Everything that we choose to take into our minds through our eyes or ears should be able to stand the Philippians 4:8 test.

Finally, brethren, whatsoever things are true, whatsoever things are honest, whatsoever things are just, whatsoever things are pure, whatsoever things are lovely, whatsoever things are of good report; if there be any virtue, and if there be any praise, think on these things. Philippians 4:8

Perhaps our pleasure reading could be better if it were centered around missionary biographies, some of which are fascinating reading. If you do read fiction, be extremely careful about the books that you choose. Don't give the devil room to fill your mind with ungodly thoughts.

We might as well tackle the T.V. while we are here. Go ahead and throw something at me, if you must. But please don't shut me off with the attitude that Mrs. Mary just hates the television. Even people who have no interest in the Gospel or Christianity are recognizing that the majority of things that come across the air waves into the minds of people is not just questionable or unacceptable - it is vile. Ladies, please, please don't poison your minds by making it a garbage receptacle for the filth that comes across the T.V. (Just recently there was a complaint lodged against the CBS news broadcasters for using blatant homosexual slang terminology on their prime time program - slinging it as an insult toward conservatives. If we can't watch the news......)

This know also, that in the last days perilous times shall come. For men shall be lovers of their own selves, covetous, boasters, proud, blasphemers, disobedient to parents, unthankful, unholy, Without natural affection, trucebreakers, false accusers, incontinent, fierce, despisers of those that are good, Traitors, heady, highminded, lovers of pleasures more than lovers of God; Having a form of godliness, but denying the power thereof: from such turn away. For of this sort are they which creep into

314

houses, and lead captive silly women laden with sins, led away with divers lusts, Ever learning, and never able to come to the knowledge of the truth.   2 Timothy 3:1-7

Examine the verse above very carefully, and consider what the content of most television programming is and you will find that the plot of it falls somewhere within these verses. The television not only reflects self-love, covetousness, pride, blasphemy, rebellion and all of the other things listed, it teaches that these things are the proper, normal way of life and that Christianity needs to catch up with the times. Yet, when a preacher preaches that television viewing is spiritual suicide, people get angry and think he's crazy - why? Honestly, it is for one of two reasons. Either they cannot figure out what else to do with their leisure time or it's because their pleasure is more important to them than being right with God.

Look what the verse says about women. This sort creeps into houses and leads captive silly women laden with sins, led away with divers lusts. Soap operas are notorious for being huge time wasters and filth providers for the minds of women. Sit coms, variety shows and "adult" cartoons are full of profanity, sexual innuendos, rock music and ridicule of morality and Christianity. There are things that are aired in prime time television, on the major networks, that are actually pornographic. They excuse themselves because the show I am referring to is animated. You cannot possibly fill your minds with those things and be as strong for Christ as you should be. In fact you can't fill your mind with that kind of garbage and be strong for Christ at all! Where does that kind of thing fit, when we are told to be **holy** even as God is holy. Would that be His viewing choice? I could give you a list of Scriptures about keeping ourselves pure before God in mind and body - but we'll just look at two.

What? know ye not that your body is the temple of the Holy Ghost which is in you, which ye have of God, and ye are not your own? For ye are bought with a price: therefore glorify God in your body, and in your spirit, which are God's. 1Corinthians 6:19-20

Neither give place to the devil. Ephesians 4:27

One more quick note: While you are considering the damage to your own mind and spiritual condition that the television causes, consider the damage to your children. So many mothers find that an easy scape goat to get out of the effort required in actual parenting is to turn on the tube and let the little ones go into the "mindless zone." They sit mesmerized in front of the thing. That way they don't bother you and you can get some stuff done! All of the things I have mentioned above are enough reason to protect your children from what comes across this destroyer of minds and morality but there are a few other things to note. Do a little research – it doesn't take much.

The National Pediatric Association has put out repeated warnings about the damaging effects of "screen time" (this includes television, computer, cell phone and video device usage) on children. Here is their recommendation: NO screen time for children under two years of age. They recommend only one to two hours per day TOTAL screen time for children between the ages of 2 and 19. I have read several articles in which the rise of autism since the 1970's and today has been linked to the rise in television viewing by infants and toddlers. It is certain that it is not good for them. The average television show changes it's scenes every three seconds. That is far too quickly for the child's brain to process what it is seeing. It throws them into a hypnotic state.

One doctor made the statement that the rapidly changing scenes and continuous input into the brain, without an outlet for the energy they are absorbing, creates an unsettled, almost explosive need for the release of energy. Hence hyperactivity, attention deficit disorder and unexplained violent outbursts by children. These are not my own statements. The information is available in libraries and on the web for anyone who chooses to do the research. In fact the Russian-born inventor of the television, Kosma Zworykin, made the statement, "I would never let my children even come close to this thing." Unless your mind is closed completely to the subject, you cannot deny that all of the facts show that T.V., internet and video games are very dangerous to the minds and development of children.

Another weight that has become an all-consuming passion for a lot of people is video games. Now, in themselves, some video games are innocent. Some are even educational. They build word skills, vocabulary, math skills, etc. But one problem is that video games can be very, **very** addicting. They are great time absorbers - and for what purpose? So many times when people get wrapped up in video games, their families take second place. Children are left to fend for themselves, the husband or the

316

wife are denied fellowship time. Especially dangerous, and in many cases satanic, are the role playing video games. There are Christians who spend literally hours a day planted in front of a computer playing role-playing video games on the internet. What a weight! What a way to waste your life! To some of these people the game becomes more real than life is. I have known of people who let their entire home life, their entire real life go, and are absorbed almost around the clock with those games.

My husband recently received an e-mail from a veteran missionary who was justifying his all-consuming involvement in a role-playing video game by saying that it gave him an outlet to witness to the other players in the game. Not exactly what the Lord had in mind when He sent out missionaries to "go into all the world and preach the gospel to every creature." There are churches supporting this Independent Baptist missionary so that he can sit in front of his computer and play video games!

Another recent outrage erupted from a role playing game that was approved for teen play which allows the character to engage in homosexual activity as one of the options during play. This option was hidden in the question/response portion of the game, not advertised ahead of time. Can you imagine allowing your youngster to play this game, only to find out later that this was a part of it? We have all been warned and warned about the violence content of video games. We have a friend in juvenile prison work who spoke with one of the boys who killed so many young people at the Columbine High School shooting. He was addicted to video games.

There is a principle of replacement in the Word of God. If you will honor God by removing these weights from your life, please replace them with something holy. Read good books, surround yourself with gospel music, spend time with your family, get involved in service for the Lord, find a creative project that you enjoy. If you don't replace a weight in your life with something that will honor Christ, you will either pick up another idle habit that is as bad or worse, or you will go back to the same one with twice the energy. God likens this Christian life to an athlete keeping himself in shape and running a race.

Know ye not that they which run in a race run all, but one receiveth the prize? So run, that ye may obtain. And every man that striveth for the mastery is temperate in all things. Now they do it to obtain a corruptible crown; but we an incorruptible. I therefore so run, not as uncertainly; so fight I, not as one that beateth the air: But I keep under my body, and bring it into subjection: lest that by any means, when I have preached to others, I myself should be a castaway.   1 Corinthians 9:24-27

When an athlete trains, his life is focused upon getting himself and keeping himself in top notch condition so that he will be a contender for the prize. He is careful about what he eats, how much sleep he gets, that he balances the right amount of practice and training with the proper amount of rest. He seeks to keep himself physically and also mentally prepared for the competition. God expects us to do the same. We are to be careful about what we feed our spirits. An athlete cannot be a contender if he feeds on junk food. We cannot be a Spiritual contender if we feed on what the world offers. He cannot be a contender if he is dragged down and out because of lack of sleep or proper rest - neither can we. We are told to rest in the Lord and wait patiently for Him, to delight ourselves in the Lord. An athlete cannot be a contender if he does not train and practice, if he doesn't know the rules for his competition. We cannot be a Spiritual contender if we do not learn the Word of God and practice it in our lives. We need, as well as he does, to be mentally prepared for the competition. Consistent prayer and Bible study is a must, as well as faithfulness to walk as close to the Lord as we can possibly get.

The other thing that the Bible likens our Christian walk to is a soldier preparing for battle.

No man that warreth entangleth himself with the affairs of this life; that he may please him who hath chosen him to be a soldier. And if a man also strive for masteries, yet is he not crowned, except he strive lawfully. 2 Timothy 2:4-5

A soldier who is preparing for battle must dedicate himself completely to the cause. He cannot be wrapped up in the things of his "pre-soldier" life, he can't spend his time concentrating on anything but the task before him. I recently asked a young man who had returned from Iraq, "What happens to the soldiers that are so wrapped up in personal problems that they cannot concentrate on the battle around them?" His answer was very short and simple, "They die." If you allow yourself to become so wrapped up in the world and the unnecessary weights that the world has to offer you,

Christ will become a faded ornament in your life instead of the main focus of your existence. He should be your all-consuming passion. His Word should be your everyday speech. His desires should be your desires.

Jesus said unto him, Thou shalt love the Lord thy God with all thy heart, and with all thy soul, and with all thy mind. Matthew 22:37

Keep thy heart with all diligence; for out of it are the issues of life. Proverbs 4:23

If we are to keep our hearts with all diligence, it does not leave any room for spiritual slothfulness or for filling our lives with empty, spiritual junk food. Am I saying that we can never do anything for pleasure - no, that's silly! But be EXTREMELY careful of the pleasurable pastimes that you choose. Give them the tests that I listed above. Make sure that the Lord is pleased. If you are not sure that the Lord would be pleased with what you are doing, then you should not be doing it.

And he that doubteth is damned if he eat, because he eateth not of faith: for whatsoever is not of faith is sin. Romans 14:23

The Lord is coming back very soon. I would not be surprised to hear the trumpet sound today. When He looks at us, on that wonderful, eventful day, will he be pleased with how we have been spending our time? He gave us, over and over again, throughout the gospels, the example of Himself as a landowner leaving a steward behind to carry out the work. And we are told each time, that He will require an account of what we have been doing. I hope with all of my heart that we will hear, "Well done, thou good and faithful servant."

This is a portion of a poem from the novel by Roald Dahl, Charlie and the Chocolate Factory written in the 1960's. (The television version of this book completely left this out, which – along with other things they changed and omitted – enraged Mr. Dahl to the point where he refused to sell television rights to any of his other works.)

The most important thing we've learned
As far as children are concerned, is never, Never, NEVER let
Them near your television set.
Or better still, just don't install
The idiotic thing at all.
In almost every house we've been,
We've watched them gaping at the screen.
They loll and slop and lounge about,
And stare until their eyes pop out.
(Last week in someone's place we saw
A dozen eyeballs on the floor.)
They sit and stare and stare and sit
Until they're hypnotized by it,
Until they're absolutely drunk
With all that shocking ghastly junk.
Oh yes, we know it keeps them still,
They never fight or kick or punch,
They leave you free to cook the lunch
And wash the dishes in the sink –
But did you ever stop to think,
To wonder just exactly what
This does to your beloved tot?
It rots the senses in the head!
It kills imagination dead!
It clogs and clutters up the mind!
It makes a child so dull and blind
He can no longer understand
A fantasy, a fairyland
His brain becomes as soft as cheese!
His powers of thinking rust and freeze!
He cannot think – he only sees!
'All right!' you'll cry, 'All right!' you'll say,
'But if we take the set away,
What shall we do to entertain

Our darling children? Please explain!'
We'll answer this by asking you,
'What used the darling ones to do?
How used they keep themselves contented
Before this monster was invented?'
Have you forgotten? Don't you know?
We'll say it very loud and slow:
They…Used….To….Read!

Oh, books, what books they used to know,
Those children living long ago!
So please, oh please, we beg, we pray
Go throw your TV set away,
And in its place you can install
A lovely bookshelf on the wall.
Then fill the shelves with lots of books
Ignoring all the dirty looks,
The screams and yells, the bites and kicks,
And children hitting you with sticks –
Fear not, because we promise you
That, in about a week or two
Of having nothing else to do,
They'll now begin to feel the need
Of having something good to read.
And once they start – oh boy, oh boy!
You'll watch the slowly growing joy
That fills their hearts. They'll grow so keen
They'll wonder what they'd ever seen
In that ridiculous machine,
That nauseating, foul, unclean,
Repulsive television screen!
And later, each and every kid
Will love you more for what you did.

Lesson Twenty Review

1) Write this lesson's Scripture passage:

_____

_____

_____

_____

2) What does redeem mean?

_____

_____

_____

3) What does slothful mean?

_____

_____

_____

4) What does idle mean?

_____

_____

_____

5) When we find ourselves bored, it is usually not because we do not have anything to do, but that we:

_____

6) What does the bread of idleness do?

_____

7) What does apathy mean?

_____

8) The bread of idleness can be physical _____ or spiritual

_____.

9) What is the difference between a sin and a weight?

_____

_____

10) List several things that can be a weight in your life

_____

_____

_____

11) The Bible says that a slothful person is brother to a great
_____ therefore he does not use the resources that he
has.

12) A spiritually slothful person will have an attitude of

_____

13) A slothful person becomes _____ and can't
_____ on things that requires any energy.

14) A spiritually slothful person easily _____ with very
little provocation, and some times_____

15) The biggest bi-product of sloth is: _____

16) Slothful people tend to be great

_____

17) When the devil attacks a spiritually slothful person, it's an easy
takeover, because:

_____

_____

18) Whereas a slothful person may just laze around, an idle person may
fill his life with activity - but

_____

19) Idleness causes us to lose _____ of our_____
and _____ things we ought not.

20) Immorality can be either in the actual _____ or it
can be _____

21) List 3 pastimes that are idle weights in many people's lives:

_____
_____
_____

22) List 2 things that the Bible likens the Christian to:

_____

_____

23) We cannot be a Spiritual contender if we

_____

24) If you allow yourself to become so wrapped up in the world and the unnecessary weights that the world has to offer you, Christ will become a _____ instead of the _____ .

25) If you are not sure that the Lord would be pleased with what you are doing, _____

A Woman Among all Those
Lessons in Christian Womanhood

Lesson 21

Scripture memory: Her children arise up, and call her blessed; her husband also, and he praiseth her. Many daughters have done virtuously, but thou excellest them all. Proverbs 31:28-29

The LORD recompense thy work, and a full reward be given thee of the LORD God of Israel, under whose wings thou art come to trust. Ruth 2:12

This part of the passage begins what I call the summary of the chapter on the Virtuous Woman. It mentions the result and reward of her lifetime of labor, and her submission to God.

What a contrast from modern, secular life! How many children in this age show that kind of respect and honor to their mother? Look! They are rising up before her in respect and calling her blessed. "I have a blessed mother!" Doesn't that sound sweet? How many husbands are praising their wives instead of criticizing them behind their backs or outlining all their faults to their working buddies. Does the problem actually lie with rebellious, unappreciative children and with selfish, complaining husbands? Could our lack of reward possibly be a result of a society of women who have not done virtuously? I believe firmly that this is exactly where the problem lies.

These verses in Proverbs 31 list each progression of a woman's life - in reverse. She is a mother, a wife, a daughter. Let's take a look at an example from the Word of God of a virtuous woman in each of these roles, and see why she was praised. Let's start with the daughter.

Esther 2:7,10,20 Esther was not actually Mordecai's daughter, but he raised her as his daughter. The Bible specifically praises the fact that Esther was submissive to Mordecai and did his commandment - even when, to the outsider's eye, it was no longer necessary for her to do so.

It is rare when a young lady takes the Bible as her guide and, in spite of the trend of society, chooses to remain at home under the protection and rules of her parents after she reaches the age that our society deems she is an adult. She is many times looked down on as "oppressed" or "strange." The Bible, on the other hand, praises that young lady. The protection offered to a young person by staying in a Christian home until marriage goes without saying. A child who jumps from the nest at the vulnerable age of 18 and runs out to start a life of their own is, in most cases, not ready for the responsibilities and headaches of maintaining their own home. Not only that, a young woman who enters a courtship without the guidance of her parents usually ends up making some very bad mistakes. In a home where God is in control, parents should be involved in the courtship process, as well as involved in guiding young people with some of their first financial decisions and most definitely in offering spiritual guidance. Whether or not the parents are involved in these things is a conscious choice that the young person themselves must make as they reach the age to stretch their wings. Of those young people of my acquaintance who have made the decision to keep themselves under the authority of their godly parents, every one of them (and I know quite a few) have later given testimony that they do not regret the decision to stay under their parents' guidance. I know a few who wish they had stayed longer but I do not know any who say that they wish they had launched themselves from the home and gone out on their own earlier.

My son, hear the instruction of thy father, and forsake not the law of thy mother: Proverbs 1:8

Hearken unto thy father that begat thee, and despise not thy mother when she is old. Proverbs 23:22

For this cause shall a man leave his father and mother, and cleave to his wife; Mark 10:7

I have mentioned before that the Bible makes no specific commandment concerning when a young woman should leave home. The reason for this is, simply, because it was an unheard of thing in Bible times for a young woman to leave her home until she became a bride. There was no issue there. It is our modern society - and only in recent years - that sends a young woman out on her own to be a "career girl." That is not the way that God set up the home. The closest thing that we have to a commandment in this respect is to look at what was done with widows.

And Naomi said unto her two daughters in law, Go, return each to her mother's house: the LORD deal kindly with you, as ye have dealt with the dead, and with me. Ruth 1:8

Then said Judah to Tamar his daughter in law, Remain a widow at thy father's house, till Shelah my son be grown: for he said, Lest peradventure he die also, as his brethren did. And Tamar went and dwelt in her father's house. Genesis 38:11

But if the priest's daughter be a widow, or divorced, and have no child, and is returned unto her father's house, as in her youth, she shall eat of her father's meat: but there shall no stranger eat thereof. Leviticus 22:13

In this case they were to return to their father's house and we see no instance in the Bible of a young, unmarried woman living alone outside of her father's house. It is a pretty sure thing that God did not intend for young women to be living out on their own outside of marriage. Does that mean that one who does is not right with God? No, not necessarily. I can think of a couple of situations that I know of where the young woman has had no choice but live on her own. What I am saying is that a young woman with godly parents should make the choice to remain under the authority of those parents for as long as she can, preferably until she is given in marriage.

Esther was praised as a daughter because of her obedience. Honest, real obedience from the heart is not only a difficult thing to find in our society, it is also a difficult thing for a woman to do. We are willing enough to obey until it pinches our desires. Then a woman who does not flare up in blatant rebellion will resort to the next, sneakier form of rebellion: manipulation and persuasion. Isn't it a universally recognized fact that a daughter has persuasion powers with her father that a son can never attain? She knows just how to turn the eyes. Even the tiniest tot figures out just the right amount of pout to give to the lips to melt a 200 pound mass of muscle into a bowl of jelly. I'm sorry to have to give you the news, young ladies, "turning on the charm" to get your way is ungodly. It is deception and unrighteous manipulation. What you are trying to do is to bend his will to yours. You are supposed to be in obedience and subjection to HIS will, not the other way around. I have known many, many girls who think this is a really funny game but the Bible doesn't consider it quite so funny.

As a mad man who castest firebrands, arrows, and death, So is the man that deceiveth his neighbour, and saith, Am not I in sport?
Proverbs 26:18-19

Deception in any form is wrong. It is deceptive to use your "womanly wiles" to get your way – with your father or with your husband.

The next step in a woman's life is as a **wife**. The virtuous woman is praised as a wife also. Her husband praises her. The Bible sets Sarah up to be the example of a wife. Why?

Likewise, ye wives, be in subjection to your own husbands; that, if any obey not the word, they also may without the word be won by the conversation of the wives; While they behold your chaste conversation coupled with fear. Whose adorning let it not be that outward adorning of plaiting the hair, and of wearing of gold, or of putting on of apparel; But let it be the hidden man of the heart, in that which is not corruptible, even the ornament of a meek and quiet spirit, which is in the sight of God of great price. For after this manner in the old time the holy women also, who trusted in God, adorned themselves, being in subjection unto their own husbands: Even as Sara obeyed Abraham, calling him lord: whose daughters ye are, as long as ye do well, and are not afraid with any amazement. 1 Peter 3:1-6

Looking at some specific things about this passage that praises Sarah, we see that the women they referred to in the old time were first of all holy women.

Holy means: Properly, whole, entire or perfect, in a moral sense. Hence, pure in heart, temper or dispositions; free from sin and sinful affections. Applied to the Supreme Being, holy signifies perfectly pure, immaculate and complete in moral character; and man is more or less holy as his heart is more or less sanctified, or purified from evil dispositions. We call a man holy, when his heart is conformed in some degree to the image of God, and his life is regulated by the divine precepts. Hence, holy is used as nearly synonymous with good, pious, godly.

Notice especially in the definition that someone who is holy is conformed to the image of God and his life is regulated by the Bible.
The next thing that we see is that they trusted in God.

They had a faith of their own. They did not try to ride in on the coat-tail of their parents' faith or their husband's faith, but they developed a relationship with God of their own.

Then that they adorned themselves with the hidden man of the heart, the ornament of a meek and quiet spirit. (which is in the sight of God of great price!) These women were not flashy and showy in the flesh. Their ornamentation was to be a modest and a godly woman. The thing that they wished to show to the world more than anything else was not their clothes or hair, but their true relationship with the Savior.

And the last thing that it mentions is that they were in subjection to their own husbands, which is where it makes the comparison with Sarah. Sarah called Abraham, "lord." The Bible tells us that our attitude toward our husbands should be not just respect, but reverence.

Nevertheless let every one of you in particular so love his wife even as himself; and the wife see that she reverence her husband. Ephesians 5:33

A lord is defined as: A master; a person possessing supreme power and authority; a ruler; a governor. Submission goes a step farther than obedience. You can obey outwardly without submitting the heart. Reverence takes it a step farther than that. Reverence means: to regard with fear mingled with respect and affection. We reverence superiors for their age, their authority and their virtues. We ought to reverence parents and upright judges and magistrates. We ought to reverence the Supreme Being, his word and his ordinances.

Ladies, "reverence" is a pretty big word. In today's society there is very little respect shown toward husbands by their wives, much less reverence. The husband is belittled and downgraded to a woman's friends. Many times mothers will even criticize their husbands to their children. He's called, "my old man," and quite a few less flattering titles. When he attempts to step into his place of God given authority in the home he is, many times, ignored by a rebellious woman who will sigh, roll her eyes at him and then do what she pleases in spite of him. That's not reverence. An irreverent, rebellious mother will sometimes even teach their children, either in action or in words, how to get around their father's rules and wishes. That is SO ungodly!

As a young wife, and a young Christian -- I had been saved for just slightly over one year when my husband and I married -- I had a large battle with subjection to my husband. I was not raised in a Christian home, and I was taught from my earliest years to be independent and resourceful, and to 'stand up and be my own person.' Every time I heard submission preached I cringed because I knew the rebellion flaring in my heart. Sometimes I would even, rather weakly, try to be submissive - until he crossed me, of course! Bless his heart, what a patient man! How he prayed for me in those early days!! It finally clicked one day as I listened to a woman teaching on submission. (Again! Sigh! Will they never shut up about that?!) I had always been of the opinion that my husband was supposed to take the reins and drive me into submission, with me kicking and screaming all the way! But she turned to the passage in Ephesians and said, "Read this out loud." "Wives submit yourselves..." "STOP," she said, "read it again." "Wives submit yourselves..." About the third or fourth time she had us do that, it finally came into focus - it's MY job, not his. Well...the Lord and I had a long, long talk. The end result was that, of my own choice, and without any prompting from anyone, I began to call my husband - no, not "lord," but "sir." For several years I called him, "sir" when he spoke to me. I received every reaction, from the women around me, from disbelief to amusement to anger when they heard me refer to him that way, but I swallowed my pride and did it anyway. Why? Because I wanted to be right with God, and I knew from the Scripture that I could not be right with God and not reverence my husband. Only God knew how deeply rooted the independence and rebellion was in my heart. Every time I called my husband, "sir," it reminded me of God's command that I "submit myself." And once the battle was fully won in my heart, the "sir" habit slipped away unnoticed by both of us, never needed again.

Praise means: Commendation bestowed on a person for his personal virtues or worthy actions, on meritorious actions themselves, or on any thing valuable; approbation expressed in words or song.

Oh, how sweet to the ears of a woman who desires godliness to hear her husband praise her!! His praise means more than all the commendation that anyone else can give. He knows her better than anyone else on earth, and his honest, sincere praise is worth its weight in gold.

A virtuous woman is a crown to her husband: but she that maketh ashamed is as rottenness in his bones. Proverbs 12:4

On the other hand...

A continual dropping in a very rainy day and a contentious woman are alike. Whosoever hideth her hideth the wind, and the ointment of his right hand, which bewrayeth itself. Proverbs 27:15-16

My mind goes back to our days in Bible school, where a young missionary was struggling to begin his deputation. His wife was young in the Lord and very rebellious and outspoken. She had made quite an impression on the folks around her. An impression anything but good! The poor man loved his wife. From time to time he would venture a word in her defense or a weak attempt to compliment something she had done. No one spoke up against her, praise God! But the looks that passed almost unconsciously back and forth reminded me every time of this verse. No matter how much he tried to sweeten the matter - she had overpowered it by her rebellious nature and complaining spirit. He couldn't hide it. On the other hand there was, in the same Bible school, another young couple. When that young man spoke out in praise of his wife every head nodded in agreement. She was, in all appearance, everything that a virtuous woman ought to be - a crown to her husband - and he loved to praise her! Even more true than with a daughter, true reverence and submission leave no place in our lives to cajole and manipulate our husbands.

The word cajole means: To flatter; to soothe; to coax; to deceive or delude by flattery.

Let's take a look at the downfall of the most physically strong man in history.

And Samson's wife wept before him, and said, Thou dost but hate me, and lovest me not: thou hast put forth a riddle unto the children of my people, and hast not told it me. And he said unto her, Behold, I have not told it my father nor my mother, and shall I tell it thee? And she wept before him the seven days, while their feast lasted: and it came to pass on the seventh day, that he told her, because she lay sore upon him: and she told the riddle to the children of her people. Judges 14:16-17

It is not submission nor reverence to pout and cry phony tears to your husband to manipulate his will. It is not submission nor reverence to attempt to get your way in an underhanded manner, any more than open "in your face" rebellion is submission. A woman should never use tears and sullenness as a weapon against her husband's will.

Another weapon that women sometimes use to get their way with their husband is the weapon that Delilah used.

And she said unto him, How canst thou say, I love thee, when thine heart is not with me? Thou hast mocked me these three times, and hast not told me wherein thy great strength lieth. And it came to pass, when she pressed him daily with her words, and urged him, so that his soul was vexed unto death; That he told her all his heart, and said unto her, There hath not come a razor upon mine head; for I have been a Nazarite unto God from my mother's womb: if I be shaven, then my strength will go from me, and I shall become weak, and be like any other man. Judges 16:15-17

"You don't really love me....if you did, you would....." Wrong! Wrong! Wrong! Notice that the Bible says that she pressed him daily until his soul was vexed unto death. A man that truly loves a woman desires to please her. When he finds out that she is petulant and difficult to please he becomes frustrated and miserable. You are not reverencing your husband if you become difficult to please and peevish if you don't get your way. You are being unrighteously manipulative.

The final weapon, that women use, is to hold their personal relationship with their husband over his head like a treat to be given to an obedient dog. It really should go without saying that this is ungodly – but we'll go ahead and address it. If you have been guilty of this wicked behavior, go ahead and be warned – you are not going to like what I have to say!

Let the husband render unto the wife due benevolence: and likewise also the wife unto the husband. The wife hath not power of her own body, but the husband: and likewise also the husband hath not power of his own body, but the wife. Defraud ye not one the other, except it be with consent for a time, that ye may give yourselves to fasting and prayer; and come together again, that Satan tempt you not for your incontinency. 1 Corinthians 7:3-5

I have always found it amusing that the Bible refers to the physical relationship between husband and wife as benevolence. But, when you think about it, in its truest form benevolence is giving – and giving from the heart because of love. Notice that the Bible says we are not to defraud one another, that's also a very interesting term.

Defraud means: To deprive of right, either by obtaining something by deception or artifice, or by taking something wrongfully without the knowledge or consent of the owner; to cheat; to cozen; followed by or before the thing taken; as to defraud a man of his right.

When you feel that your personal time with your husband is something that you can give or withhold according to your whim, regardless as to his wants or needs, you are defrauding him. You are taking something from him that is his right. If you are holding out because you want to manipulate him into doing what you please first, then mark it down – you are selling your favors to him. A woman who sells her body is a prostitute. It is never reverence, respect, or submission to manipulate your husband's will and bend it to your own, regardless of the means that you use to do so. The choice is really ours ladies. No one can conform us, it is our job to conform ourselves to God's design for our lives. The virtuous woman is also a mother worthy of praise. Her children are rising up - that's a display of respect, an expression of honor - and calling her blessed:

Blessed means: Happy; prosperous in worldly affairs; enjoying spiritual happiness and the favor of God; enjoying heavenly felicity.

Let's take a look at a couple of women in the Bible and see why they were praised as mothers.

When I call to remembrance the unfeigned faith that is in thee, which dwelt first in thy grandmother Lois, and thy mother Eunice; and I am persuaded that in thee also. 2 Timothy 1:5

Lois and Eunice were Timothy's grandmother and mother. Notice what Paul says about them here. Their faith was unfeigned.

Feigned means: Invented; devised; imagined; assumed.

Therefore, something that is unfeigned is real beyond doubt. You can never do anything before your children that is more important to their lives than to show them that your faith in Christ is real. There are parents that look at their children and say, "I don't know how in the world I managed to raise them for the Lord, because I made so many mistakes!" Haven't we all? But the difference can usually be found in that, even though they may have made more blunders than right moves in their parenting, those kids knew that when it came to God, their parents were real. The real battle with parenting, the ultimate goal in raising children, is for your children to develop their own relationship with God - God will see to the rest. If we could only get it through our heads that their salvation and their relationship with God is more important than ANYTHING else in their lives! The Bible tells us there are two important matters in our lives where we should be sure to be genuine beyond all doubt. One is in our love toward one another, and the other is in our faith. The two walk hand in hand, you cannot have one without the other.

By pureness, by knowledge, by longsuffering, by kindness, by the Holy Ghost, by love unfeigned, 2 Corinthians 6:6

Now the end of the commandment is charity out of a pure heart, and of a good conscience, and of faith unfeigned: 1 Timothy 1:5

Seeing ye have purified your souls in obeying the truth through the Spirit unto unfeigned love of the brethren, see that ye love one another with a pure heart fervently: 1 Peter 1:22

Our love toward one another is supposed to be pure and fervent. Not a façade that falls away when it does not suit our convenience to show that love any longer. Love that is feigned is love that is show only. By the same token, faith that is feigned is faith that is show only. It is really easy to put on a show of faith when things are going well but how do your children see you during the hard times? How does your faith hold up when the money's not there? When you are stretched to the max emotionally? How does your faith hold up when the whole world seems to be crashing in? Can you show them that God is still God even in those times? Do you turn to prayer in the hard times? Do you pray with your children about it? Do you rejoice openly when God answers prayer and gather your children around you to thank God for answering? How about when life becomes hum-drum and boring? Does your faith and your dedication hold up? Do you remain faithful and ask God to shake you out of your rut? Or do you display your boredom with the things of God before your children, so that they catch it from you? Children are very discerning little characters and you cannot very easily pull hypocrisy over on them. They know when you are making excuses for not serving God as you should. They know when you are pretending to love the preacher, or the brethren and yet you badmouth them when they are not around.

Our love toward one another is also to be without dissimulation. The Lord said that all men would know that we were His disciples because of our love for one another. We need to openly display our love for God's people before our children. It is that love for God and love for His church (the brethren) that will let your children know that your faith is unfeigned. Go ahead! Get involved in the lives of the people in your church. Yes, you might get hurt - in fact you probably **will** somewhere along the line. But the love of God's people is well worth the risk. Not only that, it is a direct command of God! (See that ye love one another with a pure heart, fervently.)

Let love be without dissimulation. Abhor that which is evil; cleave to that which is good. Romans 12:9

Dissimulation means: The act of dissembling; a hiding under a false appearance; a feigning; false pretension; hypocrisy.

Fervently means: Earnestly; eagerly; vehemently; with great warmth.

We need to put some eager, earnest effort into our love for the brethren and it needs to be genuine, from the heart. If you cannot love God's people in this way, ask God for the love that you should have and ask Him to make it real in your heart.

Along with the obvious reason, that God has no use for hypocrisy, a good reason for our faith to be unfeigned is what happened in the life of Timothy. It is contagious. It is hereditary. If we want our children to grow up to love and honor God, we must love and honor God openly and sincerely in our lives. Don't be a silent, underhanded Christian. Display your faith if you want it repeated in your children's lives. We've heard the old saying, "like mother, like daughter." Ever wonder where that saying came from?

Behold, every one that useth proverbs shall use this proverb against thee, saying, As is the mother, so is her daughter. Thou art thy mother's daughter, that lotheth her husband and her children; and thou art the sister of thy sisters, which lothed their husbands and their children: your mother was an Hittite, and your father an Amorite. Ezekiel 16:44-45

The word lothe means: Disliking; unwilling; reluctant.

How awful to think that your daughter would lothe her husband because she saw it in your life first! How awful to think that a mother would teach a daughter to neglect and lothe her children! We should be extremely careful about what we are teaching them through our example. Many times the spiritual struggles that children will have comes from the failures of their parents in example. We should walk circumspectly.

See then that ye walk circumspectly, not as fools, but as wise, Ephesians 5:15

Circumspect means: Cautious; prudent; watchful on all sides; examining carefully all the circumstances that may affect a determination, or a measure to be adopted.

If we are walk circumspectly before our children we are going to watch carefully what our example to them will be. This is so important, not only with our children, but with every person who sees us. We should be ever mindful of the example that we set before others. Christianity is deteriorating in character and quality before our eyes and the fault lies with Christians who will not walk in Christian character before others, so that they may follow in godly footsteps. The Lord told the Children of Israel to be constantly mindful that they kept Him before the eyes of their children. When they failed in that task, their children forgot the Lord and degraded into idolatry. The end result was that God judged his people severely, giving them over to captivity.

336

Specially the day that thou stoodest before the LORD thy God in Horeb, when the LORD said unto me, Gather me the people together, and I will make them hear my words, that they may learn to fear me all the days that they shall live upon the earth, and that they may teach their children. Deuteronomy 4:10

And these words, which I command thee this day, shall be in thine heart: And thou shalt teach them diligently unto thy children, and shalt talk of them when thou sittest in thine house, and when thou walkest by the way, and when thou liest down, and when thou risest up. Deuteronomy 6:6-7

My people are destroyed for lack of knowledge: because thou hast rejected knowledge, I will also reject thee, that thou shalt be no priest to me: seeing thou hast forgotten the law of thy God, I will also forget thy children. Hosea 4:6

One of the most important parts of acknowledging your faith before your children is to let them know that you are a sinner. Let them know that you had to be saved, just as they will have to be saved in order to go to heaven. Acknowledge that you still sin and must ask for forgiveness. They don't need to know every struggle that you have spiritually but they do need to know that you know that you haven't arrived. Some small children firmly believe their parents are perfect. When they first find out that they are not, it's devastating to them. Prepare them for it. Prepare them, too, for the idea that they are not perfect and will have to come to God again and again for forgiveness. Let them know that God is holy and that He does not approve of or excuse sin in any way. But also let them know that He is loving and forgiving and has paid every penalty for the sin for which we could never pay.

The virtuous woman's children are rising up before her in respect, they are calling her blessed (enjoying spiritual happiness and the favor of God.) Many, many a young person has given the testimony that the only reason that they came to Christ was because of the prayer of a godly mother. Many a young person has been kept from sin and harm because of the picture in their minds of a mother who was praying for them, a mother whose faith was unfeigned.

During the course of this study we've seen a lot of reasons why the virtuous woman should be praised. Here's a good example of why she's worthy that praise and respect: She chooses to be obedient, even when that obedience is not required of her in the eyes of the world around her. She chooses reverence and respect, even in the face of a world that tells her to be independent and encourages her to belittle and criticize her husband. She submits from the heart, even when her wants and desires could be granted with a little underhandedness. She displays unfeigned faith - she's completely real when it comes to her faith in God. She is displaying a life that is holy, trusting God, adorned with the hidden man of the heart, the ornament of a meek and quiet spirit.

Wouldn't it be wonderful for your children to arise up and call you blessed? Wouldn't it be a wonderful thing to have your husband praise you as the best of wives? But even more than all, wouldn't it be a wonderful thing to have the Lord look at us and say, "Many daughters have done virtuously, but thou excellest them all?"

Lesson Twenty One Review

1) Write this week's memory passages:

_____

_____

_____

_____

2) What does 'holy' mean?

_____

_____

_____

_____

3) What does 'lord' mean?

_____

_____

4) What does 'reverence' mean?

_____

_____

_____

_____

5) What does 'praise' mean?

_____

_____

_____

6) What does 'cajole' mean?

_____

_____

_____

7) What does 'defraud' mean?

_____

_____

_____

8) What does 'blessed' mean?

_____

_____

_____

9) What does 'feigned' mean?

_____

_____

_____

10) What does 'dissimulation' mean?

_____

_____

_____

11) What does 'fervently' mean?

_____

_____

_____

12) What does 'loathe' mean?

_____

_____

_____

13) What does 'circumspect' mean?

_____

_____

_____

14) The four women from the Bible used as examples in this lesson were: _____ as an example of a daughter, _____ as an example of a wife, _____ as a mother, and _____ as a grandmother.

15) A young woman who enters _____ without the _____ usually ends up _____

16) Whether or not the parents are involved in the decisions and development of a young woman's life is:

_____

17) The Bible gives no direct command concerning young women outside the home simply because:

_____

18) Pouting and "turning on the charm" to get her way is:

_____

19) _____ in any form is wrong – and it is _____ to use your _____ to get your way – with your _____ or with your

_____.

20) The Bible praised the women of "old time" because they were; _____, they _____ and they _____ and were _____

21) Even more true than with a daughter, true _____ leave no place in our lives to _____ our husbands.

22) It is not submission nor reverence to _____ to your husband to manipulate his will. It is not submission nor reverence to _____ any more than open "in your face" rebellion is submission. A woman should never use _____ as a weapon against her husband's will.

23) You are not reverencing your husband if you become _____ if you don't get your way.

24) In its truest form _____ is giving – and giving from the _____ because of _____

25) When you feel that your _____ is something that you can give or withhold according to your whim,

341

regardless as to his wants or needs you are _____ you are taking something from his that is _____

26) You can never do anything before your children that is more important to their lives than to _____

27) It is a direct command of God that we _____

28) What happened in the life of Timothy shows that unfeigned faith is _____ it is _____

29) The term "like mother, like daughter" came from

_____

30) If we are walking circumspectly before our children we

_____

31) One of the most important parts of acknowledging your faith before your children is to let them know _____

32) The most wonderful reward of a life striving for virtuous womanhood would be for the Lord to say: _____

_____

A Woman Among all Those

Lessons in Christian Womanhood

Lesson 22

Scripture memory: Favour is deceitful, and beauty is vain: but a woman that feareth the LORD, she shall be praised.   Proverbs 31:30

And let the beauty of the LORD our God be upon us: and establish thou the work of our hands upon us; yea, the work of our hands establish thou it. Psalm 90:17

Favour - means good-will, partiality, expression of favour, acclamation, applause.

Favour is deceitful, and beauty is vain: but a woman that feareth the LORD, she shall be praised. (You can't trust the partiality or applause of mankind.)

Deceitful - means tending to mislead, deceive or ensnare; as deceitful words; deceitful practices.

Favour is **deceitful**, and beauty is vain: but a woman that feareth the LORD, she shall be praised. (The favor of mankind will lie to you, it can't be trusted.)

Beauty - is an assembledgc of graces, or an assembledge of properties in the form of the person or any other object....But as it is hardly possible to define all the properties which constitute beauty, we may observe in general, that beauty consists in whatever pleases the eye of the beholder, whether in the human body, in a tree, in a landscape, or in any other object.

Favour is deceitful, and **beauty** is vain: but a woman that feareth the LORD, she shall be praised. (That which is only in the skin, in the flesh, is empty.)

343

Vain - means empty; worthless; having no substance, value or importance.

Favour is deceitful, and beauty is **vain**: but a woman that feareth the LORD she shall be praised. (The outward appearance is emptiness, real beauty lies within.)

Fear - is the passion of our nature which excites us to provide for our security, on the approach of evil. In Scripture, fear is used to express a filial or a slavish passion. In good men, the fear of God is a holy awe or reverence of God and His laws, which springs from a just view and real love of the divine character, leading the subjects of it to hate and shun every thing that can offend such a holy Being, and inclining them to aim at perfect obedience. This is filial fear.

Favour is deceitful, and beauty is vain: but a woman that **feareth** the LORD, she shall be praised. (Fearing the Lord is a choice we make. We choose to seek His approval – not the admiration of others on our outside shell.)

Praise - Commendation bestowed on a person for his personal virtues or worthy actions, on meritorious actions themselves, or on any thing valuable; approbation expressed in words or song.

Favour is deceitful, and beauty is vain: but a woman that feareth the LORD, she shall be **praised**. (What kind of praise are we looking for? And from whom?)

Therefore, goodwill, partiality, acclamation and applause tends to mislead, and ensnare; and an assemblage of graces in face or form that pleases the eye of the beholder is empty, worthless and has no value. On the other hand a holy awe and reverence of God and His laws which leads us to hate and shun everything that can offend Him and causes us to seek perfect obedience will bring commendation for our value expressed in words or song. (Oh! now that made it clearer, didn't it? It's easier to say that popularity lies and beauty is emptiness, but living to please God in all that you do will cause Him to praise and reward you.)

Popularity sneaks up on you and traps you into a role you never wanted to have to maintain. It makes demands on your time, and requires you to uphold a certain image. In the end it becomes a tyrant. It holds you as its slave, requiring that you stoop to anything, spend any amount of money, time, and energy. It requires that you sacrifice anyone and anything on the altar of popularity - lest it dump you and you become a nobody.

Beauty is empty and worthless when compared to the things that really matter. It fades with age or infirmity. It is fragile, and in itself, is a form of popularity. A woman will spend countless dollars and hours to uphold her image - only to find that someone prettier has come along and stolen the show. When a woman has lived all her life for her physical appearance, what does she have when it is gone? The phrase, "She used to be a real beauty" rings rather hollow when that is all that you had.

So...Why do we spend so much time on the things that God says are empty and worthless? We will spend literally thousands of dollars seeking to make our physical self more attractive or seeking for praise of man. Teenagers will run in gangs, fail in school, take drugs or try tobacco and alcohol - just for the approval of their peers. We grieve over them and consider them foolish but in a lot of ways we are just as bad. We get into groups and will not stand for anything that will make us look like an oddball in front of others. We will not speak out against sin and worldly behavior lest someone think we are weird. We will not dress with our minds on pleasing Christ for one of two reasons. Either we believe that godly dress will make us less attractive or make us stand out as "out of vogue" with the world around us. We seek the approval of our peers rather than the approval of God.

Nevertheless among the chief rulers also many believed on him; but because of the Pharisees they did not confess him, lest they should be put out of the synagogue: For they loved the praise of men more than the praise of God. John 12:42-43

It was okay for them to worship God - as long as they fit into the specified mold. When they took a stand for what was right they were put out of the synagogue. So they just didn't take the stand. They knew what was right, but they didn't want to lose favor with the 'in crowd.' Do we find ourselves in the same category? Probably more times than we want to admit. Whose favor are we really looking for as women seeking godliness? Of course the answer will be that we are seeking God's favor! Otherwise we would never have gotten almost to the end of this course. But what do our actions say? Do we speak with a desire to please God, or are our words directed toward pleasing those around us? Do we dress with a desire to please God, or men? Do we choose our activities and our amusements with a desire to please God, or the crowd we hang around? Are we willing to pick our standards of conduct and appearance up and lay them down according to who we are with at the time? Or are they concreted in our character with a firm dedication to the Saviour who purchased us - soul **and** body on the cross of Calvary? I cannot count for you the number of people I have seen pick up a certain Christian standard because their pastor had it or because they were surrounded by a crowd that had it, only to lay it down again as soon as their peer group changed. (We don't like to use the word "peer group" concerning ourselves and our church friendships, but many times that's exactly what we have.)

So are we seeking the praise of men? Or are we seeking the praise of God? If we are seeking God's approval, how do we get it? Let's take a look at some people who received the favor and praise of God and find out what they did to attain it. We have already studied the life of Mary but look what the Scripture says about her.

And the angel said unto her, Fear not, Mary: for thou hast found favour with God. Luke 1:30

Why did she find favor with God? Enough favor that God was willing to use her for the vessel of honor to bear His Christ? We have seen that she was of a meek and quiet spirit - God says that is in **His** sight of great price.

Whose adorning let it not be that outward adorning of plaiting the hair, and of wearing of gold, or of putting on of apparel; But let it be the hidden man of the heart, in that which is not corruptible, even the ornament of a meek and quiet spirit, which is in the sight of God of great price. 1 Peter 3:3-4

God was sure, when He chose Mary, that she would be everything that was needed to bring Christ into the world. He knew she would see to the nurturing He needed as a child. The Bible does not say so, in so many words, but I believe that He saw, in Mary, the virtuous woman. But notice that it never once says a thing about her having physical beauty. Nor does it speak about her being the most popular girl in the neighborhood.

Samuel, of course, was not a woman but the Bible says that he found favor:

And the child Samuel grew on, and was in favour both with the LORD, and also with men. 1 Samuel 2:26

Why? Because he was handsome and full current style? No, because he was such a contrast to the wickedness of the two sons of Eli. He was simple and unadorned yet he found great favor because he was faithful. Then the Bible says this of our Lord:

And Jesus increased in wisdom and stature, and in favour with God and man. Luke 2:52

All through the Word of God we see how highly God prizes and praises wisdom. We know that Jesus did not seek the praise of men. This is what the Bible says about His physical beauty:

For he shall grow up before him as a tender plant, and as a root out of a dry ground: he hath no form nor comeliness; and when we shall see him, there is no beauty that we should desire him.   Isaiah 53:2

Three examples of the favor, not of man, but of God. What did it take? Wisdom, faithfulness, and virtue. Take a look, now, at some women that the Bible refers to as physically beautiful and look at what it got them:

And it came to pass, when he was come near to enter into Egypt, that he said unto Sarai his wife, Behold now, I know that thou art a fair woman to look upon: Therefore it shall come to pass, when the Egyptians shall see thee, that they shall say, This is his wife: and they will kill me, but they will save thee alive. Say, I pray thee, thou art my sister: that it may be well with me for thy sake; and my soul shall live because of thee. Genesis 12:11-13

My! The situation her beauty got her into was less than desirable, wasn't it? How about this one?

And the men of the place asked him of his wife; and he said, She is my sister: for he feared to say, She is my wife; lest, said he, the men of the place should kill me for Rebekah; because she was fair to look upon. Genesis 26:7

Try this one:

That the sons of God saw the daughters of men that they were fair; and they took them wives of all which they chose. Genesis 6:2

Or the story of Tamar in: 2Samuel 13:1-19

We could make a list: Vashti, In Esther chapter 1 was commanded to appear before a room full of drunken men so they could gawk at her beauty. The strife between Rachel and Leah in Genesis 29 was begun because Rachel was more beautiful to look upon than Leah - causing terrible contention between sisters and a home in turmoil. Then there is Bathsheba, in 2 Samuel 11. The story of Samson's wife in Judges 14 begins because Samson was pleased when he saw her.

Now, of course, every woman in the Bible who was noted as being beautiful was not in these situations. But if you will notice - the ones who had such trouble were the ones whose beauty was the main issue, rather than their godliness, ministry or character. When you look at the beautiful Abigail who was praised - it was for her wisdom. When fair Esther is praised, it is for her courage and obedience. When Ruth is praised it is for her virtue, her hard work, and her kindness. And even though Sarah is mentioned in the Bible as a remarkable beauty, even in her old age, that's not the reason she is praised. It is for her reverence to her husband. Should we begin to get the idea we are majoring on some things that God says are unimportant and holding things in light esteem that He says are major issues?

Although a woman enjoys being admired, it is rare that you meet one who wants to be admired ONLY for her face and form (usually the ones who do enjoy it have nothing but face and form to offer - no wisdom, no morals and no character.) When we come right down to it, if we have any common sense, we know that beauty and popularity do not last. We know that a relationship that is built only on physical attraction - whether it is friendship, business relationships, or "love" is a worthless relationship. So why, why, WHY do we spend so much effort on something so worthless at the expense of the things that really matter? Why are we so careless of our testimony and so careful with our hair, face, and clothes? Why does the praise of God and the desire of the title 'Virtuous Woman' mean so little in comparison with the favorable glance of a man or the approving nod of our friends?

And he said unto them, Ye are they which justify yourselves before men; but God knoweth your hearts: for that which is highly esteemed among men is abomination in the sight of God.   Luke 16:15

We have been raised in a society that belittles the things of God and slings insults at modesty and virtue. We have been raised in a society where physical attraction, gratification of the flesh, popularity and excitement are considered of the highest worth, while character and steady faith are ridiculed. It has become so ingrained into our thinking that many times we do not even notice what we are doing. We will become embarrassed and full of shame if we think that one of our friends may be looking down the nose at an outfit or hair style. Yet, if we are caught in an ungodly act or attitude by those same friends - do we blush with shame? We will readily pick up the phrases of the world, decorations of the world, and the attitudes of the world, so that we are not left behind and considered "backward" or "out of it," (or whatever the current title is for a living fossil.) Yet, we feel no shame to admit to God that we have neglected the nourishment of our souls in prayer and Bible study. There is no remorse that we have neglected to be a witness and testimony for holiness before others. Do we really fear God?

Churches will even adopt the music and entertainment of the world in order to draw a crowd. This is just another form of seeking popularity. When you draw a crowd with entertainment, you have to keep up the entertainment to keep that crowd coming - otherwise they leave. Maintaining that popularity becomes a financial hardship on the church and a power struggle with other churches who are also seeking the same crowd. They must plan something bigger and better to get the crowd back, then we must plan something bigger than that to get them again. And the Gospel falls by the wayside as people seek to be "up with the times." So instead of winning people to Christ and teaching them to live for God we are putting on a show for them. Then we get the results of putting on a show - they don't take us seriously. We invite a nice big crowd of people who "come as they are, and leave as they were." We make no honest life changing impact on the world around us - and the devil grins. Do we really fear God?

There is also the financial aspect of keeping up the "image." We will sing with all of our hearts, "If just one more soul were to walk down the aisle, it would be worth every struggle, it would be worth every mile"... yet we will say that we cannot afford to give money to missions while we spend hundreds of dollars on clothes and makeup. Our money goes toward making sure that we, or our children, are in on all the activities that will promote popularity. Or it is spent on promotions and gimmicks in the church.

I know personally of a church that spent $50,000 on a sign for the front of their building. I met a missionary to Mexico who has a very successful Bible Institute and has trained many national pastors. I asked him, at the same time that sign was installed, how many mission churches he could have built for the same money. He said, "If I had $50,000 right now I could build 10 churches in Mexican villages and have national pastors to put in them and have them overflowing with people by the time the construction was finished. That's just one small instance of how far from seeking the lost we have gone. The same routine is repeated over and over.

I know churches that have paid huge amounts of money to have T.V. or sports celebrities come and speak from the pulpit in order to draw a crowd. Some bring in rock bands (call them what you like- they are rock bands even if the words to the song say "Jesus" now and then.) I have actually known them to have elephants walk down the aisle in the morning service - one even installed a trapeze and had acrobats perform over the heads of the congregation. These are **Baptist** churches! These things are all popularity seeking gimmicks that have nothing to do with reaching the lost and ministering to the saints of God.

I do not doubt, one little bit, that if the money that has been spent on drawing and entertaining crowds in the United States in the last 50 years had been spent instead on evangelizing the world, we would not be now facing the threat of a Muslim controlled world and the persecution of the church. Well, you say, we can't do anything about all that. True enough, in almost every instance, we cannot. But we can make sure that our own hearts are right with God. We can seek to be ready for His return. The

Bible says that if we have our hearts set on the Lord's return we will purify ourselves. We will be seeking God's favor, not the favor of man.

And every man that hath this hope in him purifieth himself, even as he is pure. 1 John 3:3

The Scripture plainly outlines some methods by which we can find favor with God, instead of seeking the favor of men -- and as usual, they are completely opposite of the world's ideas.

My son, forget not my law; but let thine heart keep my commandments: For length of days, and long life, and peace, shall they add to thee. Let not mercy and truth forsake thee: bind them about thy neck; write them upon the table of thine heart: So shalt thou find favor and good understanding in the sight of God and man. Proverbs 3:1-4

So we see first of all that God grants favor to those who keep the commandments of God and hold mercy and truth to be dear and precious commodities in their lives.

For whoso findeth me findeth life, and shall obtain favor of the LORD. Proverbs 8:35

This is wisdom talking, so seeking after wisdom grants us favor with God. He that diligently seeketh good procureth favor: but he that seeketh mischief, it shall come unto him. Proverbs 11:27

A good man obtaineth favor of the LORD: but a man of wicked devices will he condemn. Proverbs 12:2

Good understanding giveth favor: but the way of transgressors is hard. Proverbs 13:15

Fools make a mock at sin: but among the righteous there is favor. Proverbs 14:9

Thou lovest righteousness, and hatest wickedness: therefore God, thy God, hath anointed thee with the oil of gladness above thy fellows. Psalm 45:7 & 11

So those who seek good, hate wickedness and stay out of trouble will receive the right kind of favor. Look at God's promises here! What more could we ask for than the favor of God? To be anointed with the oil of gladness by our Saviour? I find this next verse kind of interesting:

Whoso findeth a wife findeth a good thing, and obtaineth favor of the LORD. Proverbs 18:22

God says that for a man to find a wife is good. It is a mark of the favor of the Lord. Are we a good thing? Did finding us, as a wife, cause our husbands to thank God for His goodness to them?....It's something to think about. Here's another one, look what God says is beautiful:

Give unto the LORD the glory due unto his name: bring an offering, and come before him: worship the LORD in the beauty of holiness.
1 Chronicles 16:29

Give unto the LORD the glory due unto his name; worship the LORD in the beauty of holiness. Psalm 29:2

Holiness is beautiful in the eyes of God. Can you imagine standing before God suddenly (remember how sudden the rapture will be - ready or not!) Now, I know that we will stand before Him clothed in HIS raiment - but picture in your minds just for a moment standing before Him dressed in your most "styling" outfit. Would He consider it as beautiful as you do? Would it not be far better to be sure that you are clothed with holiness - inwardly and outwardly, so that when He returns we will not be ashamed?

And now, little children, abide in him; that, when he shall appear, we may have confidence, and not be ashamed before him at his coming. 1 John 2:28

Remember that He said He would praise a woman who fears Him. I don't have the time or space here to do them justice but I would recommend a word study on the fear of God. I found 87 direct commandments in the Word of God to fear Him. With those commandments we are promised very precious things if we will fear Him: Wisdom, knowledge, understanding, long life, blessing, that it will be well with us, that He will be our help and shield, and we will have no want, prolonged days, strong confidence, a fountain of life....the list goes on.

Okay, that's all very desirable, you might say, but **how** do we fear Him? Over and over in these verses, these two phrases are written together - fear the Lord and keep His commandments.

Let us hear the conclusion of the whole matter: Fear God, and keep his commandments: for this is the whole duty of man. Ecclesiastes 12:13

The Word of God is a practical Book. When the Lord tells us to fear Him, He is not intending for us to run from Him or to think that He intends to do us harm. He is our loving Heavenly Father and only desires our good. So does the Scripture tell us how He expects us to fear Him? I'm glad you asked... 2 Timothy chapter two gives a detailed outline of how to live our lives in such a way that we will be an object of beauty and favor in the eyes of the Lord. It is an itemized list in how to fear the Lord.

But in a great house there are not only vessels of gold and of silver, but also of wood and of earth; and some to honour, and some to dishonour. If a man therefore purge himself from these, he shall be a vessel unto honour, sanctified, and meet for the master's use, and prepared unto every good work. 2 Timothy 2:20-21

If you are interested in becoming a vessel unto honour, sanctified (cleansed and set apart for a special purpose,) meet (right for, suitable) for the MASTER's use, then you must look back at the verses before this to find out from what you should cleanse yourself. These verses are for Christians in general, they apply to all. Man, woman, young person, old person. This is the way to obtain the favor of God. Remember that verse 21 says if you will heed to these, you will be prepared unto every good work.

2 Timothy 2:1-19

#1 - In verse 1 - be strong the grace that is in Christ Jesus. Don't be a weakling Christian. If you don't know anything else about the Word of God, make it of primary importance in your life to know the Gospel. Review your own testimony. Be ready to tell someone else about the Lord with confidence. Then make it your goal to know more about His word. Labor in the word so that you will become skillful in its use.

But sanctify the Lord God in your hearts: and be ready always to give an answer to every man that asketh you a reason of the hope that is in you with meekness and fear: 1 Peter 3:15

#2 - In verse 2 - When you know something from the Word of God, be willing to give it to others. God does not save us and leave us to enjoy our salvation in isolation. Nor does He teach us so we can have puffed up heads, enjoying our knowledge for our own benefit. We are here for the express purpose of ministering to others. Otherwise He'd have taken us home to be with Him at the moment of our salvation. Don't be selfish with what you have, be willing to give it freely.

As every man hath received the gift, even so minister the same one to another, as good stewards of the manifold grace of God.   1 Peter 4:10

#3 - In verse 3 - endure hardness. Grow up and understand that life is not fair. You are going to have to face some things in this life that are just plain hard. Make your mind up now that you are not going to let those things rob you of your godly attitude and your virtuous womanhood. Determine in your heart now that the hardness you will endure will drive you toward your Saviour, and not away from Him.

Therefore, my beloved brethren, be ye steadfast, unmovable, always abounding in the work of the Lord, forasmuch as ye know that your labor is not in vain in the Lord. 1 Corinthians 15:58

Great peace have they which love thy law: and nothing shall offend them. Psalm 119:165

I have never understood the reason why trouble and distress drive some people away from the Savior. Why blame Him for your hardships? Why blame Him when others do you wrong? He is our only source of comfort and peace. It seems like an unreasonable attempt to do yourself more harm when you allow hardships to drive you away from the peace and comfort of His arms. If you have the tendency to back away from God when trials come your way, this verse in Psalms gives the cure. Love the Word. Submerge yourself in it. Surround yourself with it. It will give you the greatest, sweetest peace available on this earth.

#4 - In verse 4 - do not become entangled in the world. You don't have time to be a servant of the world if you are a servant of the king. You cannot love and embrace the world and be a true soldier of the cross. There is no such thing as living with one foot in the world and one foot in the church. A person who tries to do so, does not really fear God.

Ye adulterers and adulteresses, know ye not that the friendship of the world is enmity with God? whosoever therefore will be a friend of the world is the enemy of God. James 4:4

#5 - In verse 5 - strive lawfully. Follow the rules. Don't try to sidestep, don't try to make your own rules. Simply follow what the Scripture says. Obedience is really kind of simple when you make up your mind to it. Very seldom do we really have to test something to see if it's the right thing to do or not. Most of the time when we are testing something in this manner it's because we want to get away with something and have God be all right with it.

For the commandment is a lamp; and the law is light; and reproofs of instruction are the way of life: Proverbs 6:23

#6 - In verse 6 - Take care of your pastor.

Let the elders that rule well be counted worthy of double honour, especially they who labour in the word and doctrine.   1 Timothy 5:17

Saying, Touch not mine anointed, and do my prophets no harm. Psalm 105:15

A person who tries to live for God and yet lives in criticism and rebellion to their pastor will not ever be a sanctified, useable vessel.

#7 - In verse 7 - Consider the Scripture. Don't just read it or listen to it, but meditate on it and apply it to your everyday life. The difference between your 'everyday' church goer and your dedicated, sold out Christian is whether or not they take the Word of God and really apply it to their lives. When the Word of God says that something should be purged from your life, don't question it or try to get around it - just do it.

But be ye doers of the word, and not hearers only, deceiving your own selves. James 1:22

#8 - In verse 8 - never lose sight of the Gospel. The death of Christ and his resurrection should be the single most important thing in your universe. Don't ever let the story grow old. If it becomes 'old hat' and stale to you, ask God to renew your vision of Calvary and what Jesus did for you. The love and devotion that springs from a heart of true gratitude for salvation will carry you through the worst of hardships and the prickliest trials of your life.

But God forbid that I should glory, save in the cross of our Lord Jesus Christ, by whom the world is crucified unto me, and I unto the world. Galatians 6:14

We need the attitude toward our Savior that was displayed by the sinful woman in Luke 7:36-50. Look at what Jesus says of her in verse 47:

Wherefore I say unto thee, Her sins, which are many, are forgiven; for she loved much: but to whom little is forgiven, the same loveth little. Luke 7:47

I believe that dear woman would have done anything in the world the Savior asked her to do, her love was so openly displayed and her gratitude for her forgiveness was so real. What about us?

#9 - In verses 9 - If you choose to wallow in the crowd of mediocre Christianity you will be just fine as far as the world is concerned. They don't mind at all if you claim the name of Christ and live for the world. But go ahead and mark it down - if you take an open stand for Christ and for true holiness, you will suffer for it in some way. You will have to put up with some ridicule, some misunderstanding and some shunning (many times from family, friends and fellow believers.) In addition, we may have to endure physical persecution before the Lord returns. A wise preacher once said, "You say you would die for your Savior? You won't even live for Him!

If you won't take a stand for Christ now, while the going is easy, you won't take a stand when persecution arises."

Yea, and all that will live godly in Christ Jesus shall suffer persecution. 2 Timothy 3:12

#10 - In verse 10 - Let the salvation of souls be your primary goal in life. If we could learn to live our lives continuously seeking souls it would make us different people. We would be always mindful of our testimony, always mindful of our attitudes, always mindful of our words.

The fruit of the righteous is a tree of life; and he that winneth souls is wise. Proverbs 11:30

Abstain from all appearance of evil. 1 Thessalonians 5:22

By this shall all men know that ye are my disciples, if ye have love one to another. John 13:35

#11 - In verse 11 - Live for Christ, die to self. Put down the flesh. Tell it 'no' sometimes. It will whine and cry and pitch a fit when it doesn't get its way but tell it no anyway. Sometimes it's a pretty good idea to deny the flesh something it wants just for practice. Part of our problem as Christians is that any time the flesh whines for something we think it has to have it. That's one of the reasons we are so quick to give in to peer pressure, preserving our 'image,' and seeking after vanity. The flesh likes those things so we make sure the flesh has them. To give in to the flesh and let it run our lives is the opposite of holiness.

And they that are Christ's have crucified the flesh with the affections and lusts. Galatians 5:24

As obedient children, not fashioning yourselves according to the former lusts in your ignorance: But as he which hath called you is holy, so be ye holy in all manner of conversation; Because it is written, Be ye holy; for I am holy. 1 Peter 1:14-16

#12 - In verse 12 - Acknowledge Christ in all that you do, everywhere that you go. Make your stand for Him plain for all to see. Not just for their sake, but for your own. Don't be a 'secret agent' Christian. Be bold and upfront in identifying yourself with Christ. It will make you a better witness, more mindful to watch the things that you do and say. By the way, most people that you are acquainted with already know that you are associated with Christ. They are standing back and watching to see what kind of a Christian you are going to be. Most of them have seen all kinds. Your testimony is going to be what they see - not what you say.

And now, Israel, what doth the LORD thy God require of thee, but to fear the LORD thy God, to walk in all his ways, and to love him, and to serve the LORD thy God with all thy heart and with all thy soul, Deuteronomy 10:12

In all thy ways acknowledge him, and he shall direct thy paths. Proverbs 3:6

#13 - In verse 13 - Seek the forgiveness of God daily. We deny Him in our actions and word sometimes, but He is always faithful, and He has promised us the forgiveness we so desperately need. We only need to seek it - don't put it off. Seek His forgiveness as soon as you sin and then strive, with all of your might, not to sin again.

If we confess our sins, he is faithful and just to forgive us our sins, and to cleanse us from all unrighteousness. 1 John 1:9

#14 - in verse 14 - Don't go around looking for an argument. Seek for peace. There's really no use to argue and fuss, even about God and religious things. Unless someone's soul is in the balance, don't bother with the fight. You don't have time, Jesus is coming back.

Let us not be desirous of vain glory, provoking one another, envying one another. Galatians 5:26

For where envying and strife is, there is confusion and every evil work. James 3:16
#15 - In verse 15 - Study the Word of God. Learn the Scripture. Let it become such a part of your life that it seems to surround you when you walk and talk.

Gather the people together, men, and women, and children, and thy stranger that is within thy gates, that they may hear, and that they may learn, and fear the LORD your God, and observe to do all the words of this law: Deuteronomy 31:12

This book of the law shall not depart out of thy mouth; but thou shalt meditate therein day and night, that thou mayest observe to do according to all that is written therein: for then thou shalt make thy way prosperous, and then thou shalt have good success. Joshua 1:8

#16 - In verse 16 - Stay away from profane and vain things. These are things that are ungodly or empty time wasters. We should shun wickedness like God does. And we should be so busy about the things of God that we do not have time for empty time wasters.

But take diligent heed to do the commandment and the law, which Moses the servant of the LORD charged you, to love the LORD your God, and to walk in all his ways, and to keep his commandments, and to cleave unto him, and to serve him with all your heart and with all your soul. Joshua 22:5

#17 - In verse 17 & 18 - Also, don't waste your time with people who teach some 'new idea' or 'new doctrine.' They will cause tremendous trouble in the church. They are usually planted there by the devil for the purpose of perverting the work of Christ and poisoning baby Christians. Avoid them, don't associate with them, refuse to argue with them, go ahead and speak to your pastor about them. If it is your place to do so – such as with your children - warn the weaker brothers of them (cautiously, you don't want to be guilty of unrighteous criticism. A good rule here is to warn them against the false doctrine and let them see for themselves about the person fostering the false doctrine.) Pray about them, in protection of those weaker brothers and the church, and eventually – unless your pastor sees that discipline is necessary - they'll get bored when they can't stir anything up and they'll leave.
But avoid foolish questions, and genealogies, and contentions, and strivings about the law; for they are unprofitable and vain. Titus 3:9

#18 - In verse 19 - If you name the name of Christ - depart from iniquity - it's that simple. Shun sin.

Having therefore these promises, dearly beloved, let us cleanse ourselves from all filthiness of the flesh and spirit, perfecting holiness in the fear of God. 2 Corinthians 7:1

The fear of the LORD is the beginning of wisdom: and the knowledge of the Holy is understanding. Proverbs 9:10

Perfecting holiness in the fear of God. It's an ongoing process that will never end until the Lord returns and presents us spotless before the Father, not clothed in our own righteousness but His. You see, doing all these things won't make us righteous. We cannot possibly take this filthy flesh controlled nature that we have and make it righteous, any more than a bride awaiting the marriage altar can change her true face and form. But just as the bride dons the appropriate gown and veil for her wedding and plans and dreams and decorates for her coming event, we should be seeking to perfect holiness in the fear of God. We are awaiting the day when we stand before our Heavenly Bridegroom hoping with all the effort of our lives to hear, "Well done thou good and faithful servant."

Once again, let me caution you against impatience. What we have been given here is a course to run, a path to follow. This is a process that will never end as long as we live here, upon this earth. Only in Heaven will we be perfected in the image of Christ. It is an ongoing process, growing step by step, each day reaching for the goal. Why? Because to please the Lord is our highest honor on this earth. Because to be truly beautiful in His eyes is a goal worth reaching for.

Favor is deceitful, and beauty is vain: but a woman that feareth the LORD, she **shall** be praised.

Lesson Twenty Two Review

1) Write this week's memory passage:

_____
_____
_____
_____
_____
_____

2) What does 'favor' mean?

_____
_____
_____

3) What does 'deceitful' mean?

_____
_____
_____
_____

4) What does 'beauty' mean?

_____
_____
_____
_____

5) What does 'vain' mean?

_____
_____
_____

6) What is the fear of God?

_____
_____
_____
_____

7) What does 'praise' mean?

_____
_____
_____
_____

8) Mary received the favor of God because:

_____

9) Samuel received the favor of God because:

_____

10) Jesus received favor because:

_____

11) What happened to Sarah because her physical beauty was the main issue?

_____
_____

12) What happened to Rebekah because her physical beauty was the main issue? _____

_____

13) What happened to the daughters of men in Genesis because their physical beauty was the main issue?

_____

14) What happened to Tamar?

_____

15) Vashti?

_____

16) Rachel and Leah?

_____

17) Bathsheba?

_____

18) Samson's wife?

_____

19) Why was Abigail praised?

_____

20) Why was Esther praised?

_____

21) Why was Ruth praised?

_____

22) Why was Sarah praised?

_____

23) A relationship that is built only on physical attraction is a
_____ relationship.

24) The Bible says that if we have our hearts set on the Lord's return we will _____ ourselves.

25) _____ is beautiful in the eyes of God.

26) Fear God and _____ are the two phrases used many times together.

27) From 2 Timothy chapter 2 give a brief idea of the18 points in the outline on how to fear God:

1- _____

2- _____

3- _____

4- _____

5- _____

6- _____

7- _____

8- _____

9- _____

10- _____

11- _____

12- _____

13- _____

14- _____

15- _____

16- _____

17- _____

18- _____

28) Perfecting Holiness in the fear of the Lord is an
_____ process that will only end _____

A Woman Among all Those
Lessons in Christian Womanhood

Lesson 23

Scripture memory: Give her of the fruit of her hands; and let her own works praise her in the gates. Proverbs 31:31

Look to yourselves, that we lose not those things which we have wrought, but that we receive a full reward. 2 John 1:8

The works of her hands are praising her in the gates. She does not have to boast and brag. She does not have to put on a show of her spiritual nature. She's just busy about the business of being who she is for God and her family. The reward comes naturally.

Let another man praise thee, and not thine own mouth; a stranger, and not thine own lips. Proverbs 27:2

A man shall be satisfied with good by the fruit of his mouth: and the recompence of a man's hands shall be rendered unto him. Proverbs 12:14

Look at the widow of Zarephath, 1 Kings 17:9-16. She wasn't looking for any particular reward. She was simply doing the best she could with the little she had. And God was watching her. He knew her need and he knew her heart. He knew that He could trust her to believe the prophet's words. By her faithfulness and her faith she gained the reward of God for her whole family and the man of God. The Lord Jesus spoke of this woman with praise for her faith and her faithfulness.

But I tell you of a truth, many widows were in Israel in the days of Elias, when the heaven was shut up three years and six months, when great famine was throughout all the land; But unto none of them was Elias sent, save unto Sarepta, a city of Sidon, unto a woman that was a widow. Luke 4:25-26

The real issue is not in seeking to accomplish great things for God so that you can gain the reward. The real issue is in seeking a right heart and a willing spirit. The real issue is trusting God to sort it all out in His time. It's a matter of honest, from the heart, surrender to the will and the way of God.

Teachers know that when a child is really motivated - whether it is for the grade they receive or for some other reward - they will achieve greater things in school. A child who is not motivated will not excel, regardless of how capable they are to learn. We are all basically the same, even as we grow older. There is no one who does not desire to be praised and rewarded. It is an ingrained part of our nature. It varies in intensity with the individual's personality but we all have a desire in some way for praise and reward. The real issue is whether or not the promised reward is worth enough in the sight of the one to whom it is promised. Will it be worth the effort it takes to gain the reward? The real issue is attitude. The battle that we face in surrendering our will to the will of God is the foundation of this entire course - and our entire Christian life. The key to the whole issue is our attitude. The question is whether or not the reward and praise of God is more important to us than giving in to the desires of our flesh. The only way that we will have the reward and praise that we seek is to surrender our will to His.

The law of the LORD is perfect, converting the soul: the testimony of the LORD is sure, making wise the simple. The statutes of the LORD are right, rejoicing the heart: the commandment of the LORD is pure, enlightening the eyes. The fear of the LORD is clean, enduring for ever: the judgments of the LORD are true and righteous altogether. More to be desired are they than gold, yea, than much fine gold: sweeter also than honey and the honeycomb. Moreover by them is thy servant warned: and in keeping of them there is great reward. Psalm 19:7-11

God has made us some promises of reward. Are they worth enough to us to make us labor for the prize? What is it worth in our sight to be called a virtuous woman? To be thought of as such by our husbands, children, and those that we have influence over, both in the church and out? Most of all, to be seen as such in the eyes of our Lord. Is it worth the change that it will make in our lives? Is it worth denying ourselves that we might be identified with Christ? Is it worth a lifetime of labor? That's really the question that we must ask ourselves as we finish up this study. We have seen, in each lesson, that it is a daily walk. It is a daily surrender of our wills and our ways to the will and way of God. It is not going to be like a finish line, where once you cross it you can sit down and rest from your labor, knowing you have accomplished the goal once and for all. It will be an ongoing process for the rest of your life. The lessons that you learn you must re-learn and re-learn as you go along. It will bring with it some victories and some great success - and it will bring some struggle, some disappointment, and some failures. Is it worth it? Does the approval of God mean enough to you to keep on and keep on? That's a question that only you can answer. To almost every woman I have ever met the answer is "no!" ..... but there are a few....

Behold, this have I found, saith the preacher, counting one by one, to find out the account: Which yet my soul seeketh, but I find not: one man among a thousand have I found; but a woman among all those have I not found. Ecclesiastes 7:27-28

The ongoing process of surrendering our wills to God reminds me of housework. How many of us at one time or another have felt frustrated with housework? We clean, pick up, straighten, arrange and organize - only to clean, pick up, straighten, arrange and organize all over again. And sometimes we put in hours of labor, then look around at what we have done and can see no difference at all! Sometimes you may work at a task endlessly in frustration and have it fail in your hands. Sometimes you accomplish so much that you feel elated, only to have no one notice it at all. Doesn't that sound a lot like what we have to face in our Christian walk? Be assured of one thing, however, God's record keeping is very accurate. There is no labor for Him that is done with the right heart and attitude - especially labor that seeks for holiness - that will go unnoticed or unrewarded by the Lord.

Behold, the Lord GOD will come with strong hand, and his arm shall rule for him: behold, his reward is with him, and his work before him. Isaiah 40:10

For the Son of man shall come in the glory of his Father with his angels; and then he shall reward every man according to his works. Matthew 16:27

And, behold, I come quickly; and my reward is with me, to give every man according as his work shall be. Revelation 22:12

And whatsoever ye do, do it heartily, as to the Lord, and not unto men; Knowing that of the Lord ye shall receive the reward of the inheritance: for ye serve the Lord Christ. Colossians 3:23-24

The Lord does refer to our lives as our spiritual house. Houses need maintenance and they need cleaning to keep them in order. Those that are not maintained fall to ruin, those that are not cleaned are uncomfortable, embarrassing and unsanitary. Keeping a home clean is the responsibility of the woman of the house. It is our responsibility to keep our spiritual house clean as well. It's a process that we will repeat over and over again throughout the rest of our lives. Have we ever taken the attitude with our housework that having a clean house was not worth the effort that it takes to keep it that way? Or have we taken the attitude that if the other members of the family want a clean house they can get in there and clean it? What of our spiritual house? What's our attitude? Let's take a look at our motives, our methods, and our means.

When you clean your house what's your motive? Why go through the effort? Of course, the first thing that comes to mind is, "Because I want it clean!" But why? We want it clean for our comfort and the comfort of our family. We want it clean because we want to be able to welcome others in and not be embarrassed by it. We want it clean because we don't want anyone to get sick because it's not.

Take a look now at your spiritual house. Do you WANT virtuous womanhood, now that you know some of the things that it will require in maintenance? Will you be willing to clean your spiritual house for the comfort of yourself and your family? So many miserable women will take the selfish attitude that if their husband wants them in submission he can drag them into it and if the Lord wanted a living sacrifice He should have called on the lady down the street! But it is a comfortable thing to be in submission to Christ and His ways. When you come to the place where Christ is the center of your life and your will is surrendered to His, He will fill your life with such joy and peace that you will wonder why you ever struggled against it. Each step you take toward victory over the flesh, each battle that you win in giving your will and way to Christ will bring with it a joy that cannot be described, because it comes from above.

Come unto me, all ye that labour and are heavy laden, and I will give you rest. Take my yoke upon you, and learn of me; for I am meek and lowly in heart: and ye shall find rest unto your souls. For my yoke is easy, and my burden is light. Matthew 11:28-30

If you will cleanse your life for Christ and surrender your will to His in the matter of Virtuous Womanhood, you will find such peace and rest in your soul! You will find, much to your amazement, that the things that you struggled at surrendering to Him will lift away, lighter than air and without regret, as you feel the elation in your soul that comes when you know you have pleased Him. You will not only find that comfort for yourself but for all of your family. What a pleasant and peaceful thing is a home where Christ is the center and the wills of those within the walls of the home are surrendered to the will of Christ and are seeking to please Him!! Even the difficulties that a family faces are lighter and easier to manage when they can be managed with prayer and seeking the will of God and the way of God. How much better (and oh! so rare and beautiful a thing,) when each family member is denying self, serving each other and seeking God's face.

Not only will it give you and your family comfort for you to surrender your will to Christ but it will allow you to open the door to your testimony wide and welcome in your friends and neighbors without having to worry about what they will see. Yes, from time to time you will fail in your attempts to be Christ like. Just as from time to time your physical house is not in perfect order. The only thing that you can do with that is to learn from experience and try again. And the Lord will smile on your efforts.

The third motive is sanitation. We keep our homes clean and in order because we want our family to be healthy. That's true also in our Christian lives. Selfish motives and sins that display themselves in our lives will spread like a virus through our family. Bad attitudes are so much easier to catch than good ones! And selfish motives are very contagious. Anyone who comes near it will be either infected by it or will have to guard themselves against it and hurry to wash themselves up (with prayer and the Word of God) to keep from catching it. Repeated exposure to such infectious sin will wear down the resistance of the strongest Christian. So in order to keep themselves pure before God, they must make the choice of giving in to the wrong attitudes or quarantining themselves from the source of the attitude. Let's not make them make that choice. Strive to surrender your will to the will of the Saviour. Seek for Christian womanhood with the right motive. Then your life will be strength giving and spiritually healthy and nourishing for those that you are living and working around.

Create in me a clean heart, O God; and renew a right spirit within me. Psalm 51:10

All the ways of a man are clean in his own eyes; but the LORD weigheth the spirits. Proverbs 16:2

When you clean your house what's your method? Surely you don't begin by vacuuming your floors and polishing your furniture. No, we begin by removing clutter, by picking up the things that are scattered.

And Judah said, The strength of the bearers of burdens is decayed, and there is much rubbish; so that we are not able to build the wall. Nehemiah 4:10

The laborers in Nehemiah were trying to build the wall around heaps of rubbish. They found the task impossible and dangerous. The same thing will happen in your life if you try to polish your life and outwardly portray Christian Womanhood without cleansing your heart first of the rubbish that collects there. In order to clean our homes we start by picking up. If you are like me you find that job, of all others, the most distasteful part of housework. I would far rather clean and shine things that walk around picking up things that are scattered.

In our spiritual lives, also, we sometimes find that cleaning out the clutter is the job that is the most distasteful. By "cleaning out the clutter" I mean removing the things that don't belong - such as worldly decorations, clothing, music, books or other objects in our lives that seem to come out of nowhere and clutter up our lives. From time to time we need to do a purging. We need to throw out the rubbish that collects in our lives. If we don't, someone is likely to come in and trip over it and get hurt.

Ask the Lord to reveal to you any object or attitude that you might have that is cluttering your life and hindering you from getting the cleanup done properly. Ask Him to show you objects in your life or home that might be damaging to your own spiritual life or the lives of others that may come in. Then take out the trash before it starts stinking.

The next thing, that a housewife would ordinarily do, is the general maintaining of the home. She makes beds and does dishes and laundry. She cleans the things that get used often, so they can be used again. She cleans the things that are of serviceable use.

We need to take a look at the things that get used most often in our lives and make sure that they are clean. Ask God to check over your speech, your attitudes and your actions toward others making sure that you are dealing with other people with a servant's heart and a Christ like attitude. There is no place in a virtuous woman's life for dealing with others with a self-centered or arrogant attitude, or with unkind or unrighteous speech. Work on the stains (some results of the sins of the past never go away completely but they do fade a great deal with continual washing) and press out the wrinkles (present yourself to others with a crisp and cheerful attitude - don't be pruney faced Christian.)

Search me, O God, and know my heart: try me, and know my thoughts: And see if there be any wicked way in me, and lead me in the way everlasting. Psalm 139:23-24

Next in our cleaning process will be the removal of dust and dirt. We'll clean and polish the surfaces, vacuum the carpets, sweep and mop the floors. When we are all through with this job, we can look around you and really see that we have accomplished something. Guess what. Tomorrow there will be more dust and more dirt. If you have ever lived on a dirt road, you know what it is to continuously wipe up dirt and dust, only to do it again and again. So why do we do it? Is it worth the effort? Why not just leave it, since it's going to come back anyway? Of course, we can't do that - it would just pile up and pile up and become horrible!

There are some sins in our lives that just keep coming back. We never seem to get complete victory over them. Even when we think we've found a way to purge them and block them out from coming back. As soon as we let our guard down - here they come again! Take a look at Romans 7:14-25. The Apostle Paul struggled with the same issue. I believe that if he struggled with it, it's a given thing that we will, too.

The temptation comes to throw up our hands in defeat and just let down all the guards and let the devil walk over the top of us. It gets so wearying to struggle against that sin. Some do cave in - but we can't do that! We've got to keep washing and wiping the dirt. Otherwise it will pile up and we will become filthy and just horrible as Christians. Keep washing. Take heart - there's no dirt (sin) in Heaven. Nothing enters in that defiles! You will please the Lord if you will just diligently keep up the cleaning process. Don't get discouraged, just confess it, forsake it, forget it and go on again.

Nevertheless the foundation of God standeth sure, having this seal, The Lord knoweth them that are his. And, Let every one that nameth the name of Christ depart from iniquity. But in a great house there are not only vessels of gold and of silver, but also of wood and of earth; and some to honour, and some to dishonour. If a man therefore purge himself from these, he shall be a vessel unto honour, sanctified, and meet for the master's use, and prepared unto every good work. 2 Timothy 2:19-21 (Notice the word 'purge' in this passage – to purge something means to clean it out of there!)

Finally, we think we've got the house looking pretty good. The clutter is picked up, the beds are made, dishes done, laundry caught up, the furniture is polished and the floors are clean. Wow! We're doing pretty good - until we open a closet! (Have you ever noticed that wire coat hangers seem to appear out of nowhere?) or a cupboard, (I know I have one of those do-dads somewhere, if I can just figure out where I put it!) or a drawer (How'd that thing get in there?) Until we look in that far away corner and see cobwebs. Until we look under the sofa and find dust. Then all of a sudden our pretty polished house doesn't look so good anymore.

When you have your life pretty well picked up and cleaned up for the Lord, you will find that He becomes very interested in your closets and corners. "Open this door, let's see how organized you are."... "Lord, I'm not so sure you want to go in there. In fact, I don't go in there too often, myself."... "That's precisely why I want to turn the light on in there. Let's do some spring cleaning."... Sigh. The closets and corners usually represent our attitudes or our hidden thoughts. Those secret sins such as pride, arrogance, conceit, vanity, selfishness, a whining and complaining or bitter spirit. These are the things that take so much work to purge from our spiritual house. So these are the things that we shove back in a corner or closet of our lives and pretend that they are not there. These too, need to be surrendered to the cleansing hand of God and worked on over and over again as we walk this Christian walk. Many times we shove those things to the back and try to forget them so often that it takes a Spirit filled preacher, tuned in to the will of God, to focus our attention to those things. Then, when they are brought into focus, God can get in there and clean it out – if we will submit. Ugly things hide in our spiritual closets - the problem is that they don't stay there. With the slightest provocation - someone makes us angry, or hurts our feelings - and that closet door will open like it's on a spring and some ugly attitude will come falling out for all to see. Or you will glance over in the corner and see some ugly attitude hanging out like a cobweb. You didn't see it forming, but all of a sudden, there it is, and you suddenly understand that it's been there a whole lot longer than you were aware of. If you will willingly pray and ask God to cleanse the secret corners of your life you will gain a great reward - and God will be so pleased! It's not necessarily easy to do. When we get into those closets and corners, we find out some things about ourselves that we had almost forgotten were there. We find things that we would really rather pretend didn't exist. But go ahead! Grab a big trash barrel and go to work!

Who can understand his errors? cleanse thou me from secret faults. Keep back thy servant also from presumptuous sins; let them not have dominion over me: then shall I be upright, and I shall be innocent from the great transgression. Let the words of my mouth, and the meditation of my heart, be acceptable in thy sight, O LORD, my strength, and my redeemer. Psalm 19:12-14

We've talked about motive and method - what about the means of our cleaning job.

The definition of means is: The instrument; that which is used to effect an object; the medium through which something is done.

So when I'm referring to the means of getting our house clean, I'm talking about what's your power source? Many years ago a woman labored from before sunup to past sundown to provide the most basic of needs for her household. My husband recently made a trip to Honduras. Some of the pictures he took showed the huge piles of wood that had to be brought in from the forest and cut up for the wood stoves for cooking and the rub-boards for washing clothes. We, in the United States, are so spoiled to modern conveniences, such as electric washers and dryers, vacuum cleaners and dishwashers, that we sometimes can't imagine living without them. They have become our basic tools. This is a far cry from a corn broom and some rags, lye soap and hot water!

What's our power source, or tools, for cleansing our spiritual house? That's not hard to answer. There is a three step basic for Christian growth and development. I have taught it, many times, to my students -- over and over again, until they mechanically repeated, "Pray, read your Bible, stay in church. Pray, read your Bible, stay in church...." The Word of God is our cleansing agent. It cleans better than the strongest soap ever known. The more of the Word of God that we get in our lives the closer we will walk to the Savior. Pray - you will never pray enough! Seek to become a prayer warrior. One of the sweetest things about being a woman is that we have the privilege of being the prayer support for our husbands. Read your Bible - not just to say that you have read your portion for the day. Seek to have something from it each day just for you. Seek for help through your day and for help to understand the mind of Christ and His will for your life just a little bit better than you did yesterday. And go to church!! You cannot be the Christian you ought to be if you do not stay in church. (How can a person possibly be the Christian they ought to be if they disobey one of the basic commands of Scripture?) Remember, it's not a spectator sport - get involved. Serve the Lord.

Search the scriptures; for in them ye think ye have eternal life: and they are they which testify of me. John 5:39

Pray without ceasing. 1 Thessalonians 5:17

Not forsaking the assembling of ourselves together, as the manner of some is; but exhorting one another: and so much the more, as ye see the day approaching. Hebrews 10:25

Now that we know the instruments used for the cleaning process, the question is - where's the wall outlet? Where do you tap in to that power source and get the cleaning power you need to keep your will and your way surrendered to God? You can push your vacuum across your carpet all day long but unless it's hooked up to the power, you are wasting your effort. You can click buttons on your washer and unless the power is hooked up, your clothes will come out as dirty as they went in. Our power source is the Holy Spirit of God. He not only has the power - He earnestly desires to use it in our lives. He wants to make us clean, usable vessels. It's no secret, no mystical, magical formula that only a few can find. It's freely available for all Christians. The problem is not that God is not willing. It is that we are not willing for Him to cleanse us for His use, because that means that we will have to throw out some things that we think we want to hang onto. It means that we will have to open the door to our secret sins and let God have His way.

If we are to receive the works of our hands and our own works are to praise us in the gates what will we be receiving? What will be said?

If we are like Ruth, as in lesson 1, we will receive rest from our labor and it will be said that we are a virtuous woman.

If we are like Bathsheba and Potiphar's wife, as in lesson 2, we will receive the shame that goes with lewd behavior.

If we are like Noah's wife, as in lesson 3, our reward may not be open and glaring, but it will be the sure saving of our homes through a quiet, supportive, faithful spirit. We will see our children grow to love and serve God. On the other hand if we are like Lot's wife, we may lose everything, children included, through worldliness and selfishness.

If we are like Rebekah, in lesson 4, we will be known for a godly work ethic and rewarded by marrying in God's will. If like Tabitha, rewarded by the praise of those we have helped and by gaining the concern of the church when in distress.

If we are like Caleb's daughter, The Shunamite woman, and the widow woman as in lesson 5, our reward will be an inheritance that will benefit our whole household. The talk will be of our prudent, generous spirit. If like Abigail, our wisdom will be noted.

If we are like Sarah and Rebekah, in lesson 6, our reward will be physical strength and health that is unusual.

If we are like Job's wife, in lesson 7, our reward will be the loss of companionship of our mate, as we have no control over our emotional strength and we will gain the title of a bitter, complaining wife.

If we are like Deborah, in lesson 8, we will do the best we can with what we've got and gain the reward of God's power in our lives. The talk will be of our wisdom and godliness.

If we are like Lydia and the wise women in Exodus, as in lesson 9, we will be known, not just for our skill, but for using that skill in the service of God. Our reward will be to see God using our lives to bless others.

If like Esther, as in lesson 10 and 11, our reward will be an impact upon our whole nation for God's will. We will be known for bravery, meekness and loyalty and compassion.

If we are like Athaliah, in lesson 12, we will be known for wickedness, selfishness, and cruelty. Her reward? Early death.

If we are like Jezebel, in lesson 13 & 14 we will be so self-absorbed that we will seek to bend other people to our will and will try to get our way using our attire for allurement. We will be known as sinful and manipulative with loose morals.

If we are like Zipporah, or Michal, as in lesson 15 we will be known for criticizing our husbands for his stand for God and our reward will be that God will not allow us to be used for His glory. However if we are like Miriam in this lesson we will be known as a leader among the women and our reward will be God's blessing on our lives.

If we are like Priscilla, as in lesson 16, we will be known as our husband's right arm, essential to his work. Our reward will be the blessing of the ministry of God and the unmatchable blessing of true companionship with our husbands.

If we are like Mary of Bethany, as in lesson 17, we will be known in the gates for our devotion to Christ. Our reward will be that He will teach us His ways and let no one deny us from our place at His feet.

If we are like Mary, the mother of Christ, as in lesson 18, we will be known as a woman of few words and fervent spirit. Our reward will be to understand more and more of Christ as we ponder the things of God in our heart.

If we are like Miriam in lesson 19, we will lose reward as our heads and hearts swell in rebellion to the man of God when we seek to put ourselves above him. We will be known and criticized for that foolishness and God will openly rebuke us.

If we are like the daughters of Lot, in lesson 20, we will let idleness and slothfulness fester in our lives. We will feed our minds on the filth around us. Our reward will be the poisoning of our minds. We will be known as perverse and ungodly.

If, as in lesson 21, we are like Esther as a daughter we will bend our will to the wisdom of our parents and we will reap the reward of the will of God and the good name of an obedient and faithful woman. If like Sarah as a wife we will gain the name of a reverent, submissive wife and the reward of being held up by God as an example to other women. If like Lois and Eunice as mothers we will receive the awesome reward of seeing our children live for God and hearing ourselves described as having "unfeigned faith."

If we are seeking to be praised for our physical beauty - we could have the reward of Vashti, Bathsheba, or Tamar, as in lesson 22 - or we could seek after Godliness instead and be praised for meekness, submission, diligence and wisdom as Esther, Sarah, Ruth and Abigail were.

Or, as in this lesson, we can be like the widow at Zarephath and be praised because we were just busy about the things that are our responsibilities, but sensitive to the call of the Holy Spirit and to the needs of others. Our reward would be the provision of God for our family and the satisfaction of nourishing the man of God.

At the beginning of this course I asked you to examine your heart and ask yourself this question: "Do I really want to be the woman that **God** wants me to be, or do I want to be the woman that **I** want to be?" The question is still there. You have seen what God requires in a virtuous woman. No, I didn't cover it all. I don't suppose that it is possible to cover it all - it remains for you to get the rest on your own, from God's Word and the Holy Spirit. But the question really lies in the attitude of your heart. 'Will I give myself to the Holy Spirit of God? Will I present myself before Him as a living sacrifice, with my will surrendered to His will and my way directed by His Word?" That is the only direction you can take if you desire to be "A Woman Among all Those." The praise and reward you will receive will be worth the effort and the time that you spend on developing your relationship with Christ. But you must choose to do so on your own. No one but God would be able to force you into such a mold - - and He **will not** do so. You must choose it of your own free will.

Who can find a virtuous woman? For her price is far above rubies. Proverbs 31:10

Lesson Twenty Three Review

1) Write this week's memory passage

_____

_____

_____

_____

2) What does "means" mean?

_____

_____

_____

3) The real issue is not in seeking to accomplish _____ for God so that you can gain the reward. The real issue is in seeking a _____ and a _____ and trusting God to _____

4) The key to the whole issue is our _____ - whether or not the_____ of God is more important to us than giving in to_____

5) What is the real question that we must ask ourselves as we finish this lesson? _____

6) It is not going to be like a finish line, that once you cross it you can sit down and rest from your labor and know you have accomplished the goal once and for all. It will be an

_____

7) God's _____ is very accurate.

8) The Lord refers to our lives as our _____

379

9) 3 motives for keeping our physical house clean are:

_____

_____

_____

10) 3 Motives for keeping our spiritual house clean are:

_____

_____

_____

11) It is a _____ thing to be _____ to Christ and His ways.

12) If you will cleanse your life for Christ and surrender your will to His in the matter of Virtuous Womanhood, you will find that they things that you _____ to him will lift away, lighter than air and _____ as you feel the elation in your soul that comes when you know you have pleased Him. You will find that _____, not only for _____ but for all of your _____

13) Even the _____ that a family faces are _____ when they can be _____ and seeking the will of God and the way of God.

14) Selfish _____ and _____ that _____ themselves in our lives will spread like a _____ through our family.

15) List the methods for cleaning your spiritual house: first you

_____

then you _____

then _____and finally

_____

380

16) Spiritual clutter could be

_____

_____

17) Those things that are of daily, serviceable use are:

_____

18) Spiritual dirt is

_____   _____

19) What kinds of things hide in our spiritual closets?

_____

20) _____ things hide in our spiritual closets – the problem is that they _____

21) If you will _____ pray and ask God to cleanse the secret corners of your life you will _____

22) What is our power source, our tools for cleansing our spiritual house?

_____

23) Where do you tap in to that power source and get the cleansing power you need to keep your will and your way surrendered to God?

_____

24) The Holy Spirit _____ to make us clean, useable vessels.

25) The problem is not that God is not _____. It is that we _____ for Him to cleanse us for His use, because that means _____ It means we will have to _____ to our _____ and let God

_____

26) The only direction that we can follow if we desire to be the virtuous woman is: _____

Made in the USA
Columbia, SC
27 March 2019